PRAISE FOR *USER R*

"This book offers a comprehensive overview of how to be a great user researcher and explains exactly how to plan, run and debrief impactful user research. This new edition is right up to date with modern research needs for ethical data handling and operationalizing research. An essential handbook for new and experienced researchers to keep by their side!"
Steve Bromley, Principal User Researcher at Reach and author *of Building User Research Teams* and *How to Be a Games User Researcher*

"For those embarking on a career in user research, research operations, or for those with experience in the fields, *User Research* is a must-have guide. Fantastically practical with all those questions you didn't even know you had already covered."
Brigette Metzler, ResearchOps Lead, Department of Agriculture, Water, and the Environment (Australia) and Co-chair of the ResearchOps Community

"A true guide as it covers the full lifecycle of user and qualitative research, from design and collection through to dissemination. Following the advice in each chapter will ensure you deliver robust research and insights. The addition of the research operations section and the prominence given to the legal and ethical considerations only further enhances the credibility and utility of this book."
Laura Wilson, Data Quality Hub Lead, UK Office for National Statistics and author of *Respondent-Centred Surveys*

"This is an essential handbook for anyone learning how to conduct user research. It's also an invaluable reference book for experienced researchers. I shall add it to my library! What stands out in this book is the excellent blending of the basic building blocks with best practice for conducting quality user research."
Karmen Guevara, human–computer interaction pioneer

"We finally have a practical and pragmatic overview of user research methods together in one book. I expect to see well-thumbed and bookmarked copies of this book on the desks of everyone who believes in the value of designing for their users."
Amy Stoks, Principal Consultant, Affinity UX

"Stephanie Marsh artfully and comprehensively describes modern user research methods and, importantly, exactly when to use which one!"
Colin MacAthur, Adjunct Professor, Bocconi University

"Empowers its readers with clear explanations and practical instructions based on Stephanie Marsh's extensive experience. If you've ever felt intimidated by the complexity and breadth of the subject of user research, this book is for you."
Amy Hupe, design systems and content design expert

•

User Research

*A practical guide to designing
better products and services*

SECOND EDITION

Stephanie Marsh

KoganPage

First published in Great Britain and the United States in 2018 by Kogan Page Limited

Second edition 2022

2nd Floor, 45 Gee Street	8 W 38th Street,	4737/23 Ansari Road
London	Suite 902	Daryaganj
EC1V 3RS	New York, NY 10018	New Delhi 110002
United Kingdom	USA	India

© Stephanie Marsh 2018, 2022

The right of Stephanie Marsh to be identified as the author of this work has been asserted by her in accordance with the Copyright, Designs and Patents Act 1988.

ISBNs

Hardback	978 1 3986 0360 8
Paperback	978 1 3986 0357 8
Ebook	978 1 3986 0358 5

British Library Cataloguing-in-Publication Data

A CIP record for this book is available from the British Library.

Library of Congress Control Number

2021950522

Typeset by Integra Software Services, Pondicherry
Print production managed by Jellyfish
Printed and bound in Great Britain by 4edge Limited, UK

CONTENTS

Preface and acknowledgements xiii

01 **Introduction: why is user research so important?** 1

What is user research? 1
Who is this book for? 1
Why do user research? 3
What will you learn in this book? 4
References and further reading 10

PART ONE
The fundamentals: what good research looks like 11

02 **Planning your user research** 13

When is the right time to do user research? 13
Be clear what your research is about 14
Planning your user research 15
References and further reading 24

03 **Best practice in user research: who, what, why and how** 26

Who should be involved in your research? 26
How do you get the right participants? 27
Incentivizing people to take part 34
Understanding the importance of observation 41
Asking the right kind of questions 44
Accessibility and inclusion 54
References and further reading 56

04 **Getting the legal and ethical stuff right** 58

Do not skip this section! 58
What is data protection? 58
What is personal data? 59

What is a data processor? 59
What is a data controller? 59
Practical things to do 60
Informed consent 61
Ethics in user research 67
Protecting people's privacy when you are sharing research results 68
References and further reading 69

05 **Setting up for success** 71
Data management 74
Communicating with participants 77
Admin 78
Tools and infrastructure 79
References and further reading 80

06 **Managing user research logistics: agencies, facilities and contracts** 82
Logistics 82
Hiring agencies, choosing facilities, signing contracts 84
Part One summary 86
References and further reading 86

PART TWO
Selecting and using user research methods 89

07 **Usability testing: observing people doing things** 97
What is usability testing? 97
The fundamentals of moderated usability testing 98
The fundamentals of unmoderated usability testing 109
Summary of usability testing 116
References and further reading 117

08 **Content testing: what do people think your content means?** 119
What is good content? 119
What content testing is good for 119
What content testing is not good for 120

Effort required to do this kind of research 120
When to use content testing 120
How to test the effectiveness of content 120
References and further reading 123

09 **Card sorting: understanding how people group and relate things** 125

What is card sorting? 125
What card sorting is good for 125
What card sorting is not good for 125
When to use card sorting 126
Effort required to do this kind of research 128
How to do card sorting 128
Tools for card sorting 136
Summary 137
References and further reading 138

10 **Surveys: how to gauge a widespread user response** 139

What are surveys? 139
What surveys are good for 139
What surveys are not good for 140
When to do a survey 140
Effort required to do this kind of research 140
How to do surveys 141
Survey tools 144
References and further reading 145

11 **User interviews: understanding people's experience through talking to them** 146

What are user interviews? 146
What user interviews are good for 146
What user interviews are not good for 146
When to do user interviews 147
Effort required to do this kind of research 147
How to do user interviews 148
Interview tools 155
References and further reading 155

12   **Diary studies: how to capture user research data over time** 156

What are diary studies? 156
What diary studies are good for 156
What diary studies are not good for 156
When to do a diary study 157
Effort required to do this kind of research 158
How to do a diary study 158
Diary study tools 162
References and further reading 164

13   **Information architecture validation through tree testing: does the structure of your information work for your users?** 166

What is information architecture? 166
What tree testing is good for 166
What tree testing is not good for 167
When to do tree testing 167
Effort required to do this kind of research 167
How to do a tree test 168
Tree testing tools 172
References and further reading 172

14   **Ethnography: observing how people behave in the real world** 174

What is traditional ethnography? 174
What ethnography is good for 174
What ethnography is not good for 175
When to use ethnography 175
Effort required to do this kind of research 175
How to do ethnography 176
Extending your ethnographic reach with mobile devices 176
Ethnography tools 177
References and further reading 177

15 Contextual inquiry: interviewing people in their own environment 179

What is contextual inquiry? 179
What contextual inquiry is good for 179
What contextual inquiry is not good for 180
When to use contextual inquiry 180
Effort required to do this kind of research 181
How to do contextual inquiry 181
Tools 184
References and further reading 184

16 A/B testing: a technique to compare options   186

What is A/B testing? 186
What A/B testing is good for 186
What A/B testing is not good for 187
When to use A/B testing 188
Effort required to do this kind of research 188
How to do A/B testing 189
Tools for A/B testing 190
References and further reading 190

17 Getting the best out of stakeholder workshops 192

What is a stakeholder workshop? 192
What stakeholder workshops are good for 192
What stakeholder workshops are not good for 193
When to use workshops 193
Effort required to do this kind of research 194
How to run a workshop 194
Face-to-face workshop tools 198
Digital workshop tools 199
References and further reading 199

18 Guerrilla research: running fast-paced research in the real world 202

What is guerrilla research? 202
What guerrilla research is good for 202
What guerrilla research is not good for 202

When to use guerrilla research 203
Effort required to do this kind of research 203
How to do guerrilla research 203
Tools for guerrilla research 205
References and further reading 205

19   How to combine user research methodologies 206
Where to start when advocating user research 206
Common research scenarios and combining methodologies 208
Part Two summary 213

PART THREE
Analysing user research data 215

20   Content analysis: understanding your qualitative data 219
How to code your qualitative data 220
How to do content analysis 222
Advantages of content analysis 224
Disadvantages of content analysis 225
Analysis tools 225
References and further reading 225

21   Identifying themes through affinity diagramming 227
How to do affinity diagramming 228
Advantages of affinity diagramming 232
Disadvantages of affinity diagramming 232
References and further reading 232

22   Thematic analysis: going beyond initial analysis 233
References and further reading 235

23   Agile analysis 236
Face-to-face synchronous 236
The rainbow spreadsheet method 238
References and further reading 240

24 Analysing usability data and cataloguing issues and needs 242

Cataloguing issues from qualitative data 242
Cataloguing issues from quantitative data 247
References and further reading 249

25 Analysing data to create personas to communicate user characteristics and behaviour 251

What are personas? 251
What to include in your personas 252
How to present your personas 254
A more advanced method: using activity theory to create your
     persona 256
How many personas? 257
References and further reading 257

26 Analysing data to create mental models: visualizing how user think and identify opportunities 259

How to create your own mental model: version one 262
How to create your own mental model: version two 263
References and further reading 267

27 Turning findings into insights 269

What are actionable insights? 270
Atomic research 272
Part Three summary 275
References and further reading 281

PART FOUR
UX storytelling: communicating your findings 283

28 Making recommendations: how to make your research findings actionable 285

What kinds of things can you recommend? 285

29   Creating executive summaries and detailed reports to present results 287

Report structure 287

30   Using video playback to present your research results 292

How to edit your user research videos 293

31   Using journey and experience maps to visualize user research data 294

How to create an experience map 295
References and further reading 298

32   Using scenarios and storyboards to represent the user journey 300

How to create scenarios 300
How to create storyboards 301
References and further reading 303

33   Using infographics to translate numerical and statistical data 304

How to make effective infographics 304
Making use of available tools 306
References and further reading 310

34   How to recommend changes to visual, interaction and information design 312

Tools 313
References and further reading 314

Conclusion 315

Index 317

PREFACE AND ACKNOWLEDGEMENTS

There isn't one way to do user research, nor is there one way of using any of the methods covered in this book. This makes doing user research endlessly fascinating, but it can also make it difficult to be confident in using these methods. I have learnt some things over the years, not only by doing user research but also from mentoring people new to it. I would like to share some of this experience and I hope it will be helpful to practitioners, particularly those just starting out. I am grateful to those who have supported me and given me opportunities to learn and gain experience (both the positive and painful). My hope is that this book does the same for others.

I am very fortunate to have spent my career so far doing work that I find interesting and fulfilling. I would like to thank those who make the time and effort to share their work and thoughts and engage in discussion about user research, and those who keep pushing forward and improving our knowledge in this field.

I am extremely grateful to the industry experts who gave such constructive feedback to make this book better and to Kogan Page for their support and hard work in making it a reality. I am eternally grateful to friends and family, who always offer their support and encourage me in my endeavours. Finally, thank you to you the readers, without whom such books wouldn't be written.

Acknowledgements for second edition.

All of the above, which I wrote in 2017, is still true. I would like to add that I am truly grateful and excited to have been given the opportunity to do a second edition of this book. For some time I have wanted to update it with new things I have learnt and be able to add detail relevant to how the field has changed in the last few years. As this book focuses on the fundamentals, to my mind all the original content is still relevant, but this has given me the opportunity to reflect on a new emphasis on data protection, the emergence of the field of research operations, and to go into analysis methodologies.

01

Introduction

Why is user research so important?

What is user research?

As you're here, reading this, you probably have a fair idea of what user research is, even if you don't know how it's done, but it's worth making sure we have a shared understanding before we continue. User research is the study of people's (users') behaviour, motivations and needs in a particular context, which affect how people understand and use things in their daily lives. It can include thinking about how these factors change over time. Market research is something different: it aims to find out what consumer preferences and wants are. Market and user research have different sets of objectives and outcomes.

Who is this book for?

The job title 'user researcher' is common in digital and service industries, even in policy making. User researchers tend to be found in organizations that have, to some extent, bought into the concept of being user centred in their ways of working. You don't need to be called a user researcher to do user research. For example, UX designers and business analysts often do user research. User research is relevant anywhere people are interacting with products and services.

I don't want you to think that anyone can jump into doing user research without training or some knowledge. You aren't 'just having a chat' with someone during a user research session. But, you can teach yourself how to do good-quality research. I did. And this book is going to show you how.

There are many reasons why you may be reading this book, including:

- You may want or need to do user research yourself, as there is no one else in your organization who is going to champion a user-centric approach.
- You may be a new user researcher looking for good practice tips.
- You may be one of the lucky ones who get to work with a user researcher and want to understand more about what user research is and how it is done; this would improve your own working practices in collaborating with the team.
- You want to be an intelligent customer when buying in outside help from specialist agencies.
- You may already be a user researcher, wanting to refresh your skills or to get a different perspective.

There are several groups of people who would benefit from diversifying their skillset with user research, such as:

- web managers and developers;
- visual and interaction designers;
- experience and service designers;
- copywriters and content designers;
- information architects;
- social media/digital communication specialists;
- digital marketing and campaign specialists;
- marketing managers;
- market researchers;
- communication officers;
- business analysts;
- digital/transformation/IT specialists;
- policy analysts;
- business development managers;
- teachers;
- gallery and museum curators;
- politicians.

Everyone is welcome here. This book is particularly useful for people who are not necessarily user research professionals; they already have a busy day job, need some user research done and are facing the prospect of having to do it themselves. This book will help them avoid common mistakes by identifying the kind of situation they find themselves in and guiding them through the process. It will explain in plain English how to:

- understand the fundamentals of research;
- choose and use the right method;
- analyse the data; and
- make practical use of the findings.

Why do user research?

Many businesses and organizations are based on creating desirable experiences for users, yet many fail to fully acknowledge users in their development processes. They do not understand:

- who their users are;
- what their users' needs are/what they're trying to do;
- how their users are currently trying to do things;
- how their users would like to do these things.

Without user input, organizations risk spending huge amounts of money creating products and services that will fail. Leaders in some organizations may think they don't need to involve users, or that they can't afford the time or money to involve users on a regular basis. This is a fallacy. You cannot presume to know what your users need: you need to really get to know them, how they think and behave. Understanding your users' circumstances, influences and expectations will help you to:

- design better products, services and experiences;
- improve your existing offerings;
- adapt to changing behaviours and expectations;
- save money by getting your offering right first time;
- make an impact by giving users what they need and want – and much more;

- influence users' behaviour by allowing them to do what they want to do and getting them to do what you want;
- influence stakeholders' decisions with options and solutions based on evidence, not opinion;
- challenge internal assumptions about the direction the organization should take.

You can use user research to achieve all of these things. You don't need to be a user research professional to take control of the situation. By following my simple rules for good research, you can truly understand your customer or audience, whoever you are. You don't need a degree in computer science, psychology or human–computer interaction; I was an environmental geologist when I started doing user research. I just happened to spend four years working out what defines good user research, and what defines bad. I taught myself these skills by reading textbooks and practising; the fact that I did it during doctoral research is beside the point. If I can do it, you can.

After getting my PhD, I left academia and started using these methods, in earnest, in anger, in the real world. I have worked for companies that are 'user research evangelists' and others that don't have a clue. In some cases I've had to build understanding and advocacy from the ground up, at the same time as delivering results. I am now 19 years into my user research career, but I have not always had the title of user researcher in the various jobs that I have had. Those non-user researcher job titles include Usability Analyst, User Experience Manager, and Head of Digital Strategy. As I write this, I am a UX Research Operations Lead. The thing that got me all these jobs? My user research skills.

User research is about putting your natural skills of observation and conversation to use in a specific way, perhaps in a way that you haven't knowingly done before. In reality, we've all tested an idea on people, seen how they react to it, improved the idea and tried it again. This is user research. This book will show you how to put your existing skills together to use them in a more structured way.

What will you learn in this book?

This book is divided into four parts. The first part outlines the essential rules for success, including making sure you are talking to the right people. I will explain how to get them and how to avoid gathering biased and inaccurate data by asking the right questions and observing people.

Part One, Chapters 2 and 3, will help you gain a better understanding of what good research looks like, no matter the methodology you might be using. This includes:

- *When you should do your research:* it's all in the timing.
- *The kinds of ethical and legal elements you need to consider:* so everything is above board and the people you choose to take part in your research will have a good understanding of what is going to happen and how you will use the data.
- *Planning your research:* choosing a location, identifying internal people who should be involved.
- *Who you should recruit to participate in your research:* we'll look at how to get this right and why this is crucial for getting good data.
- *You'll learn about observing participants:* what they do and what they say can be two different things. We'll look at the difference between behaviour and opinion, and why it is important to your research and the number of people you recruit to take part.
- *You'll understand how to ask the right questions* avoiding bias in your data and helping you get to the truth.
- *You'll understand how to set yourself up for success* doing user research now and in the future, by understanding the basics of research operations.

Part One also covers logistics (Chapter 6): hiring agencies, choosing facilities and signing contracts. Part Two will help you identify the type of situation you find yourself in and offer advice on the methods to use.

There certainly isn't one method to rule them all. In fact, there isn't always one preferred method for each situation. If this book were just a list of methods, it wouldn't necessarily be clear which was the best one to use or when. As a taster, below is a quick overview of the methods to consider. You probably have lots of questions about these methods and the various options and parameters; we'll go into each method in detail and I'll explain:

- what the method is;
- what it's good for;
- what it's not good for;

- the effort required to do it;
- how to do it;
- further reading (should you want to know more).

Usability testing – observing people doing things (Chapter 7)

Usability testing (also known as user testing) is commonly associated with but not limited to websites. A researcher observes users working through tasks on a product or service to identify where problems are encountered. Usability testing can be employed both qualitatively and quantitatively (we'll get into the detail later). It can also be done in different environments:

- *Face-to-face and moderated:* the researcher and the user are in the same room at the same time, interacting with each other.
- *Remote and moderated:* the researcher and the user are in different places but are interacting with each other, for example by using screen-sharing technology.
- *Face-to-face and unmoderated:* the researcher and the user are in the same room at the same time, but the researcher does not intervene or talk while the user is working through the tasks.
- *Remote and unmoderated:* the researcher is not involved while the user carries out the research tasks at a time and place of their choosing.

Content testing – what do people think your content means? (Chapter 8)

Content testing is a specific type of usability testing that focuses on how suitable and understandable the content is for the intended audience(s). It can be done as part of usability testing or it can be done separately.

Card sorting – understanding how people group and relate things (Chapter 9)

Card sorting is a method used to understand how people think about and associate things, ie grouping items that are related to each other. This is useful when designing or refining the structure of a website, for example: what information is closely related and should therefore be grouped together and given a label. It can be used in the same environments and manner as usability testing.

Surveys – how to gauge a widespread user response (Chapter 10)

Surveys are used frequently in both market research and user research. They have limitations, but they are inexpensive to run and can potentially reach a lot of people. UX Mastery describes surveys as typically consisting of a set of questions used to assess a participant's preferences, attitudes, characteristics and opinions on a given topic (Gray, 2014).

User interviews – understanding people's experience through talking to them (Chapter 11)

User interviews are a commonly used method. We are all familiar with interviews in some form or another, usually for a job. For the purposes of user research, interviews are useful for understanding attitudes (and how they change over time), common behaviours and how people think and associate certain things. Interviews can also be face-to-face or conducted remotely (by phone).

Diary studies – how to capture user research data over time (Chapter 12)

Diary studies are useful for understanding experience, behaviour and attitudes over time. The researcher will give users a format in which to record their observations at specified times, about particular things; users will complete the diary on their own.

Information architecture validation through tree testing – does the structure of your information work for your users? (Chapter 13)

Information architectures are structures of information. The most common example we will be using is the organizing and labelling of website (and intranet) content and functionality. A validation exercise allows you to understand if your current or draft structure is working for a group of users, using online tools to facilitate the exercise.

Ethnography – observing how people behave in the real world (Chapter 14)

Ethnography studies people and culture. It is also used in user research to study groups of people as they go about their everyday lives. Many methods take place in an artificial setting; they are still valid, but sometimes you need to observe people in their real world. Mobile ethnography makes use of communication and recording technology to capture ethnographic data.

Contextual inquiry – interviewing people in their own environment (Chapter 15)

Contextual inquiry can be seen as a hybrid of user interviews and ethnography; interviewing people in their own environment can provide insights into why people behave and feel the way they do.

A/B testing – a technique to compare different options (Chapter 16)

A/B testing compares two versions of a web page (A and B) by showing them to similar visitors at the same time to see which one performs better (VWO, 2017). Rather than choosing which to use based on opinion, data and conversion rates inform the decision.

Getting the best out of stakeholder workshops (Chapter 17)

Stakeholder workshops are a way of engaging those who have an interest in the project, including those with expertise and in-depth knowledge of the domain you are working in. Workshops can be useful for:

- Building consensus among various parties with potentially opposing views and objectives and establishing a shared understanding of what certain things mean.
- Gathering requirements: what the product/service needs to include.
- Sketching initial design ideas.

Guerrilla research – running fast-paced research in the real world (Chapter 18)

Guerrilla research is a low-cost method of usability testing or interviewing. The term 'guerrilla' refers to its 'out in the wild' approach – it can be conducted anywhere (café, library, train station, etc); essentially anywhere there is significant footfall.

How to combine user research methodologies (Chapter 19)

We'll also look at some examples of how to use a combination of methodologies during the lifecycle of a project, as different methodologies are suitable in certain circumstances and stages.

Parts Three and Four explain what to do once you've done the research. We'll look at how to analyse the data you have gathered. These parts provide an overview of analysis methods, when and where they can be used, and how to share the results of your analysis. It will explain how you can:

- *Catalogue and prioritize issues:* once you have gathered the evidence, understanding what is a serious issue and what is not.
- *Analyse your qualitative data:* making sense of and coding lots of qualitative data.
- *Identify themes:* are the problems/things you have discovered related to each other?
- *Write user needs and stories:* this is a neat way of summarizing who the users are, what they want to do and what they want to achieve.
- *Create personas and mental models:* a way of describing who your user groups are and how they think about certain topics.
- *Share insight through video playback:* creating video highlights of particular topics is another powerful way of communicating your findings.
- *Write executive summaries and detailed reports:* different stakeholders will have varying amounts of time to understand your research. We'll look at the level of detail to provide to different audiences.
- *Visualize the customer journey and experience through mapping:* plotting and visualizing a journey and user touch points, from the user's point of view.
- *Refine the design:* how to go about changing information architectures, interaction designs and visual designs.
- *Do agile analysis:* how to analyse your research data in an agile environment.

- *Turn information into knowledge:* how you can turn your findings into actionable insights.
- *Create scenarios and storyboards:* use narrative structures to share insight.
- *Visualize data:* create useful infographics.

The proof is in the evidence. People who carry out user research will identify the improvements they can make and will get results from these changes. This is something that can be done continuously and iteratively: there are different methods for different stages of the design and development cycles.

References and further reading

Gray, C (2014) Better User Research Through Surveys. UX Mastery. http://uxmastery.com/better-user-research-through-surveys/ (archived at https://perma.cc/NVW6-VMMP)

VWO (2017) The Complete Guide to A/B Testing. VWO. https://vwo.com/ab-testing/ (archived at https://perma.cc/57YH-PF3Z)

The fundamentals
What good research looks like

Part One explains how to avoid gathering biased and inaccurate data by asking the right questions and using the power of observation (you can't necessarily rely on what people are saying).

There are some things we need to think about before we delve into the nitty gritty of choosing the right research method, how to implement it and then analyse the data. There are fundamentals that go across all methodologies.

02

Planning your user research

When is the right time to do user research?

The pragmatic (and simple) answer is: any time. The ideal answer is: all the time. You can also pinpoint when user research will have the most impact and the greatest positive effect.

If you are working in a truly agile and user-centric environment, you could be planning for and doing user research on a regular, cyclical basis. Problems identified in the user research could be rectified in the next round of work, and then researched and tested again. But you aren't necessarily working in this kind of environment, and you may never work this way.

WHAT IS 'AGILE'?

Agile is a project management method, often used in software development, with short phases of work and assessment of progress.

If you are working on an entirely new concept, product or service you should start doing user research as soon as possible. You will see later on in the book that you don't need to wait to have something tangible before you put it in front of users. For example, you can use sketches on paper that describe what you intend to do.

At the inception of the concept, after some initial thinking, you should be doing research to understand whether you are going in the right direction. By understanding the way people behave and think, you will get an understanding of whether your concept is going to enhance their life somehow, or solve a problem they are experiencing. Then you will know whether or not to invest time, effort and money in the new concept, whether it needs refining (which it probably will) or whether it should be abandoned altogether.

If your product/service already exists, there is never a bad time to do user research with the aim of understanding how it can be improved. If your data/analytics/feedback shows that something isn't working, but it is not clear what the problem actually is, do user research to understand what's going on.

If a board of stakeholders disagree on the way forward, then do some research, find out what the users need and give the stakeholders the tools for evidence-based decision making. The best solutions are a balance of business and user requirements.

Part of what we will discuss in this part of the book is how long it takes to plan, execute and analyse the data from the research. This varies depending on the kind of research you might be doing. For example, if you do research before the launch of a new version, you should plan it so there is enough time to fix any issues that have been identified, before launch. If you do it too close to launch you will be told that changes can't be made; they'll have to wait for the next iteration and the potentially great solutions and ideas may never get implemented.

There is a danger, if doing the research is time-sensitive, that you will pick a method that is the quickest and easiest way to meet a crazy deadline. It may not be the most appropriate method. This book will give you the knowledge to understand if the methodology is good enough to get what you need. You will almost certainly have a number of research methods that will be applicable to what you need, but it is essential that you talk to the right people. The right people cannot be substituted for anything else.

SUMMARY

If you can, choose a point in time when the results of the research will have the most positive impact.

Be clear what your research is about

What's your problem?

To do effective research you need to be clear about the purpose of the research. Research is most effective when it is focused. *Problem framing,* also known as opportunity framing, is knowing what problem you are trying to solve or understand or, from a positive perspective, what the opportunity is that you are trying to understand and what its parameters are.

It is useful to articulate and share with stakeholders (anyone somehow involved in the project) the *aims and objectives* of your research. Get everyone to agree to them before you start putting effort into doing the research. If you don't know exactly what the problem is, that's ok: the aim of the research may be to understand the problem. Getting agreement on the aims and objectives upfront should help you avoid *feature creep*. It is best to keep the focus of the research fairly narrow, unless your aim is at first to understand the problem or context. Stakeholders will want to expand the scope – you're likely to hear: 'As you're doing some research, can you also look at x, y and z?' If it isn't relevant to the agreed aims and objectives, say no. I realize this isn't always possible, so at least make your objection known and the reasons behind it.

Part Two looks in much more depth at understanding the problem and then choosing the right method to address it.

Planning your user research

There are several factors that you need to take into account when planning your user research. How much time you need to do the research will be discussed in Part Two, looking at each research methodology in detail. How much time you need to analyse the data, understand it, draw conclusions and identify recommendations from this new knowledge and put it into an appropriate shareable format will be considered in Parts Three and Four.

If you are planning research that involves interacting with people either face-to-face or remotely, if possible your user research 'sessions' should be done consecutively (think back-to-back, with breaks in between); an example of scheduling is shown below. The people you are recruiting to take part in the research will be booked into particular time slots on a particular day. This way you, the research participants and your team all know what is happening when.

Example: scheduling

You have decided to do *remote interviews* for your user research. This means that you are staying in one place to do the interviews (ie you don't have to travel to visit people).

We'll assume you have decided to do eight interviews. Below are three different scheduling examples, depending on the length of the interviews you are conducting.

30-MINUTE INTERVIEWS

These can be done in one day. Here is how you could schedule the interviews:

Participant 1: 10:00 – 10:30

Participant 2: 10:45 – 11:15

Participant 3: 11:30 – 12:00

Participant 4: 12:15 – 12:45

Lunch: 12:45 – 13:15

Participant 5: 13:15 – 13:45

Participant 6: 14:00 – 14:30

Participant 7: 14:45 – 15:15

Participant 8: 15:30 – 16:00

Backup session (with a replacement participant if anyone drops out during the day).

Participant 9: 16:15 – 16:45.

TOP TIPS

Recruit at least one backup participant, in case someone drops out on the day the research is taking place. This will remove the stress of trying to replace people at the last minute and allow you to still have the appropriate number of participants involved. Allow breaks of at least 15 minutes between each session. This gives you:

- Leeway in case there are technical problems that need to be fixed.
- Time in case participants are late, or a session overruns as there is so much to talk about
- Some headspace. However many research sessions you schedule in a day, it is tiring work and you will be grateful to have a little time after each session. Therefore, always, always schedule a lunch break (that is my golden rule anyway).

Don't schedule your first research session at the very beginning of the day if you don't have to. This is why I suggest you start at 10:00, to give yourself some time to set things up and get everything straight before you start.

45-MINUTE INTERVIEWS

These can be scheduled to be completed in a day and a half:

Day 1

Participant 1: 10:00 – 10:45

Participant 2: 11:00 – 11:45

Participant 3: 12:00 – 12:45

Lunch: 12:45 – 13:15

Participant 4: 13:15 – 14:00

Participant 5: 14:15 – 15:00

Participant 6: 15:15 – 16:00

Day 2

Participant 7: 10:00 – 10:45

Participant 8: 11:00 – 11:45

Backup session:

Participant 9: 12:00 – 12:45

You may choose to have a backup participant for each day.

60-MINUTE INTERVIEWS

These are more labour-intensive, but are often necessary when researching complex topics:

Day 1

Participant 1: 10:00 – 11:00

Participant 2: 11:15 – 12:15

Participant 3: 12:30 – 13:30

Lunch: 13:30 – 14:00

Participant 4: 14:00 – 15:00

Participant 5: 15:15 – 16:15

Day 2

Participant 6: 10:00 – 11:00

Participant 7: 11:15 – 12:15

Participant 8: 12:30 – 13:30

Backup session:

Participant 9: 14:00 – 15:00

Again, you may choose to have a backup participant for each day.

These are only examples of how to plan your day and won't work for everyone. For example, if you need to do user research with teachers during term time, you will need to plan evening sessions. If you need to travel to people in between sessions, your day will be very different to what I have described above; you will need to factor in travel time. If possible, try to schedule visits that are close to each other. You may only be able to get two to four research session done in a day. If you are visiting people at work, for example, and if appropriate, try to schedule sessions for people in the same location. You may need to be very flexible about who you talk to and when, as their work priorities will interrupt your research plans.

Location of your research

Location affects the time taken to plan and do the research, as well as the cost. Depending on the type of research you are doing, the location will vary. Table 2.1 summarizes the advantages of different research locations you may want to consider.

(For advice on choosing a research lab, see Government Digital Service, June 2016. There is a rigorous process for UK government departments when hiring a research lab, because it is being paid for with taxpayers' money. It's also best practice and sound advice that anyone can follow to do things properly and get what you need rather than what someone wants to sell you.)

Side note: large organizations that have moved to agile and user-centric ways of working have started to build their own user research labs within their offices. There are obviously big upfront costs when doing this but, when you start doing user research on a regular basis it becomes much more cost-effective. This is probably getting a bit ahead of ourselves, but it's good to dream!

TABLE 2.1   Cost-benefit analysis for choosing a research venue for face-to-face research

Location	Advantages	Disadvantages
Your offices (or your clients')	You could simply book a room for the day; easy access for you! Hopefully booking would be simple, but it isn't always easy if space is limited. You don't have to pay for facilities. Easy access to your team members for support. Easier access to your IT, etc.	It could be intimidating for people taking part in the research. Some may not feel comfortable criticizing your things in the place where people work on them every day. Others won't care and will tell you exactly what they think. Where is your office located? Will it be easy for your participants to travel there? When using standard meeting rooms, colleagues may not be able to observe the research as it happens. You may have to think about the practicalities of getting people in and out of the building.
User research labs	These are labs designed to smoothly facilitate the research you are doing. They will record your sessions and provide you with the data. They will probably provide a person to host the participants. They will provide IT support. They generally have observation rooms, which means colleagues and stakeholders can attend.	Cost is the main consideration here. This is going to be expensive, so you will need to plan carefully when to use these kinds of facilities. Availability of the facilities is also a factor, depending on where you want to do the research. As with your offices, location of the lab is a factor to consider. Is the lab located in a place that your participants can get to?
Conference facilities and hotel rooms	Lots of options, readily available at different price ranges. They may be willing to help with the hosting of the participants.You may even get some IT support (Wi-Fi). It's a neutral venue (outside your offices). You can go to where your users are, if they aren't near you.	Unlike your office, it may not have all the equipment or IT support you need. Your team and stakeholders may not be able to observe. Although it's a neutral setting, it may not be an environment that participants feel comfortable in. It really depends on the venue.

(continued)

TABLE 2.1   (Continued)

Location	Advantages	Disadvantages
Public spaces, libraries and coffee shops	Free, but make sure you have permission from the owner/manager. It's a neutral (relaxed) setting. This is a good option if you are doing 'guerrilla research', where anyone can take part in the research, if they are places with high footfall.	There will be no privacy. This needs careful consideration depending on the kind of questions you will be asking. Background noise may become an issue in a café, for example. You may start disturbing others. There may be equipment and support issues.
Visiting people at home or work	Some research requires you to go to where your users are. It may be your only option. You can gain a deep understanding of the users' environment, making data collection more realistic. There are no venue costs.	You need to consider the travel costs (and perhaps hotel costs). It is likely that it will take longer to gather data this way. Particularly if you are going to people's homes, for safety you should go with a colleague. You should let the participant know beforehand that there are two people coming, so they are prepared and it is not unexpected, which could be uncomfortable for them.

Options for remote research

Remote research simply means that the researcher and the participants are in different places. Table 2.2 summarizes the advantages and disadvantages.

There are two main modes of remote research: moderated and unmoderated. Moderated remote research includes telephone interviews and video and screen sharing, which means the researcher and participant are interacting in some way. Unmoderated remote research includes online surveys and information architecture validation; participants complete the research without any contact with the researcher, in their own time. This means lots of people can do the research at the same time. Time and money are saved by not requiring a location to do the research, but you will still need to recruit the right people to take part.

If you are reading this second edition close to the time it was published, that means you have lived through the coronavirus pandemic, which started in 2020. The pandemic impacted how user research is done, with all research being done entirely remotely at certain points in time. The benefit of this is that there are a lot more tool options and lots of good guidance online to help you set up and do remote research.

TABLE 2.2 Cost-benefit analysis for remote research

Advantages	Disadvantages
You can access a wide geographical spread including international audiences	You exclude users that do not have easy access to the internet.
It is cheaper to run these types of research	You exclude users that have low digital/IT literacy.
It can be quicker to plan and do remote research	You will miss some of the detail gained by observing people in real life (face-to-face).

The importance of pilot testing

If you have some flexibility and you aren't sure at the beginning how long the research session should be, you can do some pilot testing. It is considered best practice to pilot your research methodology before you do the research for real.

By pilot testing I mean creating a draft outline of how you want to run your research session: the things you want to say to the participants, the tasks that you want them to do, any questions that you want to ask them, etc. Do a dummy run session (ideally with someone who is similar to your participants, otherwise get a colleague to role-play a participant). Doing a pilot test means that you can identify what does and doesn't work with your draft document: you can edit questions and tasks that cause confusion or are too leading, etc, and refine the draft until you are comfortable that it is the best it can be.

Inviting people to observe research sessions

In the right circumstances, if you are doing face-to-face or remote moderated research, there is the potential to invite people to observe. The best example (an ideal scenario) of this would be inviting stakeholders to observe some usability testing, ie observing participants interacting with your product or service.

SCENARIO

The scene: you are improving your website. You are in a user research lab with an observation room. Various stakeholders are watching (on a large screen) as a participant struggles to complete a task. The participant becomes frustrated and annoyed, and eventually gives up. This is a very powerful way for stakeholders to see what it's like to use your product/service in real life, in real time.

GETTING OBSERVERS INVOLVED IN THE RESEARCH

If you are lucky enough have people from your organization/project team observing the research, it's a good idea to get them actively involved in notetaking. It is useful to have multiple perspectives on what is going on if you can get them! If you do have several observers, it's worth having some ground rules to be shared before they start observing and writing things down; ideally the rules will be visible wherever the observation is happening. For example:

- Note each observation down separately, whenever a participant says or does something interesting or relevant.

- For each observation, note which participant it was (using the participant ID), so you can tell which participants said what. If possible note down the time for your observations.

- Avoid interpreting what you have seen or heard. Just take notes of what you see and hear.

- Try to write your observations in a sharable format, eg, on a Post-it (one observation per Post-it).

- If doing remote research you may ask observers to write notes in a spreadsheet, for example.

If the observers see five different participants struggling five times in one day, this is hard evidence that something needs to be fixed. It's not just you telling busy people that something isn't working: it's showing them that it's not working. Video highlights (which we'll discuss in Part Four) for those who can't attend are also powerful.

Government Digital Service in the UK (https://gds.blog.gov.uk) have a mantra for observing user research: each team member should observe two hours of user research every six weeks. This may not be realistic for you, but it demonstrates how important it is to have stakeholders observe.

Recruiting people to do the research

The main question here is: how easy or difficult are these people to find and get some of their precious time? For example, if you are building a legal research database you will want to talk to lawyers, barristers, paralegals, law students, judges – a prime example of a specialist audience. They are a relatively small group (compared to people who listen to music online, for example) and they are time-poor. For these kinds of people, you will need a long lead time, before the research happens, giving plenty of notice for them to make time in their diary for the research, especially if you are asking them to travel to a different location during their day.

If you are looking for people who shop online, these are much easier to find. It will take less time, but it still takes time. From the moment you have decided exactly who to include in the research, the general advice is to give at least two weeks to allow for recruitment, longer for specialist audiences. There are multiple ways that you can recruit people; see more on this in Chapter 3.

Planning for analysis and sharing of work

The research process does not finish once you have gathered the data: you need to plan time and resource for analysing it and sharing the outcomes. The time it takes to do analysis will depend on the amount of data (Part Three will give you some insight into this).

If you can get others involved in the analysis that will help. In the same way as having people observe the research, multiple perspectives will improve the insight gained. In many cases, you can involve people in the analysis even if they haven't observed the research, if they have a good enough understanding of its aims, objectives and context.

If you've had people observing the research, schedule in a group analysis and debrief as soon as you can after it's completed (see Part Three for more on this). You'll also want to schedule in time with the relevant people to share the outcomes of your research. If you have a clear plan and timescale, it's worth planning this well in advance to get the right people in the room, especially when some of the stakeholders may be very time-poor.

Planning for user research when working agile or lean

The first thing I want to say is that using agile and lean UX (user experience) approaches does not mean excluding users and user research. I have seen more than one presentation that adopted the 'no users' approach to lean UX. In my opinion there is no UX without the users.

If you're working in an agile environment, hopefully you are also working in a multidisciplinary team and ideally a multidisciplinary team with a dedicated user researcher. If you are that dedicated user researcher, great! If not, it's a challenge to take up that responsibility within the team, but it's certainly worth it and I salute you!

The lean approach is similar to agile in its principles. Lean methods are more holistic across the business, and agile is more focused on software development (Stockwell, 2016). There are many useful resources in lean UX and agile user research, which you can find in the further reading section at the end of this chapter.

There are a few things that I want to highlight before you delve further into this area. The first is to get user research into the planning phase, so that it has committed time and resource. It will depend on the way your organization is doing agile, but ideally you won't develop, design or progress anything for more than two to three weeks at a time without putting it in front of users. Part Two will identify the few methods that can't be adapted to lean and agile approaches.

Getting user research into the plan also includes the data analysis and sharing insight. In an agile environment (or whenever timescales are tight), group analysis is useful, not only because it shares the workload but it also helps others in the team incorporate the insight into the next phase of work (you can find out more about group analysis in Part Three). Not everyone will be able to be involved in the research and analysis phases. You can share the insight with them through retrospectives and 'show and tells' to spread the word; agile is all about being collaborative and not doing things in isolation. There is less documentation, less taking time to make things look pretty in agile; Part Four will highlight which methods are useful for sharing insight in an agile way.

The type of research you do in each sprint will depend on the focus of that sprint. Having team-wide agreement of the aims, objectives and scope will help you do useful and actionable research. The focus of your research is likely to be narrow and the number of participants relatively small to fit into agile ways of working, but it is still valid.

References and further reading

Gothelf, J (7 March 2011) Lean UX – Getting out of the deliverables business. Smashing Magazine. www.smashingmagazine.com/2011/03/lean-ux-getting-out-of-the-deliverables-business/ (archived at https://perma.cc/ZFK4-AJ7Z)

Gothelf, J and Seiden, J (2016) *Lean UX: Designing great product with agile teams,* O'Reilly Media, New York

Government Digital Service (24 May 2016) Getting users' consent for research. Service Manual (for further information on gaining consent for your research). www.gov.uk/service-manual/user-research/getting-users-consent-for-research (archived at https://perma.cc/QQF3-BCEF)

Government Digital Service (16 February 2017) How a knowledge Kanban board can help your user research. GDS User Research Blog. https://userresearch.blog.gov.uk/2017/02/16/how-a-knowledge-kanban-board-can-help-your-user-research/ (archived at https://perma.cc/X6SE-H5HF)

Hall, E (September 2013) *Just Enough Research: A book apart.* www.abookapart.com/products/just-enough-research (archived at https://perma.cc/MGG8-QJY2)

Hands, A and Vashisht, K (21 November 2016) Agile development is no excuse for shoddy UX research. UX Matters. www.uxmatters.com/mt/archives/2016/11/agile-development-is-no-excuse-for-shoddy-ux-research.php (archived at https://perma.cc/HYY9-3VY7)

Interaction Design Foundation (July 2017) A simple introduction to lean UX. www.interaction-design.org/literature/article/a-simple-introduction-to-lean-ux (archived at https://perma.cc/5R7U-3VZV)

Sharon, T (2016) *Validating Product Ideas Through Lean User Research,* Rosenfeld Media, New York

Stockwell, A (26 June 2016) How to adapt UX research for an agile environment. UX Mastery. https://uxmastery.com/how-to-adapt-ux-research-for-an-agile-environment/ (archived at https://perma.cc/T5JT-MTCP)

Survey Monkey Inc (2017) Consent form. www.surveymonkey.com/r/consent (archived at https://perma.cc/Q7NQ-TAXS)

03

Best practice in user research

Who, what, why and how

Who should be involved in your research?

There are many different ways to describe people who use your products, services and content: users, audience, customers or consumers. Involving the right people is one of the fundamentals of doing good research: if you don't understand who 'they' are, you won't be able to provide 'them' with the right thing.

Whatever your organization does, there will be a particular group of people who are interested in what you do or provide. Very few organizations have 'everyone' as their users. Even if you are a national government or an international business such as Amazon or Facebook, not everyone is going to be interested in everything about you. This might seem a little abstract, so let me give you an example. A government does technically have everyone in the country and many people outside it as its audience, but it is not useful to see them as one massive group of people. Where would you even start when trying to understand them? You need to break down the large group into smaller, manageable chunks. If you try to cover everyone and everything in your research, generally you won't get very far. So continuing with the government example, if you are focusing on a particular kind of government service, you will do research with the type of people who need to use that particular service. The fundamental question is: who do you need to understand?

You can involve your current and potential users. Users who have similar behaviours and needs can be put into a group together, known as a 'user group'. Depending on what you are working on, you are likely to have several different types of user group.

> QUICK FACT
>
> Different user groups do not 'perform' consistently, so who you choose to include in your research will affect your research results.

Scenario

If you are working in a university, building software for academic mathematics experts to use, you cannot do user research with English literature undergraduates to improve the software. This is an extreme example, but it clearly highlights my point. English literature undergraduates have very different knowledge to draw on when interacting with the world compared with academics with PhDs in maths. Substituting one for the other is not appropriate. You have to involve the people for whom you are building that software. It seems obvious when it's laid out in this way, but there are many reasons why researchers recruit the wrong people:

- They don't know who the users are.
- The users are difficult to gain access to (lawyers, doctors, CEOs of large corporations, people in intensive care and their families, etc).
- It would be expensive to include them in the research.

> TOP TIP
>
> *To achieve useful and usable results, having a small number of intended users is preferable to having a lot of inappropriate ones.*
>
> There are times when the rules should be broken, such as when you are doing guerrilla research (see Chapter 18), but we'll get into that later. For the purposes of doing research, we are going to start thinking about the users/audiences/customers as participants.

How do you get the right participants?

There are agencies that specialize in recruiting for user and market research. They have databases of people who have signed up to do various types of research. These people have shared a certain amount of detail with the agency about who they are and what they like, allowing the recruitment agencies to find the right people to do your research. This can be costly, but it might be the right choice for you, depending on your budget, time, resources and intended participants.

You may have access to subscribers to your organization's newsletter or your customer database, which you can draw upon to recruit for your research, if you have permission to use the databases in this way. Whether you are recruiting the participants yourself or working with a recruitment agency, you are going need two things: *a recruitment brief*, which sets out exactly who you want to be involved in the user research (and how many); and *a recruitment screener*, which is a questionnaire to find out whether or not they are suitable to take part in the research. The intricacies of getting these two things right could be the subject of a whole other book. However, I will give you enough knowledge to successfully recruit your participants or be an intelligent customer when working with a research recruitment agency. (There are ways of calculating the numbers you need; see Survey Monkey, 2017.)

Writing a recruitment brief

To write a recruitment brief you will need to include:

- dates of the research;
- location;
- length of the research session;
- the number of participants needed;
- the times at which you want to schedule people;
- the incentive (amount of money you will pay each participant to take part in the research);
- a list of demographics and characteristics you want the participants to have.

It's essential that you don't just include the demographics of the participants. They are useful but they are only one dimension. There is a well-known example that has been doing the rounds for years, shown in Table 3.1. As you can see, on paper Prince Charles and Ozzy Osbourne look like the same person, based on their demographic profiles.

TABLE 3.1   The limitation of demographics

Person 1 Demographics	Person 2 Demographics
Born 1948	Born 1948
Grew up in England	Grew up in England
Second marriage	Second marriage
Two children	Two children
Successful business person	Successful business person
Wealthy	Wealthy
Spends winter holidays in the Alps	Spends winter holidays in the Alps
Dog owner	Dog owner
Prince Charles	Ozzy Osbourne

SOURCE Brian Solis (briansolis.com) inspired by Dr Peter Gentsch

When you search for advice on how to get the right participants for your user research, you will come across all sorts of tips, including avoiding recruiting introverts, shy people, non-talkative and 'inarticulate' people. *Please ignore this advice*. Almost everyone has something worthwhile to contribute to your research, if they have the right characteristics and behaviours that make up your user groups. With some participants, it will be more difficult to get a response, but with patience and skill you can coax valuable information from them. If you start screening for particular personality types, you are in danger of skewing your research data and results.

There will be times when you will have difficult or unhelpful participants; they are rare but are simply a part of life. Generally, it is my experience that people want to be helpful. In Part Two we will learn about the importance of observation and asking the right questions, so that we get to the truth and don't allow participants simply to tell us what we want to hear. When you are thinking about who your users are, don't exclude certain people because they are harder to recruit or are in some way disadvantaged. This can include people with low literacy or digital skills, or those with permanent or temporary impairments to their cognition, hearing, sight, speech, movement, etc.

RECRUITMENT BRIEF EXAMPLE

Table 3.2 is an example of a recruitment brief written to recruit participants for an imaginary online travel company. Tables 3.3, 3.4 and 3.5 detail the participants' characteristics that the brief is asking the recruitment agency to focus on. These characteristics aren't mutually exclusive. For instance, one of the frequent travellers may always book his or her train tickets online while the other may always buy tickets at the train station.

TABLE 3.2   Summary of logistics to include in a recruitment brief

Organization	The Online Train Ticket Vendor
Date of research	22 October
Location	Central User Research Lab The Street AW1 JHD
Number of participants needed	6
Length of session	45 minutes
Research session schedule	Participant 1: 10:00 – 10:45 Participant 2: 11:00 – 11:45 Participant 3: 12:00 – 12:45 Participant 4: 13:15 – 14:00 Participant 5: 14:15 – 15:00 Participant 6: 15:15 – 16:00
Incentive amount	X per participant

TABLE 3.3   Participants' characteristics included the recruitment brief

Who you want to talk to	Characteristics to include in the brief	Number of people to include in the research
You want to talk to people who travel by train. You want a mixture of those who travel frequently and infrequently. For this piece of research each type of traveller is equally important.	Frequent travellers (several times a week)	2 participants
	Occasional travellers (a couple of times a month)	2 participants
	Infrequent travellers (a couple of times a year)	2 participants

It can be useful to clarify who you don't want to talk to, ie those who don't currently travel by train or those who don't plan to travel by train in the future.

Recruitment screening

Screener questions Below is an example of a screener questionnaire for a group of possible participants. At this point you don't want to give too much away about the purpose of your research. We are trying to avoid potential participants guessing at the type of person you want to recruit and then skewing their answers. Obviously once they have been selected to participate

TABLE 3.4 The range of online experience wanted in the research participants

Who you want to talk to	Characteristics to include in the brief	Number of people to include in the research
Experienced and inexperienced in using the internet.	*Very confident online:* Does as many tasks online as possible Happy to try new things online	1 participants
	Confident online: Does most tasks online Sometimes reluctant to do new things online	3 participants
	Not confident online: Does some things online Reluctant to increase the number of tasks they do online	2 participants

TABLE 3.5 Mixture of travel booking habits wanted in the participants recruited

Who you want to talk to	Characteristics to include in the brief	Number of people to include in the research
Book travel online and offline.	Book all their travel online	1 participants
	Mixture of online and offline travel booking	3 participants
	Book all their travel offline	2 participants

you will share more details about the nature of the research (but not all the details, to avoid biasing the participants).

TOP TIP

- Be aware that you are asking people to self-assess their behaviour, which can be difficult, so provide clear descriptions of what you mean.
- Use neutral questions that give the potential participants options that will allow them to reflect their behaviours, rather than just the ones you are looking for.
- If you are working with a recruitment agency you won't necessarily need to include demographic questions as the agency may already have this some of data. If you are recruiting yourself, it is worth including some demographics to allow you to select an appropriate range of participants.

The questionnaire, which can be sent by email, put on a website or social media, done over the phone or face-to-face, has the following main elements (adapted from Lewes, 2015):

- introduction;
- logistics;
- demographics;
- behaviour;
- confidence levels;
- technology and devices usage;
- confidentiality and disclosures;
- accessibility.

INTRODUCTION

Here you introduce both you and the project to the participant. The introduction is your opportunity to explain to participants that the screener is to ascertain whether they are eligible to participate, and to make it clear that they may not be able to take part (Lewes, 2015).

LOGISTICS AND TIMINGS

Share location and schedule details. It is best to do this at the start, so that if participants aren't available on the specified days and times of the research they will have avoided completing all the other questions for no reason.

DEMOGRAPHICS AND BEHAVIOUR

These are the questions that will help you identify the type of user you require. The options you give at this point should include demographics and behaviours that you both *do* and *don't* want to include in your group of participants. Including options you are not currently interested in will help filter out people that are not appropriate for this research (this will become clearer when you read through the example screener below).

I totally agree with Lewes' (2015) suggestion that as a default you should screen out participants who work in the same industry as you/your client, or for competitor organizations, and those working on website or app design and usability. However, this will depend on the specific nature of the testing session or research.

CONFIDENCE LEVEL

This part of the screener asks potential participants to self-assess their levels of confidence related to the topic being researched. The example screener above uses digital confidence questions as the imaginary organization is an online travel booking company.

TECHNOLOGY AND DEVICES

Understanding what technology and devices participants use is useful for two main reasons. 1) If you intend to support multiple devices, you may want include the devices your participants are using in the research sessions. 2) This can be grouped with the information the potential participants have shared on their digital confidence to ensure there is a mix of experience levels, so that the outcomes of the testing aren't biased.

CONFIDENTIALITY AND DISCLOSURES

If participants are required to sign a non-disclosure document or similar, it makes sense to mention this at the screener stage. It is best practice to make sure participants are aware that they may be asked to sign something and – most important – why they are being asked to sign it (Lewes, 2015).

ACCESSIBILITY

If the research location is not fully accessible, this should be made clear at the start of the process, and alternative arrangements made to accommodate participants who have access needs that mean it's difficult to travel/get around. Include a question in all screeners to check whether participants require additional hardware or software in order to participate (Lewes, 2015).

Incentivizing people to take part

The easiest way to persuade people to take part in your research is to pay them. This persuasion is twofold: they will agree to be scheduled into the research and they will turn up on the day.

   The amount you should offer depends on the type of person you trying to recruit and the type of research you are doing. It will also depend on the country, culture and economy in which your research is taking place. If you are unsure about the amount of incentive to pay, contact research recruitment agencies in the area in which you intend to do your research and ask for some advice. These examples are UK-specific, as this is where the majority of my experience lies:

30 minutes	£30
45 minutes	£45
60 minutes	£60

The incentive amount will also depend on how long the session is. You should at least pay for travel expenses, where these are incurred. Participants will expect a higher amount in big cities than in small towns. People with well-paid or specialist jobs will expect a higher amount to give up some of their time, even if the user research is not related to their work. It sounds unfair to give different people different amounts and you may feel uncomfortable doing this, but it is worth noting that some groups place a higher value on their time, and incentive amounts usually reflect this so as to encourage the people you want to take part.

   If you are asking people to fill in an online survey you can incentivize using a prize draw for vouchers; for example, first prize: £50 voucher x 1, second prize: £20 voucher x 2. However, incentives shouldn't be related to the product, service or experience being researched. Beyond questions about the ethics of this, it will also affect the results of your research. If you are paying participants in vouchers to spend with your organization, they are likely to be more positively inclined to anything you show them.

Screener example

The titles of each section of the screener for our imaginary online train ticket company, above, don't correspond exactly to what has been discussed; they have been changed to be more appropriate and understandable for the potential participants, helping them to more quickly comprehend what will be asked of them in each section. People from all and any backgrounds and experience could be completing your question, so it is best to use plain English whenever possible. Table 3.6 shows how the screener sections and the topics we discussed relate to each other.

INTRODUCTION AND WELCOME
We are looking for people to take part in some research for a travel ticket vendor, which is seeking help in improving how it provides services.

TABLE 3.6   The headings for the recruitment screener and how potential participants correspond

Our topics	Screener sections
Introduction	Introduction and welcome
Logistics	Research details
Demographics	About you
Behaviour	How you book travel
Confidence levels	Online experience
Technology and device	Your technology and device
Accessibility	Your access needs
Confidentiality and disclosures	Confidentiality and disclosure

NOTE Demographic questions are mostly optional; only include those that are relevant to your research. There will be other questions that I have not included in the demographics that may be relevant to you. Below is the recruitment screener for the imaginary online travel company.

RESEARCH DETAILS

TABLE 3.7

Date of research	22 October
Location	Central User Research Lab The Street AW1 JHD
Length of session	45 minutes
Incentive	£45

WHAT SESSION TIMES ARE YOU AVAILABLE FOR?

TABLE 3.8

Time	Availability	
10:00 – 10:45	Yes	No
11:00 – 11:45	Yes	No
12:00 – 12:45	Yes	No
13:15 – 14:00	Yes	No
14:15 – 15:00	Yes	No
15:15 – 16:00	Yes	No

ABOUT YOU
Please tell us a bit about yourself.

TABLE 3.9

Age	Under 18 years 18 to 24 years 25 to 34 years 35 to 44 years 45 to 54 years 55 to 64 years 65 or older

(continued)

TABLE 3.9 (Continued)

Gender	Woman Man Transgender woman Transgender man Non-binary Pangender Prefer not to say
Education	No formal qualifications GSCEs BTEC GNVQ/NVQ AS Levels A Levels Bachelor's degree Master's degree Doctorate Training through apprenticeship Trade/technical/vocational training Other (please specify)
Marital status	Single (never married) Cohabiting Married Civil partnership Separated Widowed Divorced
Are you a parent or guardian?	No children 1 child 2 children 3 children 4 or more children
Ethnicity	**White** British/Irish/Gypsy or Traveller Other White background, please describe **Mixed/Multiple ethnic group** White and Black Caribbean White and Black African White and Asian Other Mixed/Multiple ethnic background please describe **Asian/Asian British** Indian Pakistani Bangladeshi Chinese Other Asian background, please describe

(continued)

TABLE 3.9 (Continued)

	Black/African/Caribbean/Black British African Caribbean Other Black/African/Caribbean background, please describe **Other Ethnic Group** Please describe
Employment status	Employed full time Employed part time Self-employed Out of work and looking for work Out of work but not currently looking for work A homemaker A student Military Retired Unable to work Volunteer
[If relevant] Job title	[Open text field or specify particular industries]

(For further discussion on inclusivity and diversity when designing forms to capture information, see Fonseca, 2017. Our understanding and language are constantly evolving in these areas.)

HOW YOU TRAVEL

Please tell us your preferred modes of transport.

TABLE 3.10

Transport	Frequency
Car	Frequent traveller (several times a week) Occasional traveller (a couple of times a month) Infrequent traveller (a couple of times a year) I never travel this way, and don't intend to I currently don't travel this way but intend to in the future
Motorbike/ scooter	Frequent traveller (several times a week) Occasional traveller (a couple of times a month) Infrequent traveller (a couple of times a year) I never travel this way, and don't intend to I currently don't travel this way but intend to in the future

(continued)

TABLE 3.10 (Continued)

Transport	Frequency
Bicycle	Frequent traveller (several times a week) Occasional traveller (a couple of times a month) Infrequent traveller (a couple of times a year) I never travel this way, and don't intend to I currently don't travel this way but intend to in the future
Bus	Frequent traveller (several times a week) Occasional traveller (a couple of times a month) Infrequent traveller (a couple of times a year) I never travel this way, and don't intend to I currently don't travel this way but intend to in the future
Train	Frequent traveller (several times a week) Occasional traveller (a couple of times a month) Infrequent traveller (a couple of times a year) I never travel this way, and don't intend to I currently don't travel this way but intend to in the future
Tube	Frequent traveller (several times a week) Occasional traveller (a couple of times a month) Infrequent traveller (a couple of times a year) I never travel this way, and don't intend to I currently don't travel this way but intend to in the future
Tram	Frequent traveller (several times a week) Occasional traveller (a couple of times a month) Infrequent traveller (a couple of times a year) I never travel this way, and don't intend to I currently don't travel this way but intend to in the future
Taxi/Uber/cab	Frequent traveller (several times a week) Occasional traveller (a couple of times a month) Infrequent traveller (a couple of times a year) I never travel this way, and don't intend to I currently don't travel this way but intend to in the future
Flying	Frequent traveller (several times a week) Occasional traveller (a couple of times a month) Infrequent traveller (a couple of times a year) I never travel this way, and don't intend to I currently don't travel this way but intend to in the future

HOW YOU BOOK YOUR TRAVEL

Please tell us how you prefer to book your travel.

TABLE 3.11

I book all my travel online (or as much as I possibly can)	Websites Apps
I book some of my travel online and some offline	Websites Apps Ticket machines Ticket counters Travel agents in person Travel agents over the phone Inspectors on the transport
I book all travel offline	Ticket machines Ticket counters Travel agents in person Travel agents over the phone Inspectors on the transport

ONLINE EXPERIENCE
How do you prefer to do things online?

TABLE 3.12

What kind of things do you things do you *tend to do* online?	Shopping Booking Banking Watching TV/film/videos Social media Administrative tasks Email (corresponding) Listening to music Research Other; please specify
What things do you prefer *not to do* online?	Shopping Booking Banking Watching TV/film/videos Networking Administrative tasks Corresponding Listening music Research Other; please specify

YOUR TECHNOLOGY AND DEVICES

TABLE 3.13

What devices to do you use to go online?	PC Desktop
	iMac Desktop
	Laptop
	MacBook
	iPad
	Tablet
	Smartphone
	iPhone
	Smart TV
	Smartwatch
	None of the above
	Other; please specify

YOUR ACCESS NEEDS

Please tell us if you will have any access needs once you have arrived at the venue, for example wheelchair access or assistance with stairs. Please tell us if you use any assistive technology, for example, a screen reader.

CONFIDENTIALITY AND DISCLOSURES

You will be asked to sign a non-disclosure agreement if selected to take part in this research.

NEXT STEPS

If you are eligible to take part in this research you will be contacted by one of our recruiters by (date).

If you are creating a recruitment screener, you can take this example and adapt it. If you are asking a recruitment agency to draft the screener, you can use your newfound knowledge to review what it has done.

Understanding the importance of observation

What people say and what people do are two different things

If you are looking to understand how people behave you can include a much smaller number of people in your research. Behaviour in the context of services and products (digital or not) is often about how people undertake and complete tasks; groups of people with a similar background and motivations for doing something are usually quite consistent.

We all like to think we are very different and unpredictable as people. This is simply not true. We all have a lot of learnt behaviour, shared cultural and societal understandings of how things work on both a macro (society) and micro (families, individuals) level. As you drill down (moving towards the micro level), smaller groups (user groups) that have been segmented in the right way will have similar/shared experiences and therefore understanding of how things work. Designers will already know this. This shared understanding is why we have design patterns for how to build things.

> Opinion varies much more widely between people (compared with behaviour) and also within one person over time. Therefore, you need to ask more people when considering opinions.

If you are doing usability testing, after a few sessions observing people doing the same tasks you will start to see a lot of repetition in how people behave and how they get tasks done. However, there might be quite a lot of variation in how they feel about it and what they think of the experience. Some of the difficulty with opinion is that people aren't always willing to tell you what they actually think or they don't really know what they think. I have often heard in user research, when asking people what they think, something along the lines of: 'Most people will struggle to buy gloves from this website and they won't like it, but I found it easy and enjoyed it because I am an internet expert.' The truth is most of the time we don't really know what other people think.

Self-reporting is difficult as people find it hard to be objective when analysing themselves and their behaviour. You are also relying on people to tell the truth and be honest about who they are, when filling in a survey, for example. Online surveys in particular are completed by a self-selecting group of people who aren't necessarily going to be representative of a group as a whole.

When collecting preference data, you must take human nature into account. When talking about past behaviour, users' self-reported data is typically three steps removed from the truth (Nielsen, 2001):

- In answering questions (particularly in a focus group), people bend the truth to be closer to what they think you want to hear or what's socially acceptable in the group.

- In telling you what they do, people are really telling you what they remember doing. Human memory is fallible, especially regarding the small details. Users cannot remember some details at all.

- In reporting what they do remember, people rationalize their behaviour, explaining away mistakes, or take responsibility for something that isn't their fault.

TOP TIPS

When you are asking for people's opinions, make sure you are asking the right kind of questions so as to avoid gathering biased or poor quality data.

CASE STUDY
The difference between behaviour and opinion

When I was a consultant, I worked closely with the UK Houses of Parliament. What parliament does and the content of its website is fascinating; if you're interested you can find out more at www.parliament.uk.

I was observing a participant complete a task on the UK Parliament website during a usability testing session. I watched her complete various tasks and noted down when and where she struggled and what she did to successfully complete all the tasks. Some tasks were easier to complete than others, as is often the case. The participant was talking to me as she went along and I was asking appropriate, timely questions. At the end of the session I asked her to reflect on her overall experience of doing various tasks on the website. She told me it was a really terrible website, extremely difficult to use or find anything, and went on to tell me how much she hated the Prime Minister and all the awful things he had done in his tenure.

I am highlighting another extreme example to demonstrate my point. This participant could not separate her feelings for the Prime Minister and his politics from her experience of the website. If I had not observed her using the website and just surveyed her opinions, I would have got a very biased and inaccurate view of what her experience was. This perfectly illustrates the importance of observation and not just listening to what participants say.

This example is contrary to the normal: often people are too polite and can feel uncomfortable criticizing. They will say that something is fine to use and they like it, when you have observed them struggle and fail to complete tasks.

Here's another point to consider: sometimes it is obvious to participants when they have correctly completed a task, sometimes it is not. This will also affect their opinions and views on what they have done. If they don't know exactly what success looks like, for example it's not as clear cut as 'buy a pair of gloves from this website', they may not know they have failed the task and may feel they've had a very positive experience.

A final thought: if people can't be objective about what they have just done, don't ask them to predict what they might do in the future! Users don't know what they want. Many of you will already know the infamous Henry Ford quote about cars and horses (Nielsen, 2001).

Asking the right kind of questions

Whatever research method you decide to use, a key component of good quality results is asking the right questions.

The first rule is to be inclusive

Avoid jargon and technical words. Use as much plain English as possible. If you do need to use technical words, be sure to explain exactly what they mean: don't assume people will understand what you are talking about. If you don't, two things could happen: 1) they may ask you to explain, which is fine, but doesn't necessarily help the participants feel at ease during the research; or 2) they will not ask you to explain and they will simply guess or make up answers to a question they haven't fully understood; giving you inaccurate data. Even when doing research with technical and expert audiences you need to establish a shared understanding of terminology. Keep in mind that even among experts there is a range of knowledge, experience and 'expertise'.

Using plain English will help you be inclusive. Using clear, simple language not only helps people understand you but also makes them feel more comfortable and included in whatever is going on during the research session.

The second rule is use neutral open-ended questions in exploratory research

There are times when closed questions with yes/no type answers are necessary and valid. However, if you are doing any kind of exploratory research, interviews, usability testing, etc, you'll want to use open-ended questions as much as possible. By 'open-ended' I mean questions that don't assume a certain answer and don't elicit one-word answers.

There is definitely good and bad practice when it comes to question format. A very simple example to demonstrate this is the question, 'Do you like this?' It might seem like a perfectly reasonable question to ask people when you are showing them an example of your product/service, but it will influence the participants to give a positive or at least less negative answer than they may have given naturally. People essentially don't want to hurt other people's feelings, so they will worry about telling you that they don't like what you are offering.

Such a simple question could elicit a yes or no answer with no elaboration. To create open-ended neutral questions, you need to give respondents options and avoid influencing them. We are all much more susceptible to being influenced then we like to think, so I would try to make preference questions more balanced; for example: 'What, if anything, do you like about this?' I would always follow this up, for balance, with: 'What, if anything, do you dislike about this?' Asking if someone likes something may seem innocuous on the surface, but subconsciously it can influence them. Simply adding 'if anything' to 'do you like about this', gives the respondents a get out clause to say they did not like it.

If you can, avoid using positive and negative words altogether, but I know this often isn't possible or appropriate. Some examples are:

> What is your experience of xxx?
> How did you find doing xxx?
> Do you feel this is something that is designed for you, or is it not relevant to you?

When you first start writing your questions, for whatever research you are doing, practise asking them and see what responses you get. This will help you refine your questions to be most effective. It's worth spending time formulating your questions in the most neutral way possible.

EXAMPLE

Imagine you have just asked a participant to read some content. You want to know if the content is written clearly (see Chapter 8 for more on this) but for now we'll keep it simple, by considering the three questions below and their connotations:

1 *Do you understand (the content)?* This question subtly assumes that the participant has understood the content, and is likely to get a yes or no

answer. Without further questioning you cannot know for sure that this is the case or why.

2 *What do you understand about (this content)?* This way of phrasing the question still subtly assumes that the participant has some kind of understanding of the content, which may not be the case. However, asking the question in this way encourages the participant to describe what has been understood.

3 *What does (this content) mean to you? How would you describe it to a friend?* This way of phrasing the question is most neutral. It does not make any suggestion as to whether the participant has 'understood' anything; it simply asks how they would describe what it means to them. During analysis, you will be able to identify how well participants have understood the question.

The third rule is avoid key words

Another useful technique for avoiding influencing the results of your research is to limit the use of key words in your questions and tasks. This can be applied to anything you may be researching. The easiest way to explain it is with an example.

SCENARIO
Figure 3.1 is a screenshot of the home page of a charity website that I have made up, named 'Support Charity'. Let's imagine that you are doing some usability testing on this website. You think there are some problems with finding and signing up to events and activities that raise funds for the charity; Figure 3.2 shows the events landing page.

To explore how participants find and sign up to take part in an event, you can set them an open-ended task. You could phrase it as follows:

Option 1 Please imagine that you want to get involved with raising money for Support Charity by taking part in a sports event. You want to look for when and where an event is happening in your area.

Option 2 Please imagine that you want to do a sports activity to raise money for Support Charity. You want to find out when and where something is happening that is local to you.

There are differences in the language used but it is the same task. Let's look at why the differences are important. Option 1 uses key words and option 2 doesn't (here, by 'key words' I mean words that are used as navigation labels

FIGURE 3.1 Support Charity website homepage

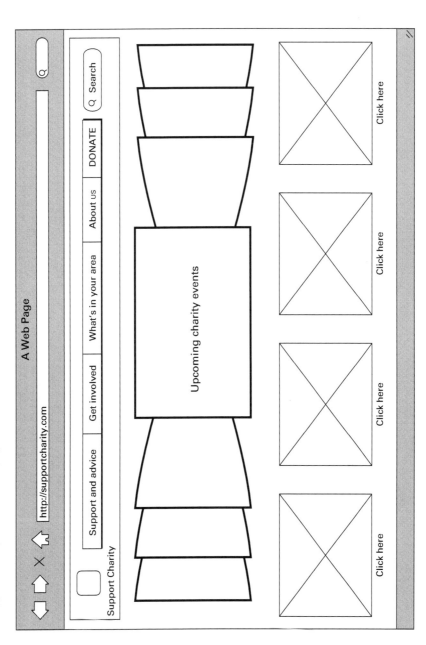

FIGURE 3.2 Support Charity website events page

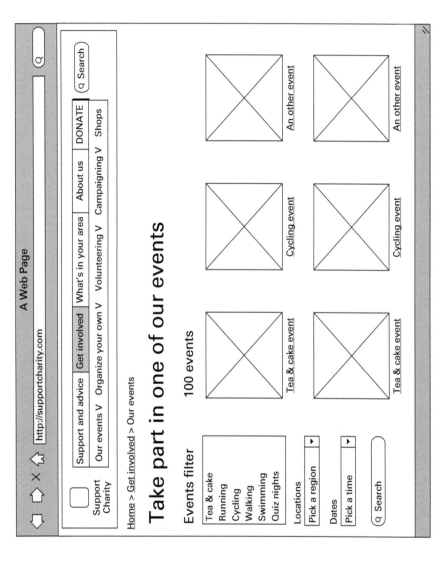

FIGURE 3.3 Step 1 in completing the task

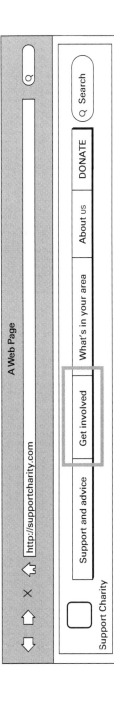

FIGURE 3.4 Step 2 in completing the task

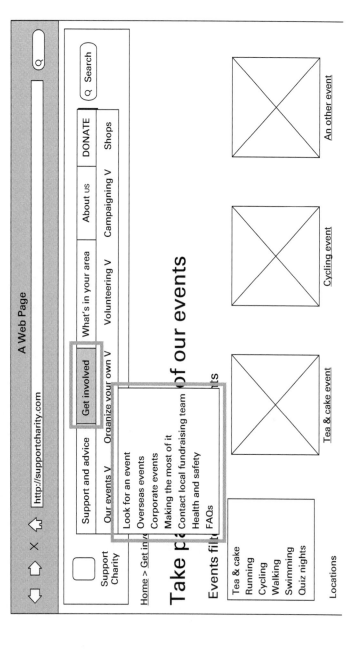

FIGURE 3.5   Step 3 in completing the task

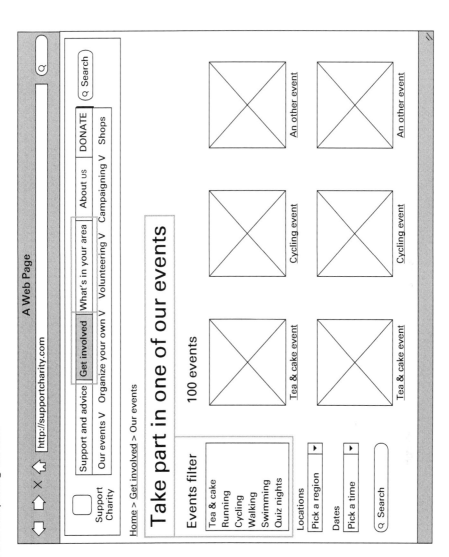

on the website itself). Figures 3.3 to 3.5 show the three steps you could take to get to all the fundraising sports events:

1 Click on 'Get involved' on the main navigation of the homepage (Figure 3.3).
2 Click on 'Events' and 'Look for an event' in the second-level navigation dropdown menu (Figure 3.4).
3 You would then look for a sports event in your area (Figure 3.5).

Let's look back at Option 1: 'Please imagine that you want to *get involved* with raising money for Support Charity by *taking part* in a sports *event*. You want to look for when and where an *event* is happening *in your area*.' I have highlighted all the *key words* that can be found in the task. The effect of including the keywords in this example is twofold: 1) when participants are looking round the website, working out how they are going to complete this task, they will spot the key words quickly and focus on clicking these to get to the next step in the task: 'Get involved', 'Look for an event', 'Take part in one of our events', 'Filter events'. This means they could complete the task more quickly and easily than if they were doing it at home on their own. 2) You may inadvertently take them off track in a way they may not have done on their own, by mentioning '*in your area*', which has a different function on this website. They may notice it because it is mentioned in the task and start to explore this instead. Of course, they may have done this anyway, but we want to avoid being the cause of an effect.

Option 2, 'Please imagine that you want to do a sports activity to raise money for Support Charity. You want to find out when and where something is happening that is local to you' – this doesn't contain any of the key words and therefore leaves the participants to their own devices to work out how they want to do the task, avoiding potential false positives and false negatives.

This is a digital example, but the same rules could apply to non-digital things such as paper forms. If you are trying to find out where people are struggling to complete a form, avoid using any key words on it.

The fourth rule is know when to break some of the rules

The Dalai Lama XIV has been reported as saying something along the lines of, 'Learn the rules so you know how to break them properly.' It sounds like something a wise person might say. Once you are familiar and comfortable with these rules, you will understand when you need to break them. It's important that you make a note of when you have 'broken the rules' and in what way you needed to break them as this will have to be considered during your analysis.

SCENARIO 1: THE NON-RESPONSIVE PARTICIPANT

No doubt if you do enough research you will meet some participants who aren't willing to say much. Some do not naturally elaborate on their answers. They may have a wealth of insight to offer you, but they don't know how to express it. It takes a lot of skill and practice to get to their answers; sometimes you will have to ask direct, leading questions. Here's a very simple example:

Question: Tell me about your experience of buying train tickets from the Imaginary Train Companies app.

Answer: It was fine.

Follow up question: Was there anything you found difficult about it?

Answer: It took a few attempts to enter my credit card details; that was frustrating.

Follow up question: What did you think was good about it?

Answer: Choosing the right train times was easy.

You can see from this very simple exchange that leading questions were used to get some insight about the participant's experience that would have not been obtained otherwise.

SCENARIO 2: USABILITY TESTING INTERVENTION

If a participant is really struggling with something it may cause them a lot of distress and frustration. If it is not appropriate to stop the research session at this point, for the wellbeing of the participant you may need to assist them in the task, to allow them to progress (this is discussed further in Chapter 7 on usability testing).

SCENARIO 3: SURVEYS

Surveys are different and benefit from using closed questions; they still have to be well crafted questions (we'll cover this in more depth in Chapter 10). You can give people options with closed questions; for example, to say whether they agree or disagree with a statement, such as: 'Here is a statement about our service. How much do you agree or disagree with this statement?' (see Table 3.14). Whichever technique you use, always give participants the opportunity to express themselves in the way they want.

TABLE 3.14

Strongly agree	Agree	Neutral	Disagree	Strongly disagree	Not applicable

Accessibility and inclusion

I have already mentioned that your products/services are unlikely to be for everyone – but you do need to be as inclusive as possible with your intended audiences. Even in a specified group of people there will be a lot of diversity and a wide range of human capability, so you'll want to be thinking about accessibility and inclusion from the beginning. I'm not going to cover accessibility and inclusion fully here as they deserve their own book to do them justice, but I can give you just enough information to get started. Making your offering accessible can take on several different meanings, so here is a brief overview of what you can do.

Automated accessibility testing

There is a variety of automated tools that can be used while designing, developing and improving your product, to help you check how accessible it is. W3C (2017) has a helpful list of web accessibility evaluations tools; using them will identify 20–30 per cent of the issues (Government Digital Service, 2017).

Manual accessibility testing

During the development cycle designers and developers can use assistive technologies (eg, screen readers, screen magnifiers and speech recognition software) to see if what they are building is compatible with them. You may need to purchase some assistive digital technologies; doing so is a worthwhile investment. Other accessibility considerations include:

- Allowing people to change the colour contrast of your digital item to suit their needs.
- The size of targets, such as buttons and check boxes, used to select items. Can these be used by people with a motor impairment?
- Can your digital item be used with a keyboard only, without a mouse?

Getting specialists to audit your work

You can get your digital products/services audited by technical accessibility specialists, and you should do so as early as possible in your work. The later you leave it the harder any problems will be to fix (Government Digital Service, 2017). Specialists will be able to review the full range of potential problems for visual, hearing, cognitive and motor impairments. This will uncover a lot of issues and it is always worthwhile investing time and money; however, these specialists are experts and do not replace the users themselves.

Usability testing with assistive technologies

As with all kinds of user research, you need to include the users themselves in the process. Usability testing your digital offer with users of assistive technology is a great way to uncover issues. It's a good idea to not only test with a range of assistive technologies but also a range of experience with those technologies: a user new to a certain assistive tool will experience different problems to those who have been using it for a long time.

Inclusion

Inclusion isn't just about 'technical digital accessibility'. If we're going to think about the full range of human capability we need to think about literacy and (digital) skill levels as well as temporary and permanent impairment.

When developing or improving your offering, consider how you can support those with low literacy and digital skills (or whatever skills are applicable for your product/service). Making accessible products and services isn't just about coding, screen readers and choosing the right colour palette: inclusion can take many forms. Use plain English, and clear and descriptive content that works for a range of abilities (see more in Chapter 8 on content testing). Clarity is important for everyone, whether they are just learning to read or are highly educated. As someone with dyslexia, I can very much appreciate this.

For digital, you may need to consider how you can meet the needs of those who do not have easy access to a computer or have low digital capability. If you have a multi-channel approach to your work, you may want to do some research to understand if each channel has the same quality of experience to help users achieve what they want and need to do. Those with low literacy and digital skills will experience different issues and barriers to using your product than an expert user: getting the balance right for supporting both ends of the spectrum is hard work but worth the effort.

References and further reading

Cunningham, K (2012) *Accessibility Handbook*, O'Reilly Media, Sebastopol

Digital Accessibility Centre (2017) http://digitalaccessibilitycentre.org/ (archived at https://perma.cc/A3Q4-YNH9)

Featherstone, D (October 2015) UX foundations: accessibility course. Lynda.com. www.lynda.com/Accessibility-tutorials/Accessibility-user-research/435008/446206-4.html (archived at https://perma.cc/2BDC-5P7S)

Fonseca, S (25 April 2017) Designing forms for gender diversity and inclusion. uxdesign.cc. https://uxdesign.cc/designing-forms-for-gender-diversity-and-inclusion-d8194cf1f51 (archived at https://perma.cc/FXJ6-TUWB) (last accessed 11 July 2017)

Government Digital Service (August 2016) Assisted digital support: an introduction. Service Manual. www.gov.uk/service-manual/helping-people-to-use-your-service/assisted-digital-support-introduction (archived at https://perma.cc/D7EV-8Q99), and Understanding users who don't use digital services. Service Manual. www.gov.uk/service-manual/user-research/understanding-users-who-dont-use-digital-services (archived at https://perma.cc/8FR8-VDTU) (last accessed 26 August 2017)

Government Digital Service (2017a) Digital Inclusion Blog. https://digitalinclusion.blog.gov.uk/ (archived at https://perma.cc/R9NQ-7KFX) and Accessibility Blog. www.accessibility.blog.gov.uk/ (archived at https://perma.cc/P7B6-EAJR)

Government Digital Service (2017b) Making your service accessible: an introduction. Service Manual. www.gov.uk/service-manual/helping-people-to-use-your-service/making-your-service-accessible-an-introduction (archived at https://perma.cc/2RWJ-D6Z9)

Henke, A (27 March 2017b) How users change colours on websites. Government Digital Services Accessibility Blog. https://accessibility.blog.gov.uk/2017/03/27/how-users-change-colours-on-websites/ (archived at https://perma.cc/Q2HF-RLDR)

Horton, S and Sloan, D (March 2014) Accessibility in practice: a process-driven approach to accessibility. Paciello Group. www.paciellogroup.com/blog/2014/03/accessibility-practice-process-driven-approach-accessibility/ (archived at https://perma.cc/8PM5-KX4X)

Horton, S and Quesenbery, W (2014) *A Web for Everyone: Designing accessible user experiences*, Rosenfeld Media, New York

Hurt, S (12 February 2015) How we recruited people with low/no digital skills on carers allowance. GDS User Research Blog. https://userresearch.blog.gov. uk/2015/02/13/how-we-recruited-people-with-lowno-digital-skills-on-carers-allowance/ (archived at https://perma.cc/LC59-B2VG) (last accessed 26 August 2017)

Kalbag, L (September 2017) *Accessibility for Everyone. A book apart.* https:// abookapart.com/products/accessibility-for-everyone (archived at https://perma. cc/5ULR-63G5)

Lazar J, Goldstein, D and Taylor, A (2015) *Ensuring Digital Accessibility through Process and Policy,* O'Reilly Media, Sebastopol

Lewes, J (May 2015) Top tips for writing an effective participant recruitment screener – Part One. People for Research Blog. www.peopleforresearch.co.uk/ blog/2015/05/top-tips-for-writing-an-effective-participant-recruitment-screener-part-1/ (archived at https://perma.cc/AGJ5-G3HV) (last accessed 8 July 2017)

Nielsen, J (5 August 2001) First rule of usability? Don't listen to users. Nielsen Norman Group. www.nngroup.com/articles/first-rule-of-usability-dont-listen-to-users/ (archived at https://perma.cc/4J2E-JJNC)

Solis, B (29 May 2014) The limitation of demographics. Social Media Today. www. socialmediatoday.com/content/connected-customers-are-invisible-those-who-value-demographics (archived at https://perma.cc/FZ5E-K872) (last accessed 8 July 2017)

Survey Monkey Inc (2017) Consent form. www.surveymonkey.com/r/consent (archived at https://perma.cc/64F6-V43T) (last accessed 8 July 2017)

W3C (2017) Accessibility. www.w3.org/standards/webdesign/accessibility (archived at https://perma.cc/TX28-K8QZ)

04

Getting the legal and ethical stuff right

Do not skip this section!

Since the first edition of this book was published in March 2018, new data protection laws have come into effect in many parts of the world, such as the General Data Protection Regulation (GDPR) that protects citizens of the EU and UK, and the California Consumer Protection Act (CCPA). You may be in a part of the world that doesn't have the same kind of data protection legislation, but I would recommend taking on data protection practices as they are also part of ethical practices in research and practical habits such as making sure data is findable in case you ever need to delete it. Some international organizations have adopted such laws as GDPR as a global standard; this has been done where I currently work (in 2021), Springer Nature.

Let's start with a few definitions.

What is data protection?

Data protection is the fair and proper use of information about people. It's part of the fundamental right to privacy. Good practices in data protection are vital to ensure public trust in data use in both the public and private sectors (Information Commissioner's Office, 2020). GDPR, for example, isn't a set of strict prescriptive rules, but it's about using principles to assess data protection risks (Information Commissioner's Office, 2020).

In essence, personal data should be kept:

- accurate and up to date;
- secured;

- transparent about how it's going to be used;
- restricted to the minimum needed to do the job (Buckbee, 2020).

It is inevitable that you will collect (and create) personal data in the course of doing user research. You'll collect, for example, by capturing details about the participant in order to understand if they are suitable to take part in the research. And you'll create personal data by recording the participant during a research session and in order to store that personal data you will then need their informed consent.

What is personal data?

Anything that identifies a person. It can be an obvious, single piece of information such as a person's name. Personally identifying information can also be cumulative. Cumulative personal data is when several pieces of information are combined to identify a person. For example, combining such information as listed below, it could be possible to identify someone if they have a specialist job:

- job title;
- organization;
- location.

What is a data processor?

The data processor is often referred to in data protection content and contracts you/your organization may sign with suppliers. Data processors are organizations or persons (not you or your organization) that process data on your behalf as agreed between you, complying with data protection laws.

What is a data controller?

Data protection content also often talks about data controllers – generally, that is you on behalf of your/an organization. A data controller decides why and how data will be collected and is responsible for complying with data protection laws. It's best to consider everyone responsible for taking care of data.

Practical things to do

You'll need to consider how you handle data throughout the research process, including collecting, recording, storing, using, analysing, combining, disclosing or deleting it (Information Commissioner's Office, 2020).

TOP TIPS

Here are some practical tips:

- Only collect the personal information that you really need.
- Store it in a consistent place – it also needs to be secure and only accessible to those who need it. Ideally in the cloud, and not on a laptop that could potentially be stolen.
- Set restrictions for internal users who can view research data files but not download, print or copy the files.
- Make sure that anyone who is collecting personal data about participants knows where to store it.
- Have consistent naming conventions for user research files – this will make them easy to find when they are needed, either for research purposes or if a participant requests that their data be deleted.
- Have a policy about when you will delete data, for example, if the participant hasn't signed a consent form or after not being used for three years etc.
- If using internal data, only contact people to invite them to research if you have permission to contact them. If you don't, collaborate with colleagues who do have permission to contact them on your behalf.
- Work with your legal and data protection teams to make sure you are using tools that comply with your organization's policies for data protection and security.
- It's useful to have templates (eg research session schedules) to keep data in a consistent way each time you do user research.
- If you are 'cold' calling or emailing someone to recruit them for your research, explain clearly where you got their contact details and why you are contacting them; what is it about their expertise, for example, that means it will be useful for them to take part in your research.

When things get complex:

- If you have included clips of audio or video (for example) in presentations, then these clips will need to be deleted if a person has requested it; you need to be able to track and trace each piece of data. This is where consistent storage places and naming conventions really are invaluable.

Informed consent

Informed consent is key to collecting data and retaining that data for a certain amount of time. Consent is participants giving you permission to collect and use data about them.

For consent to be informed, participants must understand:

- Who is doing the research.
- The purpose of the research.
- What data you're collecting.
- What will happen during the research.
- How will you use and share the results of the research, for example, with people in your organization or people outside your organization?
- Participation is voluntary – they can withdraw consent at any time before or after the session.
- How long their data will be kept.

You must also let participants know:

- Whether the session is being observed.
- That the session is being recorded.

For participants to be able to give informed consent the information must be shared with the participant in a clear and understandable way. If they don't understand the information they cannot give informed consent.

Other informed consent considerations

People who are aged 16 and older can give their consent. If the participant is considered an adult, then they need to give consent themselves and not by proxy. In the UK, for participants under 13 years old, you'll need their parent or guardian to give consent; in other countries it's often under 16 years old, but you'll need to double-check with local regulations (Information Commissioner's Office, 2021; Buckbee, 2020).

You can get people to read and sign their consent form at the beginning of a research session, but this takes up valuable research time in the session, so, if possible, send it to them digitally a few days before. This will give them time to read it and sign it or ask any clarifying questions first.

You can use services such as DocuSign or HelloSign that allow for digital signatures. These tend to work with PDFs. If you are doing research with people who have vision access needs, for example, where PDFs aren't appropriate, you'll need to find an alternative. I've seen effective examples of consent forms using survey tools. In these circumstances, it may be best to ask the participant what their preference is.

If you are doing international research in different languages, it's useful to have material on consent translated into those languages.

In the organization I work for currently, Springer Nature, we have a policy for a consent form to be signed before a research session takes place. These are stored in a consistent place. In moderated sessions, we also confirm verbally at the beginning that participants have understood the content and give them an opportunity to ask questions.

Different ways to ask for consent

There are a variety of ways that you can obtain informed consent from participants:

- Remote or face-to-face research: digital forms or paper forms.
- Pop-up research: survey consent forms, digital form that allows multiple simultaneous signatures (both available through services such as DocuSign and HelloSign) or paper forms.
- Research with deaf people: video in BSL (or ASL etc). For an example read about how the service design agency Snook went about it: https://wearesnook.com/inclusive-design-learnings/
- Research with visually impaired people or those who have difficulty reading: consider using a video or audio consent form.

These are just a few examples and there are many other ways to ask for consent, depending on the kind of research you are doing.

You may have a fair amount of information that you need the participants to know before taking part in the session so it's important to consider how you present this information to make it easy to understand. This may mean breaking the information down into small chunks, perhaps more than one document; you may want to consider if you can use images, icons, etc, to better signpost information. You may also want to separate user research terms and conditions from the consent form itself to make it less overwhelming and more easily digestible.

Consent information includes terms and conditions. These are a contract between participants and you or your organization if you represent one and therefore protect both parties. They contain details that are always true of user research, for example:

- Participants must be over 16 or 18, depending on whether there are any location restrictions.

- Any restrictions such as not allowing agencies or third parties to take part in unmoderated remote research.

- Anything unacceptable from the participant, which means the research would be stopped and the incentive not paid. For example, offensive behaviour, language constraints, too much background noise, false representation of knowledge, skills, or other characteristics that would make them suitable for the research.

- Information about confidentiality and nondisclosure.

- Legal and compliance information about incentives.

- Privacy policy content or a link to the organization's privacy policy.

- Data protection information (eg storage of data).

- Any necessary exemptions.

Don't worry if you are unsure of some or a lot of the details of this kind of information. Speak to your legal, data protection, and compliance teams to get the information you need – they are the experts. For organizations not experienced in doing user research, there is plenty of supportive content out there to help you and your teams to figure out the content you need.

*

When you don't need a consent form

The consent form is used to obtain users' consent when collecting personal data. There are certain kinds of research where you don't need to collect personal information and therefore you don't need participants to sign a consent form for you to store that data. This tends to be unmoderated research, where participants voluntarily take part in short sessions, without an incentive. For example:

- short surveys (not collecting any personal data);
- first click, first impression tests;
- card sorting;
- tree testing;
- very short usability testing tasks captured by screen recording only (not video and audio recordings of people's faces or voices).

If you want to incentivize unmoderated research whether individually or through prize draws you'll need to collect at minimum contact details (usually an email address). You don't necessarily have to ask them to sign a consent form, but you do need to provide a data privacy statement of how you intend to securely store and use their data.

As part of the research planning process, you will need to write your statement of data collection, storage and processing. It is helpful to put in a little context on what is going to happen during the research session. At the beginning of the research session, read this statement out. It is worth reading it out every time you do a research session, so that everyone will have the chance to get the same understanding. Doing this at the beginning of the research can help reassure people and help them settle in. Other things you need to tell people during an interactive session include:

- your name, role and who you work for;
- why you're doing the research (the basics only);
- what you're going to ask them to do (again, only the basics);
- whether the session is being observed (and who's watching).

Make sure the consent information is in plain English so it is easy to understand.

In the box below is an example of 'consent explanation' for research where you are interacting with people.

CONSENT INFORMATION SAMPLE

First off, thanks for agreeing to help us out. Today we are going to be looking/ doing [xxx]. I'll be asking you to [xxx] and answer some questions along the way. This isn't a test so relax as you can't get it wrong! Please let me know if you want to stop and take a break at any point, or if there is anything that you really don't want to talk about. This session will last no longer than [xx] minutes.

I will be recording the session, by using [xxx] to help me with my note-taking but any information you provide will be kept confidential, so don't be afraid to speak openly to me. Just so you know, there may be people [from xxx] observing in another room, but you won't see or hear them.

May I remind you that everything you see in this session is confidential, so by agreeing to the terms on our consent form you agree not to discuss it with anyone after this session. This works both ways – we also protect your anonymity and will not discuss anything that may identify you.

Any data collected will be stored [on/in] a secure [server/computer/ cupboard]. The data will be shared with [the project team/etc] only for the purpose of [xxx]. The data will be held only for a period of xx months, after which it will be destroyed.

I have a consent form for you to read and agree to before we can continue. I appreciate that you are doing this on a voluntary basis and you can withdraw your consent at any time. Please let me know if you have any questions.

TOP TIPS

- If someone does not give consent before or at the beginning, the session needs to be terminated.
- If someone withdraws consent, you need to stop the session immediately and ensure that you destroy/delete any data that has been collected. You should not use this partially collected data in the research analysis.
- Keep the consent form for as long as you are using and storing the information.

Example explanation for online surveys and other unmoderated research

If the research is in the form of an online survey that asks participants to share personal data or some other kind of unmoderated research where the participants' image and voice are recorded as part of the process you will need to ask for consent. It can be disruptive to the research process if you require the participant to sign a consent form in one tool and do their survey or tasks in another tool. In these situations, it's advisable to include the consent wording and a way to acknowledge that the participant does consent. It could be the first question in your survey or the first task in your unmoderated research. This will limit the number of barriers for people completing your research.

You need to be able to prove consent was given for data to be collected and used (Buckbee, 2020), so it's a good idea to get it in writing and store the information somewhere consistent and secure. You need to document what you're doing to comply with GDPR and be able to prove that in cases where it's not self-evident. Keep a record of GDPR training, procedures, steps taken, etc (Buckbee, 2020).

This is not exhaustive in terms of data protection but should be a good start. In the event of a data breach, you will need to do further reading to find out what you'll need to do.

Finding your participants in an ethical, legal way

Chapter 3 gives an example of creating a recruitment brief to send to a recruitment agency. Experienced and high-quality research recruitment agencies will have their own policies and procedures for data protection of participants' personal information.

Working with (and paying) an agency isn't the only way to recruit research participants. There are many potential sources for such data internal to your organization, for example customer services, sales team, marketing teams, subscriber lists to name a few. The important thing to understand is, do you have permission to contact them? It will depend on what these people have signed up to with your organization. Have they given agreement to only be contacted in specific circumstances, or to generally be contacted by your organization? The agreement will determine whether you can contact them or not. It may be that you can contact them yourselves, or the team that holds the data can contact people on your behalf, or you may not contact them at all. It's entirely possible that each department that holds people's data has a different agreement in place, so don't assume because you can contact one department's list that you'll be able to contact others.

You can recruit directly by using intercepts such as pop-up surveys on your digital products and services. If you are recruiting for unmoderated research which doesn't capture personal information and doesn't offer an incentive you will not need to display a data privacy statement or ask for informed consent. If you are recruiting for any other kind of research that requires you to capture personal data then you will need to incorporate data privacy and informed consent into the recruitment process.

Over time, as you continue to do user research, it may be worth building up your own participant database, where you can securely keep the details of people who are in your target audience groups and have consented for you to hold their data and contact them to invite them to research that is relevant to them. For advice on building your own participant database see Lamb (2020).

Ethics in user research

To think about the ethics of your user research, it's useful to make time and space at the beginning of (and throughout) the research process, so you can be critical, ask the right questions and make the right considerations. There are various ethical frameworks that you can use to discuss the ethics of the user research you are considering doing. For a simple example see Marsh (2020).

The Market Research Society (MRS) is the world's leading research association. Their code of conduct and set of principles are very relevant to those of us doing user research activities.

High-level MRS principles

For research to be done with integrity:

- research activities are transparent and reputable;
- teams and participants understand what data you are collecting and why you are collecting it;

- you balance the needs of participants, the organization and yourself during the research process;
- you give proper credit to other people's work.

Do no harm to participants by respecting:

- people's rights;
- their wellbeing;
- their right to confidentiality.

Get informed consent; let participants know their rights with regards to:

- anonymity;
- being deleted;
- being forgotten.

Handle data in the right way:

- data collection and storage is fit for purpose, eg secure;
- data is only used for its intended purpose.

Meet your legal and ethical obligations:

- comply with the law:
  o data protection;
  o GDPR;
  o human rights (protected characteristics);
- do DPIAs (data processing impact assessments) for high-risk participants;
- inform observers of their legal and ethical obligations.

Protecting people's privacy when you are sharing research results

Often the most powerful way to show stakeholders the struggles your users are experiencing is to share quotes, images, video and audio clips. You should have included in your consent form/terms and conditions that you will share some of the data in this way internally. But that doesn't mean you can or should share the participants' personal data around your company. You still need to do some work to protect the participants' privacy. The good news is that it's possible and you can share the powerful data you have collected. The Government Digital Service provides an outline of how to do so.

When including participant clips and quotes in your work, anonymize them wherever possible. Anonymizing the data means that you edit it in a way that accurately reflects what happened but the participant cannot be identified (Government Digital Service, 2018a).

If participant clips can be fully anonymized then you can share your work widely without concern. You will not need to remove these clips from work if the participant exerts their right to be forgotten or withdraws their consent (Government Digital Service, 2018a).

The UK Data Service also have a lot of useful guidance on how to anonymize your research data: https://ukdataservice.ac.uk/learning-hub/research-data-management/#anonymisation

However, some participant clips can be difficult to fully anonymize or can lose much of their meaning and therefore value when they are fully anonymized, for example, if using a video clip of the participant talking, or doing a task that includes their face. You can remove, blur, bleep things like names, contact details, and sensitive information like credit card details (Government Digital Service, 2018a).

Super quick summary

I appreciate there is a lot to consider for data protection and ethics in user research, it can feel daunting, especially at first. But it is doable and the more you do it, the more it becomes a normal part of your research practice and process.

References and further reading

Bowman, N (26 August 2014) The ethics of UX research. UX Booth. www.uxbooth.com/articles/ethics-ux-research/ (archived at https://perma.cc/E63F-RXG7)

Buckbee, M (14 May 2020) GDPR requirements in plain english. www.varonis.com/blog/gdpr-requirements-list-in-plain-english/ (archived at https://perma.cc/LJ7G-D9DC)

Government Digital Service (5 November 2018a) Managing user research data and participant privacy. www.gov.uk/service-manual/user-research/managing-user-research-data-participant-privacy (archived at https://perma.cc/JFM2-PBA4)

Government Digital Service (5 November 2018b) Getting users' consent for research. Service Manual. www.gov.uk/service-manual/user-research/getting-users-consent-for-research (archived at https://perma.cc/THE8-EFT9)

Government Digital Service (2019) Researching emotionally sensitive subjects. Service Manual. www.gov.uk/service-manual/user-research/researching-emotionally-sensitive-subjects (archived at https://perma.cc/N85C-69V3)

Information Commissioner's Office (nd). Key data protection themes: Children. ICO. https://ico.org.uk/for-organisations/guide-to-data-protection/key-data-protection-themes/children/ (archived at https://perma.cc/23JX-2RR2)

Information Commissioner's Office (2020) Guide to data protection. https://ico.org.uk/for-organisations/guide-to-data-protection/introduction-to-data-protection/some-basic-concepts/ (archived at https://perma.cc/5UEE-KPRR)

Intersoft Consulting (25 May 2018) GDPR: Consent. https://gdpr-info.eu/issues/consent/ (archived at https://perma.cc/76AS-2Q72)

Intersoft Consulting (25 May 2018) GDPR: Right to be forgotten. https://gdpr-info.eu/issues/right-to-be-forgotten/ (archived at https://perma.cc/XC22-5YJ8)

Kidder, RM (2009) *How Good People Make Tough Choices: Resolving the dilemmas of ethical living*, HarperCollins Publishers, New York

Lamb, N (18 August 2020) A blueprint for sourcing user research participants. UX Collective. https://uxdesign.cc/a-blueprint-for-sourcing-user-research-participants-7b8824ae0ae6 (archived at https://perma.cc/PL8Q-LV4T)

Marsh, S (30 November 2020) A way to start thinking about ethics in user research. UX Collective. https://uxdesign.cc/a-way-to-start-thinking-about-ethics-in-user-research-bfdde538261b (archived at https://perma.cc/T482-JW4D)

Mortensen, DH (December 2020) Conducting ethical user research. Interaction Design Foundation. www.interaction-design.org/literature/article/conducting-ethical-user-research (archived at https://perma.cc/6MWH-BDG6)

Office of the Attorney General (2021) California Consumer Privacy Act (CCPA). https://oag.ca.gov/privacy/ccpa (archived at https://perma.cc/D2HW-9ML4)

Yousef (30 November 2015) Ethical decision making: Right versus wrong and right versus right. Life is Life Blog. https://blogs.lt.vt.edu/yousef/2015/11/30/ethical-decision-making-right-versus-wrong-and-right-versus-right/ (archived at https://perma.cc/M26D-LB6A)

05

Setting up for success

An important development since the first edition of this book was published is the emergence of the field of research operations, often referred to as ReOps (https://researchops.community). This field has come to prominence as the field of user research continues to mature. ReOps focuses on all the stuff that researchers do around the 'doing' of research, all of which is important for undertaking and sharing high-quality research but is an additional burden to the already busy and challenging job of doing user research.

Research operations is now the field that I work in (in 2021). I will outline the basic research operations practices to set up when you are starting out that will help you out immensely, as user research is not only done but also (hopefully) expands, scales and matures. Setting up for success from the very beginning will help make your research practice sustainable and ultimately more effective not just for you doing the research, but for those around you who are making use of it.

Please read the data protection section (Chapter 4) as this is an important part of what to do when setting up a successful research practice, and is a key aspect of research operations. Many organizations with user-centred design and user research functions will now have research operations roles. These are people who manage the tasks that enable user research to be done. Having another person do these tasks allows the researcher to focus on the research, free of the burden of administration and infrastructure work. There are many organizations where these roles don't exist yet or they are very new, which means the researchers will most likely be doing both the research and the operations side of the work. There is always room to improve your practice, whether it's user research or research operations. Whether research operations aren't established, it's in progress or already a key part of the organization, it's always useful to go back to the basics.

FIGURE 5.1   The eight pillars of user research

Research Operations

Environment	Scope	People	Organizational context	Recruitment and admin	Data and knowledge management	Governance	Tools and infrastructure
People silos	Cadence	Community of practice	Space	Incentives	Research library	GDPR	Procurement
Education	Sharing insights	Professional development	Time	Scheduling	Data silos	Legal	Software
Value of research	Prioritization	Staffing	Resources	Logistics	Data gardening	Information security	Hardware
Buy in	Integrating insights	Mature career paths	Budget	Panel management	Document templates	Risk assessments	Labs
Push back	Processes	Leadership	ROI	Participant coordination	Knowledge management	Consent	Systems
Internally focused	Methods	Organization design	Business constraints	Paperwork		Ethics	Technology
Stakeholders	Protocols		Market forces	Timesheets			Networks
Executives	Research as a team sport		Organization maturity				
Colleagues							

The rest of the chapter will cover the foundational, fundamental basics that will be useful to consider from the start or to change if you aren't using them (it's never too late to implement such things). There are likely other things that you should be considering for your organization, and I recommend reading Emma Boulton's work on getting started in research operations to help you with that (Boulton, 2019a). The places to start are usually around the areas of:

- participant recruitment;
- research admin;
- data management;
- tools and infrastructure.

ReOps is relevant to each aspect of the research process, and this is explained particularly clearly by Emma's work on the eight pillars of user research (Boulton, 2019b). This helps us understand what a research practice entails, in order to be able to understand what ReOps support is needed. I recommend looking at the advances in the field that the global research operations community continues to make (https://medium.com/researchops-community).

FIGURE 5.2   Things included in the user research scope pillar: guidelines and templates

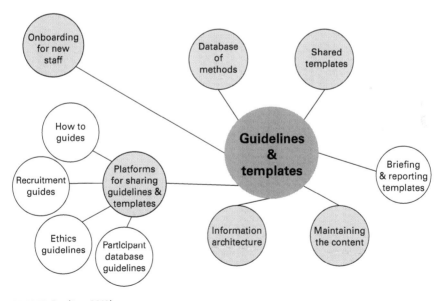

SOURCE Boulton, 2019b

Research operations go across all eight pillars of user research, which is a lot for any one person to deal with!

Each element on each list has a whole host of things underneath it. For example, Figure 5.2 shows the items included in the scope pillar.

See the references and further reading section to find more sources on all the things currently included in the research operations framework.

Showing you this isn't meant to scare you or overwhelm you, although it is understandably overwhelming. This is to show you that there are a lot of things to consider when doing user research, but don't let that put you off. You won't need to consider everything within the framework and eight pillars, especially if you are a one-person user experience team (see Leah Buley's 2013 book about this). Even organizations with dedicated research operation roles won't necessarily take on all aspects of the framework, depending on the structures and needs of the organization and those doing user-centred work within it.

I want to make you aware of the pillars and the framework, to enable you to select the aspects that are important for you and your organization to consider, to best support a research practice.

Understanding your organization's context and any constraints to doing research will help you understand what to focus on when getting started. How research is done will require more careful consideration if any of these areas need to be considered:

- sensitivity of the work, eg using health or national security data;
- vulnerability of the target audience;
- budget constraints;
- extreme internal resistance;
- perceived (or real) time constraints in the development or launch of your product or service.

Data management

Data management is an excellent place to start as your data is highly valuable and some of it will be sensitive (eg personal data).

Naming conventions

The data protection section in Chapter 4 refers to file-naming conventions; here are a few suggestions as to how to name your files consistently. This will make files easy to find in the future, which is helpful for GDPR reasons (for example, the right to be forgotten, which is the legal term for your right to have your data erased) and also for colleagues who may want to make use of some of your artefacts in the future. This can help reduce both effort and redundancy in future research and avoid repeating research that doesn't need to be done again.

Both the folder and file names for research data should clearly identify:

- what service, product or project the data was collected for;
- (if doing iterative design and research) the round of research the data is from;
- the participant's name, or unique identifier, if the file contains participant data (eg video recording of research session);
- date the data was collected;
- perhaps the type of research done.

Example of shared drive folder and file names

Let's imagine that the Support Charity website (as we discussed in Chapter 3) is redeveloping its payment function for online donations. Start by creating folders somewhere you and those who need to, can access them. For example, within your shared drives set up these folders:

Shared drives > User research data > Website > Payments

All the research data for a recent round of prototype testing research might be stored in a folder, which would live within the Payments folder, as shown above, called:

> 2021-06-25 - prototype usability testing round 1

The research data, consent form and research extracts for a participant in that round of research might be named:

2021-06-25 - Payment prototype - round 1 - Sam Smith - session notes.docx
2021-06-25 - Payment prototype - round 1 - Sam Smith - screen recording.mp4
2021-06-25 - Payment prototype - round 1 - Sam Smith - consent form.pdf
2021-06-25 - Payment prototype - round 1 - analysis.xlsx
2021-06-25 - Payment prototype - round 1 - write up.pptx

There is no one right way to structure the storage of your research data. You can use a structure like the above to keep all files in one place that are related to the project. You could also structure things by the research process, having different folders for:

- plans;
- recruitment and admin;
- research data;
- results.

You will still need clear file names to understand what the files contain and which project they are related to. In fact, it's more important to have clear and understandable file names if they aren't all in the same folder. Not having everything in one place is useful if you don't want all the artefacts to be accessible to all. You may not want everyone to have access to the raw data or all the details you have collected about the participants.

Helping your colleagues keep track

You may want to have some way that people can easily access certain things from the research process, eg the plan, the schedule, the write-up of results, without them going through all of your files and folders. Using something like a Trello board will allow interested parties to track the progress of the research and will allow you to give them access to the assets that you want them to have access to.

Sorting out infrastructure related to participants is key to do at the beginning. This is important for data protection reasons, but also to make sure that the participants have a positive experience of participating in your research and you create a consistent experience between participants.

Participant data management

For moderated research, it's useful to have a table or spreadsheet set up for the times and dates your research sessions will take place and which participants are doing those sessions. Having a schedule template will help you keep the participant information in schedules to a minimum. You can share the schedule with colleagues to help gain agreement that the participants are from the target audience, and encourage them to observe sessions, to see for themselves the users' behaviour and attitudes, etc. Whether you are sharing the schedules or not, in GDPR terms it is important to keep participant

TABLE 5.1   An example of what you can include in your participant schedule

Participant number	Participant name	Contact details	Other important details	Session date	Session time	Consent form signed	Incentive sent

TABLE 5.2   An example of what you can include in your participant schedule, with reduced personal information

Participant number	Participant details	Other important details	Session date	Session time	Consent form signed	Incentive sent
	<link>					

information to a minimum, and in as few places as possible. An example of what columns to include in your schedule is shown in Table 5.1.

If you are concerned about sharing personally identifiable information with colleagues, you can keep this information securely elsewhere (for example in a CMS) and link to it within the schedule (Table 5.2).

It may be easier to control who can access participants' personal details in a CMS or something similar.

Communicating with participants

If you intend to build up an iterative research practice, it's useful to create templates you can use from the outset. When it comes to interacting with the participants, this will help with the efficiency of communication and each participant will also receive the same information. Templates can be adapted where necessary, but an adapted template is better than entirely individualized communications for each and every participant, which takes a lot of time and effort and risks each participant having a different understanding of the research and research session.

There are various stages in the research process and where you are interacting with participants where you can create templates such as:

- The initial stage for all potential participants:
  - screening.

- For people selected to be participants:
  - o invitation;
  - o confirmation of scheduled session;
  - o thanking and incentive confirmation.
- For those who don't take part in a session:
  - o 'Sorry you didn't get selected, you don't have the right profile' messages.
  - o 'Sorry our sessions are fully booked' messages.

You could work with your marketing department, for example, to make sure any communication templates you create are in the organization's tone of voice.

Other templates

Other parts of the research process you can make templates for in the future as your research practice matures include:

- research plans;
- research session scripts/protocols;
- result reports.

Admin

Incentives

See Chapter 3 for more information on incentivizing participants. From the point of ReOps, you need to take into consideration what approvals you may need for the incentives budget. If this is a lengthy process, you'll need to factor this into your planning and proposed timescales.

Budgeting for research

It is entirely possible to do user research without a budget, but this is obviously not ideal, and doesn't consider the cost of your time and effort, and that of colleagues who may be supporting your efforts.

Things that you may need to pay for:

- participant recruitment;
- participant incentives;
- research tools and infrastructure (hardware, software, networks);
- facilities (such as a lab or conference room).

A remote-first mindset has become more prominent in the last few years, as the way we work changes. Certainly, in the Springer Nature Digital department, we have internationally located teams and an international customer base, so it makes sense to be remote first. This then impacts what you require budgets for. For example, facilities don't need to be considered in a remote-first workplace, but the digital tools you use are critical for success. They need to meet data protection regulations, work in all the countries where you have colleagues and customers, and support the types of research you are doing.

Tools and infrastructure

If you don't have the budget to buy specialist research tools, your organization may already have tools you can make use of to conduct your user research, such as video conferencing software for conducting remote research interviews. You'll need to talk to the data protection team to make sure that the data processing agreements (DPAs) in place will cover utilizing tools for research purposes. If the agreements don't cover this, there may be steps you can take to be data protection compliant, such as not storing research videos within your video conferencing tools, but storing them securely somewhere the organization has a DPA to cover the storage of personal data of people outside the organization.

If you have the budget to make use of specialist tools, you'll need to get to know procurement teams and data protection teams, if you don't already. These teams will need to be consulted in the procurement of tools that will gather and store people's personal information. It depends on the size of the organization you are in; for example in a start-up you may be doing the procuring yourself, or you may be in a large organization where a team does it for you. Make sure you consult a data protection officer (DPO) about contracts and agreements to ensure they comply with any data protection regulations you may have internally as well as international standards.

Reputable suppliers will cover the necessary things such as GDPR and CCPA. Data protection impact assessment and risk assessments may also need to be done, so consult with your DPO.

Chapter 4 covers the importance of getting informed consent from your participants covering what the research will entail and how you will use and store their data. Assuming you don't already have a consent form, work with your data protection and legal teams to create one that everyone is happy with – it will protect the participants and you/your organization. For further advice on what to include, and how to structure your consent form see:

1 Anatomy of a user research consent form: Travis (2018).

2 Consent forms for user research: Data Transformation Agency, Australian Government (2021).

This is not a comprehensive look at ReOps, which is vast, but it's a good high-level start. Kate Towsey is currently writing a handbook on research operations for Rosenfeld, which I am very much looking forward to.

References and further reading

Boulton, E (8 October 2019a) Getting started with research ops. https://medium.com/researchops-community/getting-started-with-researchops-f77cd6779554 (archived at https://perma.cc/836L-X4V4) (last accessed: 27 March 2021)

Boulton, E (11 July 2019b) The eight pillars of user research. https://medium.com/researchops-community/the-eight-pillars-of-user-research-1bcd2820d75a (archived at https://perma.cc/XX95-VNM6) (last accessed: 27 March 2021)

Buley, L (2013) *The User Experience Team of One: A research and design survival guide*, Rosenfeld Media, New York

Data Transformation Agency, Australian Government (2021) Consent forms for user research. www.dta.gov.au/help-and-advice/build-and-improve-services/user-research/consent-forms-user-research (archived at https://perma.cc/PU5U-A4G3) (last accessed: 27 March 2021)

Sergeant, S (28 May 2020) 5 baby steps on the path towards a research repository. https://medium.com/researchops-community/5-baby-steps-on-the-path-towards-a-research-repository-1179b35cbad0 (archived at https://perma.cc/R5VR-3H2E) (last accessed: 27 March 2021)

Towsey, K (24 October 2018) A framework for #WhatisResearchOps. https://
medium.com/researchops-community/a-framework-for-whatisresearchops-
e862315ab70d (archived at https://perma.cc/XZ2H-9DVQ) (last accessed: 27
March 2021)

Travis, D (2 July 2018) Anatomy of a user research consent form. www.userfocus.
co.uk/articles/anatomy-of-a-consent-form.html (archived at https://perma.cc/
R6JF-WJ83) (last accessed: 27 March 2021)

06

Managing user research logistics

Agencies, facilities and contracts

Logistics

Safety first

I don't want to scare you before you've even started, but it's important to consider your own safety and the safety of others when doing user research. Wherever the research is taking place, make sure that your team/colleagues know the location and timing of the sessions. If you can have someone help you out, even better. For example, ask someone to escort the participants in and out of the building, get them a drink, and pay their incentive. This will make everything run much smoother and it's someone to call upon if something doesn't feel right. If participants are rude or aggressive (which is rare and unlikely), don't grin and bear it. It sounds obvious but it's worth stating: this is not acceptable behaviour and you should stop the session immediately and ask them to leave.

If it is obvious that a participant has lied about who they are, for example you are working on a teacher's resource and from the participant's answers it is clear they know nothing about teaching, stop the session and ask the participant to leave. This has to be done tactfully and calmly, and should be done in the presence of a colleague. Sometimes the participant will go willingly; sometimes you have to pay them for their time anyway. There is no point wasting your time and energy on someone who is not giving you useful or truthful data.

• For research where you are visiting people in their own environment, it is advisable that two people do the research together. It is a two-way trust contract if people are letting you into their house, and everyone needs to feel safe. Let the participant know upfront that two people will be visiting (this is discussed in more depth in Chapter 15 on contextual inquiry). For example, if you are bringing a colleague to take notes, it is more comfortable for the participant if the roles and reasons for being there for both of you are clearly defined.

You can ask people if they have any medical conditions that you should be aware of before a research session starts, and whether there is potential for a medical emergency. (You can, of course, remind them they are fully entitled to not answer the question.) For example, if someone starts having difficulty breathing and you know they have asthma, you can help in finding the inhaler or call for medical assistance.

Appearance and perception when doing face-to-face research

It is inevitable when you and the participants are together in the same room, at the same time, that they (and you) will make snap judgements about each other. Therefore, you need to consider what kind of impression you want to make.

Dress in a similar way to the participants if possible. If in doubt, dress neatly and avoid standing out. In many contexts, it won't be appropriate to be suited and booted, as you don't want to appear overly authoritarian and you want to make the participant feel at ease, but there will be situations where this could be necessary.

Make sure your equipment is ready and working before you start and you have everything you need. If participants are travelling to you, have everything set up and ready to go before they arrive. If you are travelling to the participant, you want to have everything in easy reach and be well organized to set up as quickly as possible when you arrive.

Be aware of cultural differences

If you are going to be doing research in a context that is culturally different to your own, it's a good idea to familiarize yourself with the differences you could encounter. You could be undertaking international research, or research in a different industry, or different socio-economic groups to your own. You may need to consider language barriers, local customs and expected behaviours, for example. Being aware of potential differences will help you:

- plan your research appropriately;
- prepare for differences in what is deemed acceptable and unacceptable behaviour, for example;
- start to understand the context of data you are gathering.

Doing user research with children

If your product/service is for children, there are additional considerations for planning and doing user research. Briefly, the main things to consider are:

- If you are in the UK, you'll need to be CRB-checked (by the Criminal Records Bureau). If you are working outside of the UK, it's worth checking if there are similar regulations involved.
- You will need to have the permission of the parents/guardians and an adult will need to be present when you are doing the research.
- In the UK, you cannot pay a child a cash incentive, but vouchers are a good alternative. It's worth checking, wherever your research is taking place, what the rules are.
- Consider the length of the session and the likely attention span of the age of child you want to involve in your research. You'll need to be very focused in what you want to achieve.

Hiring agencies, choosing facilities, signing contracts

Depending on the budget available for your research, there are different ways to spend it.

Very small budget

You must spend this on participants' incentives, unless you can persuade participants to do the research for free. Essentially you will be doing the whole project yourself.

Small budget

Consider hiring a research participant recruitment agency to find the right people for your research. This will be money well spent, as it can be very time-consuming to find and schedule participants. By outsourcing recruitment, you can concentrate on the rest of what is required for good research.

Medium budget

This could be spent on a combination of:

- specialist facilities in which to conduct your user research;
- specialist agencies/contractors to do the research for you;
- participants' recruitment and incentives;
- iterative rounds of research.

Choosing whether to spend your money on facilities, skills or more research depends on your requirements and chosen methodology. By the end of Part Two you should have a better feel for which will be the right choice for you.

Large budget

With a large budget you will be able to outsource all aspects or carry out more research yourself, spending money on:

- participants' recruitment and incentives;
- specialist facilities in which to conduct your user research (depending on your requirements and chosen methodology);
- specialist agencies/contractors to do the research;
- iterative rounds of research and more in-depth research.

If you have a large budget, I still advise that you read this book to understand what good research is and then read guidance from Government Digital Service (2016) on how to procure services in a structured way. This guidance will help you to:

- describe your requirements;
- communicate effectively with suppliers;
- evaluate suppliers' proposals;

- choose the right supplier for you;
- draw up a good contract that protects you and the supplier.

You don't need to follow the government advice to the letter: the government understandably has strict criteria for spending taxpayers' money, but it will give you an idea of how to structure your selection process, buy the right product or service, and spend your money wisely if you haven't procured specialist services before.

As a final note on this subject, I think it's worth acknowledging that professional facilities and services are rarely available outside of major cities, so money could be better spent doing the research yourself and going wider and deeper, as appropriate.

Part One summary

The main things to remember are:

- Be clear about what your research is for.
- Get the right people involved.
- Be aware of ethical issues.
- Organize and plan your research in a way that works for both you and the participants.
- Remember the importance of observation: what people say and what they do are two different things.
- Ask the right kind of questions.
- Don't forget about accessibility and being inclusive.
- Safety is important to smooth running research.
- Spend your money wisely and negotiate good contracts.

References and further reading

Arnould, K (2015) Recruiting your target audience for UX testing with screener questions, User Testing Blog. www.usertesting.com/blog/2015/01/29/screener-questions/ (archived at https://perma.cc/D5NN-JG54)

Government Digital Service (August 2016) Writing your requirements for digital outcomes and specialists services. www.gov.uk/guidance/how-to-write-your-requirements-for-digital-outcomes-and-specialists-services (archived at https://perma.cc/V4WM-4XV4)

Government Digital Service (2017) User research. Service Manual. www.gov.uk/
service-manual/user-research (archived at https://perma.cc/2DCU-Z5BX)
UXPA Code of Professional Conduct, User Experience Professionals Association
(October 2016) https://uxpa.org/resources/uxpa-code-professional-conduct
(archived at https://perma.cc/CWF9-699Y)

PART TWO

Selecting and using user research methods

Overview

We've had a brief look at the various user research methods available to us in Part One. In this section, we'll look at selecting the right method for your current research question/UX problem, and learn how to choose and use each method effectively. There are many situations where you will need to use multiple methods to get the answers you need. For example, if you are looking to understand who your users are, you may want to start with interviews to get an in-depth understanding of your users, particularly how they think and behave. And then do a survey to assess the scale of the problems, attitudes, behaviours etc you identified during the interviews.

The first thing to do is to identify your current research question(s). Which scenario (as shown in Table 7.1) do you find yourself in at work? If there isn't an exact match, is there a scenario that approximates your situation? You may recognize yourself in more than one of these scenarios. I advise you to focus on one problem at a time, or a handful of clear related problems.

There isn't one particular method for each scenario, as much as we'd all like it to be that simple. There are likely to be multiple methods that could be useful to you. You may need to read through a couple of different user research method chapters before you decide which one is most appropriate. The more research you do, the easier it will become to understand the most appropriate research method(s) to use for any given scenario.

TABLE 7.1 Problem scenarios you may be experiencing at work

Generative	Formative and summative
We have a concept that's new to our industry	Why isn't xxx working?
	What do the analytics mean?
The CEO has an idea...	There are several solutions to this issue...
Who are our users?	Why is there such poor conversion on xxx?
We need to get to know our users	What do our users think about xxx?
How do users really use our stuff?	Our digital stuff reflects the organization's
What are our users experiencing?	structure
We need to change the way we work	We need to rebrand
The stakeholders can't agree	The stakeholders can't agree
We need to rebuild	We need to rebuild

You may be experiencing several of these scenarios at the same time – such is life. It may be tempting to choose a method that could solve all your problems at once. I would try to refrain from going down this road; it is better to prioritize the questions that you want to focus on. It may be that some of your questions are interrelated and you can group them and research them together, but I would avoid trying to research multiple problems that are not obviously related at the same time. It will take longer and require more effort to do separate pieces of research, but as I have mentioned, user research isn't a one-time thing and you will avoid confusing issues and diluting the results of the research and the impact of the conclusions and recommendations that come out of the research if you don't try to do too much at once.

The user research methods

Figure 7.1 shows the user research methods covered in this book.

We've gone over the foundations and now, for each research method, this section will explain:

- an overview of the research method;
- when and where you can do this kind of research;
- the time required to prepare and run the research;
- how to prepare for the research;
- how to do the research and gather the data.

There are different types of research that you can do depending on where you are in the product or service lifecycle (design, develop, deliver) as shown in Figure 7.2.

The research questions covered in Table 7.1 are grouped into generative and summative/formative questions. This starts to help us narrow down which user research method(s) is the best fit for the work you need to do.

FIGURE 7.1 User research methods

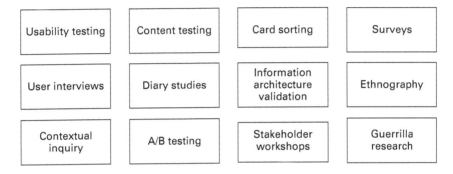

FIGURE 7.2 The types of research you should do at each stage of the user-centred development cycle

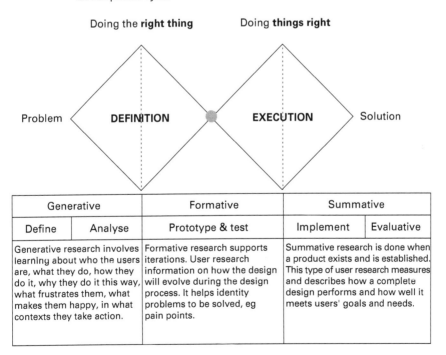

Generative		Formative	Summative	
Define	Analyse	Prototype & test	Implement	Evaluative
Generative research involves learning about who the users are, what they do, how they do it, why they do it this way, what frustrates them, what makes them happy, in what contexts they take action.		Formative research supports iterations. User research information on how the design will evolve during the design process. It helps identity problems to be solved, eg pain points.	Summative research is done when a product exists and is established. This type of user research measures and describes how a complete design performs and how well it meets users' goals and needs.	

Always start with the question that you need answering rather than the method you are thinking of using when you are planning research.

Figure 7.3 will help you decide which methods you may want to read about first. Hopefully, the scenarios covered will approximate what you experience and help you narrow down your research method of choice.

A useful way to think about selecting a method is to think about the four-step process below; answering a few questions will help us identify the method:

1 What is your research question?

2 What phase of the product/service lifecycle are you in?

3 Do you need subjective (attitudinal) or objective (behavioural) data, or both, to answer your question? See the top tip below for a definition of each.

4 Do you need quantitative or qualitative data or both?

TOP TIP: DEFINITIONS

Objective data: behaviour/achieving goals/increasing effectiveness and efficiency/increasing engagement/reduce number of queries/task success/findability

Subjective data: attitude/opinion/perception/expectations/sentiments/feelings/motivations/satisfaction

---

Gathering data is about taking people's (colleagues and stakeholders) opinions out of the equation as much as possible when making a decision about the product/service. I've seen people ignore the data because they know better than the evidence, with disastrous consequences. If you want to meet your users' needs, then you need data both quantitative and qualitative, depending on the situation, to make good decisions. One type of data isn't better than the other, it's using the right data at the right time. You need both to build the right thing and to build the thing right.

Why combine quantitative and qualitative data?

Quantitative data is really good at telling you what is happening, what has happened; how your products and services are being used; what people's attitudes and opinions are about the things they are using; what's going well and what isn't, and at what scale all these things are true. But it doesn't tell you why.

That's where qualitative data comes in. You can use qualitative user research techniques to understand your users and why they are behaving the way they do. And where their attitudes and opinions come from.

Combining quantitative and qualitative data enables us to zoom in and out, to have different perspectives, look at the bigger picture as well as the detail and go back and forth to create that holistic view of what's going on.

The macro might be understanding the landscape – the context your users are living and working in, the context that they're using your product or service in. What their needs are, what their goals are – what is helping them and what the barriers are to achieving their goals.

The micro can zoom right down to 'Does the interaction on this component in this step of the digital service work?' 'Is it accessible?' 'Do people understand it?' 'Can they use it?' And you need to iteratively go back and forth to make sure you are doing the right thing and you are doing the thing right.

You need to prioritize what you gather; minimize noise to maximize the signals, so only gather the data you need. Because it can be time-consuming to gather and analyse data. There is also an ethical consideration: don't gather data you don't need. For a product or service to meet its users' needs and business goals, it's important that teams can use the data they gather in meaningful ways.

A general rule is that attitudinal is almost always better answered with quantitative data, and behavioural can be a combination of qualitative and quantitative. Because opinions and attitudes can vary so much from person to person, it's important to get a large sample. Behaviour is much more consistent and we can work with smaller sample sizes in qualitative research, for example, usability testing with five people. There is an excellent article by Jakob Nielsen about this that I highly recommend reading: https://www.nngroup.com/articles/why-you-only-need-to-test-with-5-users/

FIGURE 7.3   Cheatsheet for picking the right research method

Development phase	Define	Analyse		Implement		Evaluate		
Intention / Type of info		Generative		Formative		Summative		
	Attitudinal	Behavioural		Behavioural		Attitudinal	Behavioural	
Question	Quant	Qual	Quant	Quant	Qual	Quant	Qual	Quant
Method	Surveys	User Interviews, Diary studies, Ethnography, Contextual inquiry, Stakeholder workshops, Guerrilla research	Analytics	A/B testing, Tree testing, Card sorting, Content testing, Analytics, Metrics	Usability testing, Content testing, Card sorting, Guerrilla research	Surveys	Usability testing, Content testing, Contextual inquiry, Ethnography, Diary studies, Guerrilla research	Usability benchmarking, Analytics, Metrics, Content testing, A/B testing

SOURCE Based on Baliani (2021)

CASE STUDY
Why it's useful to combine quantitative and qualitative data

You can watch five people drive over a pothole, identify that it is a problem and why it's a problem – this is your qualitative research. You've observed in usability testing that people struggle to do a task when using your product or service. But what is the scale of the problem? Should we invest in fixing the road? The interaction in the product/service?

Quantitative data can tell us about the amount of traffic on the road: is it heavily used? Or are there only a couple of cars a week? Is the task people are struggling with on your product/service getting a lot of traffic? Is this one of your most common tasks? You can also do this the other way round. You can see in your analytics that something untoward is happening, for example poor shopping cart to purchase conversion. But it isn't clear why this is happening.

Quantitative insights come from things like page views, events, and internal search results. Those user interactions and metrics tell a story. Qualitative data is described in words rather than measured in numbers. As user researchers, we interview and observe people in order to better understand how they use the things that we make and why they might have problems.

Once you've got the answer to the four questions, you can use Figure 7.3 to identify what method(s) are best suited to your needs: consider this a cheat sheet for selecting your research method.

Important notes

Don't use guerrilla testing in isolation, this is a useful quick and dirty method to help make some decisions and uncover certain issues, but it's not rigorous enough to be used alone.

If you're working in an agile or lean way, most methodologies can be adapted to be used in short timescales, other than ethnography and diary studies, which are methods used to understand change over time.

Hopefully you've now narrowed down your potential methodologies – let's move on to finding out how to conduct the research itself.

Reference

Baliani, E (6 January 2021) How to pick the right UX research method. Boot
     Camp. https://bootcamp.uxdesign.cc/how-to-pick-the-right-ux-research-method-
     d8b08a881c0 (archived at https://perma.cc/8NZU-7FDZ)

07

Usability testing

Observing people doing things

What is usability testing?

Usability testing (also known as user testing) is a commonly used method, where a researcher observes users who work through tasks on a product or service to identify where problems are encountered. Usability testing can be employed in different ways, both qualitatively and quantitatively, and be moderated or unmoderated.

MODERATED
Face-to-face: the researcher and the user are in the same room at the same time interacting with each other. Remote: the researcher and the user are in different places but are interacting with each other by using screen-sharing technology.

UNMODERATED
Remote: the researcher would not be involved while the user does the research tasks at a time and place of his or her choosing. Face-to-face: the researcher and the user are in the same room at the same, but the researcher does not intervene and converse while the user is working through the tasks (the least common approach).

In Chapter 2 (the section on planning) we thought about the logistics of session length. Purists will tell you that the only consideration is how best to research the issue thoroughly, but in the real world this may not be the (only) deciding factor, and here we are pragmatists. For example, you may need to talk to a specific number of people on a particular date. Or the budget you have available will determine how long you can spend with participants; for example the budget will only cover 30 minutes of 'high value' participants' time, such as lawyers or doctors. This means you may have to tailor your research to fit your current parameters. It's best to pilot test your research to make sure you can cover the priorities in the time available.

The fundamentals of moderated usability testing

What moderated usability testing is good for

Moderated tests give you more control. Moderators can answer questions posed by the participants if appropriate, or be able to note questions that participants have, which can be very insightful for uncovering what is happening. Also, you are able to have an in-depth conversation with the participants. Asking follow-up questions allows you to understand what they have said and done, and how they feel about it.

It gives you the ability to adapt the research based on your findings. It's common for this kind of research to reveal something you haven't consid-ered before. Moderating the session will allow you to go off on necessary tangents to pursue it. If warranted you can adapt subsequent research sessions to revisit the new item with other participants. This should be done with caution: it is not advisable to change the tasks and research questions after each session as you will have no consistency in your findings, but sometimes the magnitude of what you have discovered makes it necessary.

It is relatively cheap. No special equipment is needed; you can simply sit next to users and take notes as they talk. It takes about a day to collect data from a handful of users, which is all that's needed for the most important insights (Nielsen, 2012).

Results are robust. As long as you avoid bias questions, you'll still get reasonably good findings; also, the results are convincing. Feedback from customers can be more powerful than you delivering the same feedback to your team. Getting the rest of your team (and management) to sit in on a few thinking-aloud sessions doesn't take a lot of their time and is the best way to motivate them to pay attention to usability (Nielsen, 2012).

Where you need to include accessibility usability testing with assistive technology users. This should really be part of any digital development or improvement project, and it should be done iteratively as development progresses. You should be aware, if you are asking users of assistive technology to visit you in your work place or a user research studio, that the set-up of tools you have is going to be different to the participants'. This means you'll need to include time for them to set up their tool of choice in a way that is suitable to them. It is preferable, if possible, to visit assistive technology users in their own environment (see Chapter 15 on contextual inquiry).

What moderated usability testing is not good for

It is a time-consuming research method. It's more difficult to schedule research with the participants, restricting when and where they do it. It may therefore not be your first choice if your timescales are very restricted and planning ahead is difficult.

Moderated testing uses small samples of people and so is *not statistically significant*. Stakeholders new to user research sometimes distrust insights that have 'only come from five people', without understanding the background to the differences between behaviour and opinion. It can be difficult for stakeholders to agree to spending money on making changes based on the 'opinion' of five people. (We'll look at this more in Parts Three and Four on analysing and presenting your data). The way the work is presented can help, giving some context and background; and getting the stakeholders to see for themselves can be useful. Sometimes it takes some additional research (such as a quantitative study) to convince those new to user research.

This may not the method for you if you want to understand 'natural' behaviour. Most people don't sit and talk to themselves all day: it can feel very strange at first to talk continuously about what you're doing and thinking. Participants are typically willing to try their best, and they quickly become engaged in the task. I would add that most people soon get used to thinking out loud and some appropriate prompting from you during the session will help keep the momentum going.

Effort required to do this kind of research

Usability testing is one of the easiest methods to practise and learn. It is relatively easy to learn the basics and if you are aware of the fundamentals of good practice, you can start doing usability testing straight away. But it does require some time and effort to become a skilled moderator.

The results are affected by the method. This is known as the 'observer effect', a phenomenon well known in physics: observing changes the act that is being observed and measured. You can't get around the fact that watching and talking to the participants will change what they would have done if you weren't there. Be aware that the less experience you have at moderating, the greater the observer effect is likely to be. It will decrease as you become more experienced, but it will always be a factor in moderated user research, so don't let being new to usability testing put you off.

CASE STUDY
Example of usability testing

Usability testing was the first user research method that I taught myself when doing my doctoral research. I was testing some highly interactive software that combined multiple geographic datasets, to help graduate students understand what was happening environmentally in a specific part of the Lake District in England.

Because I had read about the fundamentals of best practice, I was able to not only use this method to identify usability issues with the software, I could also show the different kinds of issues identified by different user groups, in this case Master's and Doctoral students and experienced academics. This demonstrated the importance of including relevant user groups in research.

When to use moderated usability testing

It is a flexible method that you can use at any stage in the development lifecycle, from early paper prototypes to fully implemented running systems, services and experiences. If it's possible, use face-to-face qualitative usability testing (this will always be my preference), because observing facial expressions and body language can help you understand what is happening. If your participants are international, or you aren't able to travel to where they are and they can't travel to you, remote moderated usability testing is a great option.

How to do moderated usability testing

We've already covered what 'usability testing' means. Now let's outline what the rest of these words mean:

- *Moderated:* you are talking to the participants during the session and they are talking to you while they undertake the various tasks you have given them.
- *Face-to-face:* you are in the same room at the same time.

- *Remote:* you and the participant are in different places.
- *Qualitative:* this means your findings won't be statistically significant. It also means you won't be counting things like the number of clicks it takes a participant to complete a task or timing how long it takes to do something.

We have already considered a few of the preparation aspects of doing user testing (or any other research) such as choosing the problem/issue that you want to research and your participants (and how you will incentivize them). You also need to set the dates, times and location of the research, then draft and pilot test the protocol and finally, do the research!

Creating a protocol or a script

A protocol or a script lists all the things you want to say to the participants, the questions you want to ask, the tasks you want them to do and reminders of certain things that you may want to observe. Various resources describe this document in different ways. It could just be semantics but there are subtle differences in the terms so I'll share my understanding to clarify. This understanding came from when I was working for the agency Bunnyfoot (www.bunnyfoot.com) as a user experience consultant.

A 'usability testing script' is a document where you follow what is written down exactly, saying and doing everything in the order in which it is written. Confusingly, a 'usability testing protocol' looks exactly the same as a script but it's used in a different way. You don't have to do everything in the exact order it's written down. During the research session, it may become clear that certain questions and tasks are not relevant to a particular participant, so you may cut them out completely; or you do some of the tasks in a different order, because it makes sense at the time. One of the most useful things about using the document in this way is that when a participant has covered two tasks in one go, you can feel free move on.

Whether you use your document as a script or a protocol is entirely up to you. Both are legitimate. My preference is for the protocol approach, but when you are just starting out with usability testing you may feel more comfortable with the script approach, to make sure you have covered everything you need to. If you are going to use your document as a protocol, it is worth putting a small disclaimer at the bottom of your first page, for the benefit of anyone you are sharing it with and for anyone observing the research session and using a protocol document to follow progress. For simplicity's sake I am going to refer to the usability testing document as a protocol from now on.

HOW TO EXPLAIN YOUR PROTOCOL TO OBSERVERS

There will be an opportunity to make small changes to the protocol based on observations of the test sessions. Note that tasks are normally used as a *guide* throughout the testing sessions, rather than being entirely set. The moderator may decide during the testing session that the undertaking of an upcoming scheduled task may be pointless based on a user's performance on a preceding task. Task schedules are therefore flexible; altering the tasks according to user responses allows us to record more realistic responses.

What should a protocol contain?

1 Introduction and the ethical/legal issues discussed in Part One (5 minutes).

2 Short pre-task interview questions (5 minutes).

3 Research tasks.

4 Short post-task interview questions (5 minutes).

As this list suggests, you should leave about 5 minutes for the introduction, pre-task and post-task interviews. You can extend these if you need to but I wouldn't go beyond 10 minutes, as you really want to focus on the research tasks.

1 INTRODUCTION

In Part One, in the discussion on being aware of ethical and legal issues, I gave an example of how you can start your research session, explain to the participants what the research is about, what's going to happen, how the session is being recorded if at all, and how you will use the data. Giving some context is a good way to start a research session. When writing the interview questions and research tasks you can refer back to Part One and the section on asking the right kinds of questions.

2 SHORT PRE-TASK INTERVIEW QUESTIONS

You will have learnt a little about the participants from the screener questionnaire (see Part One on who should be involved in your research). Asking some preliminary questions is a chance to get to know the participants better and make them feel comfortable, before diving into the tasks. The questions can focus on gaining some insight into the participants' experience related to the tasks or area that you are researching. This will help you understand some of the observation you make during the session: how and why the participants behave the way they do, how they complete tasks, have certain issues, solve problems, etc.

It's difficult to say what questions should be included without knowing the industry you work in or the area you are researching, but here are some examples of digital experience questions to help you get the idea:

a What, if any, devices do you use at home (desktop, laptop, tablet, smartphone, smartwatch, smart TV, games consoles, etc)?

b What, if any, devices do you use at work (desktop, laptop, tablet, smartphone, etc)?

c Which of the following tasks, if any, do you like to do online: researching, booking tickets and travel, gaming, social media, banking, shopping, corresponding, reading, listening to music, watching TV, films, vlogs, other videos, etc?

d Which of the following tasks, if any, do you prefer not to do online: researching, booking tickets and travel, gaming, social media, banking, shopping, corresponding, reading, listening to music, watching TV, films, vlogs, other videos, etc?

C and D prompt: Can you tell me a bit about why you like/dislike to do these things online?

QUICK NOTE ON PROMPTS

You will have noticed the use of 'prompts' in the questions above. Prompts are clarification and follow-up questions and can be used at any time during the research session. They can help you delve a bit deeper into participants' answers or they can provide examples if participants are struggling with something. Examples can be useful but should be used sparingly as they are leading by nature and could skew the participants' answers.

You won't always be able to anticipate when you need a prompt, but you'll get used to using them the more research you do. It's worth noting down the unanticipated prompts during a research session as you may need to use them again. It may also show you an issue that needs to be rectified that is relevant to one of the tasks you have set.

3 RESEARCH TASK

There are a couple of different kinds of research task that you can make use of during a usability testing session depending on your objectives: specific and open-ended. You can use specific tasks and questions if you want your research to focus on a precise issue or range of issues, for example, why there is a high rate of shopping cart abandonment or users leaving a journey at a particular point. Being specific gives users clear guidance on what actions to take and what features to speak about. There are various reasons why you may want to be specific:

- You may want to test a particular feature or function, either a new or suboptimal one, for example.
- If you know there's a specific point in a journey or experience where people are dropping out, you can ask participants to do this journey to see the context and insights to understand why.
- If your product is complex and has a learning curve associated with its initial use you may want to use specific tasks that will guide users through it and explain the context (for example investment banking, stocks and shares apps).

You will still want to avoid bias in questions by suggesting a specific response or giving exact instructions; let them work things out for themselves.

Open-ended tasks involve you giving participants a minimal amount of information and explanation about how to perform the task, allowing them to uncover the answer or solution on their own. If you are developing something new and are testing a prototype, it is likely you have a broad focus to your research; you are interested in how people use and experience it. You won't necessarily want to be too specific about what participants do.

You can use open-ended tasks to find topics of interest. When you're not sure where to focus your test in the beginning, you will be able to narrow down you field of focus in subsequent tests. Open-ended tasks and questions lend themselves to exploratory research as you can observe how people are using your product or service, rather than you specifying how to use it and the kinds of problems they're running into. You can find things that are broken or cause friction for your users: letting them explore freely will uncover issues you may not be aware of.

Remember that open-ended tasks and exploratory research still need clearly defined objectives, as discussed in Part One. Open-ended and specific tasks can both be defined in two different ways: 1) pre-defined tasks: ones you have selected to ensure that you cover the topics and issues that you need to during the session; or 2) user-defined tasks: ones a participant self-selects or you help the participant select. The questions you include during the initial interview phase can help with task selection, for example if a participant has stated they have already carried out a task with your or a competitor's product/service.

You can use all these task types during one research session, or just one particular type of task depending on the focus of your research. The main bulk of your protocol will be your list of tasks that you will read out (if they are predefined) to the participants so they can do the tasks. If they are not predefined, make a note of what they are when the participants do these tasks.

USING 'THINK ALOUD' IN MODERATED USABILITY TESTING

Think aloud is the main method used for doing moderated testing. Think aloud is when the participants verbalize what they are doing, what they are thinking and feeling while they are undertaking the tasks you or they have defined.

Think aloud is useful for getting deep insight into participants' mental processes while doing tasks. On the 'positive side' there is what they like, what delights and surprises them, what they can get through easily. On the 'negative side' you can identify when they are struggling, what they dislike and what frustrates them, and their misconceptions. It is particularly useful to identify when participants have a different understanding of something to the one that you intended. To help you identify what practical changes can be made to content, designs and processes, it is important to gain insight into both what is and isn't working.

The main thing to remember is that you need to learn to combine think aloud with observation, as discussed in Part One. Although most of the time people will be honest and truthful, this is not always the case. People won't always admit to struggling or finding something difficult, for example, or they will down-play it when they are.

When you first start using think aloud in usability testing, it is tempting to fill in all the gaps with probing questions when participants stop talking. In filling the silence you run the risk of going off the topic of the research, asking leading and biased questions and potentially preventing the participants saying things they had intended to before you leapt in. It can be useful to occasionally leave an awkward silence; most participants will endeavour to fill the void with commentary and thoughts. You'll also get used to using 'mmm' and 'uh-ha' a lot to encourage participants to keep talking, without leading them astray. With experience, you will get a feel for when it's right to talk because the participants needs encouragement to verbalize their thoughts and when to remain silent.

The participants will ask you questions when they are struggling, which can feel like a dilemma at first: it's common to want to ease participants' frustration/anxiety/stress, but it will introduce bias. Here are few tips on how to handle these situations:

- Immediately note down their question and at what point in the task they asked.

- Before answering the question, ask them what they would do if they were doing this by themselves. This is useful for seeing if they can solve the issue on their own or identify at what point in the process they would have actually given up if you weren't there observing them.

- If it's not critical to the research session, do not answer the question. Simply ask them to move on to whatever is next. You may want to tell them you'll answer outstanding questions at the end of the session.

- If it is critical to the research session that they progress at this point, do offer assistance, but be sure to note down that you helped out and they could not progress on their own, as this is a serious usability issue.

4 POST-TASK INTERVIEW

Once you have completed the tasks that you need to cover, or as many as possible in the time available, it's worth leaving 5 minutes at the end to conclude the research session with a few final interview questions. These questions should continue to adhere to the rules we've already set up, in terms of being neutral and open. You can ask anything you want, but it's useful to have a few questions in mind, such as the ones I've suggested below. You may want to tweak, add or remove certain questions depending on what you've observed and heard during the session. As long as it's relevant to the research session, it's all good.

It's worth keeping in mind that the final statements that the participants make may not always accurately reflect the experience they've just had. Sometimes they can be overly positive or negative in their assessment (which is interesting in itself). Here are some examples of post-task interview questions you could pose:

- Overall, how would you describe your experience of the website today?

- Was it what you expected? Did anything surprise you?

- Was the __ easy or difficult to find?
- Was the __ overall easy or difficult to understand?
- Having seen what is currently available on the site, is there anything else that you would like to see, or is it all covered?
- If you could change one thing about what you have seen today, what would it be?
- Is there anything else you would like to mention?

It's nice to finish on a statement of thanks such as: 'Thank you very much for your participation. It will help us in the process of improving X to make it easier to use.' If there is any follow-up to the session, now's the time to remind the participants and also pay them (if appropriate).

POST-TEST CRIB SHEET

In between research sessions, if you have time, it can be useful to note down the most important things about the session while they are still fresh in your mind. You could use these headings:

Participant name/number

Task name

Task completed/partially completed/failed

Top three issues

Top three positive things

Useful quotes

Remote testing considerations

Remote moderated testing can be set up in a similar way to face-to-face usability testing, in terms of drafting your protocol. The main difference between remote and face-to-face usability testing is the technology involved in letting people in different locations connect, so you may need a few more prompts and questions as you cannot observe body language and facial expressions so easily. When considering the timings for your research session, you need to bear in mind that it will take a little longer to start the session, because of setting up and logging into whatever tool is being used, for both you and the participants. The same rules apply to remote testing as face-to-face testing. You'll need to remind the participants if you are recording the research session and if there are people observing.

Tools for moderated usability testing

EQUIPMENT CHECKLIST

- Protocol (one or one per participant).
- Something to take notes on.
- Devices (desktop or laptop, tablet, smartphone) if what you are testing is digital or has digital aspects. For mobile devices it's beneficial to have more than one for participants to use, as operating systems are quite different (eg, Apple vs Android). It's worth having a device the participants are somewhat familiar with otherwise the results will be skewed.

Note: I like to write my notes on the protocol next to the particular task or question they are related to, so I print out one protocol per participant. Others will print off one protocol then write their notes on a pad of paper or laptop, etc.

OPTIONAL ITEMS

- A second screen that is mirroring the device the participants are using so you don't have to look over their shoulders too much.
- A way to record the session (a video record if not on a traditional computer). If you are on a desktop or laptop you can use screen recording software; there is also specialist software such as Morae and Camtasia from TechSmith (https://www.techsmith.com) that has been specifically built to record and edit usability testing sessions.
- If testing on a mobile device there are various rigs which have a web camera mounted that can be used.

Eye tracking equipment is expensive to own, but often available in specialists labs. It can be a useful addition to your user research, but is not essential. Eye tracking is useful for observation as it allows you to see what the participants are looking at, what they are focusing on and what they are ignoring. If you do have access to this equipment, it's worth reading up on it.

TOOLS FOR REMOTE TESTING

At the time of writing, video conferencing and screen sharing tools are freely available and easy to use. Your organization may already have tools for remote testing, but consider whether your participants have access to these tools and the limitations of their technology.

There are different ways to utilize these tools depending on the setup of the product/service you are testing. For instance, if it's a live website, ask the participants to access the website and share their screen with you. This is the quickest and easiest way for the remote testing to happen. If it's a prototype on a secure server, you will need to access the prototype on your computer and then give the participants control of your screen so that they can interact with the prototype directly. Sometimes the participants can experience some lag, but generally it's ok. You may have to talk to your IT department about access.

EXAMPLE OF REMOTE TESTING

I once worked on a project with tight timescales, looking at education software resources for teachers. I needed to do the testing in the space of a couple of days, during term time. That meant that some participants (the teachers) were taking part in remote moderated usability testing at school during their lunch breaks and free periods. I had to make sure the day before the research sessions happened that the teachers were able to download software (the remote testing tool) on the computer to allow them to take part in the session.

There are lots of options and they are changing all the time. Look for an option that allows control of the screen to be shared between you and the participants, which will let you and them interact with each other's screens (if permission is given).

The fundamentals of unmoderated usability testing

What is unmoderated usability testing?

Unmoderated usability testing means participants complete specific, defined tasks without the presence or intervention of a moderator, mostly researching digital items. As with moderated testing, unmoderated testing can be done both face-to-face and remotely.

What unmoderated usability testing is good for

In remote unmoderated usability testing, participants can complete the research essentially at any time, in any place and on any device, giving both you and the participant flexibility. Some suggest that it is more realistic and unbiased than moderated usability testing (Zurb, 2017). While it is true that thinking aloud and asking questions can affect the way a task is completed, the benefits of capturing this in-depth qualitative data can outweigh this, depending on the objectives of your research.

Unmoderated usability testing is effective at understanding, through observation alone, how participants actually complete a task; you aren't able to talk to the participants while they are undertaking the task, or ask what they are doing and why. It is a useful method to use if:

- *You need a large sample of data.* A small sample of face-to-face usability test sessions is enough to understand behaviour from a design perspective. However, some stakeholders are uncomfortable making decisions on such small numbers. Doing research with lots of people may be simpler than trying to convince others of the value of the small sample (below we will talk about increasing stakeholders' confidence).

- *Where the audience is hard to access.* They may be geographically dispersed or time-poor or have other reasons why they cannot travel to you. The research can still be done, without great cost.

- *Where timescales are tight.* An example would be working in an agile environment, but we all know what it's like to work on a project with tight timelines or one that is running behind schedule – getting research done quickly may be the only option. An unmoderated study can be run in its entirety in a couple of days. However, you shouldn't have this as your only method for iterative testing; you can work towards building different kinds of research into the work schedule.

- *Where a specific context is critical to getting valid insight.* Some products/services are used or happen in environments that cannot be replicated in a lab/office setting; for example, an app used outdoors for orienteering or a service being used by emergency medical staff.

- *Where budgets are limited.* Remote unmoderated tests don't require a reserved location and the cost of these tools is scalable, so you can pay whatever amount you deem appropriate.

What unmoderated usability testing is not good for

As with all methods there are limitations to its application:

- *Can you recruit the right people?* By choosing unmoderated testing you are excluding participants who don't have easy access to computers and the internet or who have low digital literacy. The range of participants you need should be a consideration in the methodology you choose. Also, unmoderated testing runs the risk of participants being motivated purely by the incentive payment.

- *There is a lack of in-depth conversation.* While you can include forms for open-ended questions to users, you won't get the depth of insight that can come from a conversation between moderator and participant.

- *You have less control of what happens.* Because it's up to the user to decide when a task is complete, participants may move onto the next task prematurely.

Effort required to do this kind of research

As with moderated usability testing, you can get to grips with the basics of unmoderated testing relatively quickly. The main thing is to keep in mind best practices in task writing; otherwise it's pretty easy to set up most kinds of unmoderated testing. If you are testing remotely, depending on what you are testing and the tool you have chosen, you may need some technical help setting things up. It's probably a good idea to pre-warn the technical folk when this will happen (if you aren't the technical folk in question).

When to use unmoderated usability testing

Remote unmoderated usability testing is used when quantitative data is important and therefore a large number of participants are needed to take part in the research. In both remote and face-to-face usability testing, the actions of the participants are tracked/recorded in some way so that they can be analysed after the data has been captured.

How to do unmoderated usability testing

Running good quality unmoderated usability testing starts with the set-up, and the first question is about format, which can be low- or high-fidelity:

- *Digital/paper prototypes:* take photos of your drawing on paper or use simple wireframes with no functionality built into them (digital sketches).

- *Low-fidelity prototypes:* these are black and white wireframes with some simple functionality (eg, some buttons are clickable and something will happen when you press them).
- *High-fidelity prototypes:* these are interactive wireframes that have visual design built into them; they could closely resemble a finished website.
- *Live testing environment:* working version of a website that isn't fully finished or publicly available.
- Live publicly available website.
- Any other relevant assets, including physical artefacts if doing face-to-face unmoderated testing.

Choosing the type of unmoderated testing you want to do

Decide what observations you want recorded. For remote testing, this could affect the tool you chose (for example, one that allows qualitative notes to be added by the participant). For face-to-face testing this will help you with instructions for observers. You also need to identify the metrics you want to record:

- task completion rates;
- time on task;
- time on pages;
- clicks per task;
- web analytic data (eg, browser, operating system, screen resolution, device).

Draft your unmoderated protocol

The opening statement: have a statement for participants to read and agree to before they start doing the tasks. This will explain what to expect (in terms of tasks and session length), what the research is about, how the data will be captured and what you'll do with it, how you'll store it and for how long. You may also want to ask a couple of survey questions about the participants after the opening statement but before they undertake the tasks.

Set up your tasks. You should have well-defined specific tasks. As there is no moderator, tasks should be succinct and easy to follow. Avoid conflating two tasks into one question, as this will lead to confusion. It's important that participants complete one task at a time.

Run pilot tests to see how long it will take on average to complete the number of tasks you want to include in your research. I think that shorter sessions (up to 15 minutes) work better for unmoderated testing, as you are relying on the self-motivation of the participants.

Post-task/test questions: you can ask the participants questions after each task and/or at the end of the session when all the tasks have been completed or attempted. After each task, you could ask the participants about their satisfaction at doing the task. There are various methods you can draw upon to measure such things, such as the Net Promoter Score, which is a paid-for solution to track customer experience (Satmetrix Systems, 2017). There is also the System Usability Scale (SUS; Usability.gov, 2017). When a SUS is used, participants are asked to score the following 10 items (see Thomas, 2015) although you can use any relevant questions you want:

1 I think that I would like to use this system frequently.

2 I found the system unnecessarily complex.

3 I thought the system was easy to use.

4 I think that I would need the support of a technical person to be able to use this system.

5 I found the various functions in this system were well integrated.

6 I thought there was too much inconsistency in this system.

7 I would imagine that most people would learn to use this system very quickly.

8 I found the system very cumbersome to use.

9 I felt very confident using the system.

10 I needed to learn a lot of things before I could get going with this system.

You can find tools online to help you calculate your SUS score.

While the participants are working through the tasks, give them closed questions with a choice of relevant answers rather than requiring them to type an answer to an open-ended question (which is more difficult and takes longer for the participants to complete and for you to analyse). Sometimes the rules need to be broken: if researching the participants' understanding of something you may need to include open-ended questions with open text fields for the participants to describe what they have understood.

You can ask the participants to complete a survey afterwards, but research shows that people find it difficult to recall actions accurately. Some remote unmoderated testing tools do allow participants to make notes and annotations as they complete the task. In a similar way to a moderator asking the participant a question (the observer effect), making notes about the task will interrupt the natural flow, to a certain extent. It really depends on your objectives for how you want to run your research; each method has its pros and cons. You need to decide whether you want accurate observation (allow participants to make notes during the task or record them thinking aloud to themselves), or realistic and naturalistic task completion (give participants a post-task survey if you want to know their thoughts).

Thank you statement

This can be served as a final page to close a remote research session or as a follow up email, depending on how the tool you are using works. If it is face-to-face you can say this to the participants at the end. You can include a short statement that may cover your appreciation for their participation, reminders if anything is going to happen next, and contact details if the participants have questions.

Face-to-face unmoderated usability testing considerations

During face-to-face unmoderated research, the participants are left alone in the research lab (or wherever you are doing the testing) with a series of tasks to complete. You could observe from somewhere else or sit next to them. Participants can think aloud or not, depending on your objectives. This methodology is more unusual and not used as often, but is worth considering as it allows for more naturalistic behaviour when interacting with your product or service, compared with moderated testing, although it's likely to be a relatively unnatural setting if it's not the participant's home or workplace.

If you are using a research lab, you can employ eye tracking technology to aid your observation. Unmoderated testing with eye tracking will allow you to ask questions such as:

- Do participants notice the xx?
- Are participants able to use xx?
- What is the cognitive load of having xx on the page? Does xx make it harder or easier for participants to navigate to what they need? (Richardson, 2014)

As you have the participants in close proximity, after the task(s) is finished you have an opportunity to ask them questions about their experience. There are several ways to do this:

- *Online or paper survey:* participants to complete a few questions after each task. This is less disruptive but you will get less in-depth answers.
- *Short interview(s):* ask a few questions/have a short discussion about the participants' experience. You are relying on them accurately recalling what they have done and how they felt about it.
- *Post experience eye-tracked protocol (PEEP):* in this instance, you and the participants watch a video of the participants completing the task. You can pause the video at relevant points to ask them what they were doing or thinking about at that particular point. This method is labour-intensive as the observer/moderator will need to keep accurate times-tamped notes of what they want to ask the participants about. It is more disruptive to the flow of the session if you do this for multiple tasks and you will only be able to complete a few tasks in one research session. The major benefit of this method is that you are not relying on the recall and memory of the participants, which will allow for a more accurate and in-depth discussion about their experience (Ball et al, 2006).

EXAMPLE OF FACE-TO-FACE UNMODERATED USABILITY

I have used face-to-face unmoderated usability testing to see how participants go about finding online guidance and resources to support them in their role in an agile working environment. It was useful to see how they did or did not complete the tasks depending on their knowledge of agile ways of working and agile jargon. If they did not understand the terms used in the guidance, this became clear when they were persistent or when they would give up and go elsewhere to find what they were looking for. In combination with other user research methods it helped identify when too much jargon was being used. It also gave insight into what language would help both those new to agile and those who are experts, which is a difficult balance to strike.

Tools for unmoderated remote usability testing

Find a tool that will allow you to do the kind of test you want to conduct with the assets you have available. Most tools will give a live demonstration if you ask, or will allow you to trial it for free to make sure it's the right tool for you.

Summary of usability testing

It's not really moderated versus unmoderated

Moderated and unmoderated testing are complementary: you can run both kinds of research. For example, you can run a moderated test on your prototype, then iron out any major usability issues; further on in your development cycle, you can run an unmoderated test to gauge how it performs 'in the wild'. If possible, run both kinds of research for true confidence in your results.

Building confidence in small samples

If you've already had some experience of doing or commissioning user research, it's likely that you have come across stakeholders' resistance to and lack of confidence in the small numbers involved in qualitative testing compared with the large sample sizes gained from unmoderated usability testing and surveys. Building stakeholders' understanding of qualitative usability testing will help gain their trust in the results and confidence in the decisions on the next step to take. Reichelt (2014) advocates that if you're doing qualitative design research, you shouldn't worry about sample size or statistical significance. The only thing that matters is how confident your team members are about the next decision they need to make.

Reichelt (2014) advises that everyone making and signing off decisions should watch user research sessions on a regular basis. This can be difficult to schedule with busy stakeholders, so video playback could help. As soon as you start doing user research, you'll be so busy working out what to do with everything you're learning. You'll know what is broken and what is not, and you'll know what you need to spend more time learning about.

References and further reading

Ball, L, Eger, N, Stevens, R and Dodd, J (2006) Applying the post-experience eye-tracked protocol (PEEP) method in usability testing, *Interfaces, 67,* pp 15–19

Bojko, A (2013) *Eye Tracking, the User Experience: A practical guide to research,* Rosenfeld Media, New York

Bolt, N and Tulathimutte, T (2010) *Remote Research. Real users, real time, real research,* Rosenfeld Media, New York

Cao, J (2017) Moderated vs. unmoderated usability testing: Which is better? UX Pin. www.uxpin.com/studio/blog/moderated-vs-unmoderated-usability-testing-better/ (archived at https://perma.cc/62RG-HN5X)

Dumas, J S and Redish, J C (1999) *A Practical Guide to Usability Testing,* revised edn, Intellect Ltd, Bristol

Gray, C (7 October 2015) How to run an unmoderated remote usability test. UX Mastery. https://uxmastery.com/how-to-run-an-unmoderated-remote-usability-test-urut/ (archived at https://perma.cc/Y7HB-DA2E)

Lanoue, S (18 May 2015) Writing your user test plan: Open-ended vs. specific tasks and questions. User Testing Blog. www.usertesting.com/blog/2015/05/18/open-ended-vs-specific-tasks-and-questions/ (archived at https://perma.cc/X52B-6QYU)

Nielsen, J (16 January 2012) Thinking aloud: The #1 usability tool. Nielsen Norman Group. www.nngroup.com/articles/thinking-aloud-the-1-usability-tool/ (archived at https://perma.cc/FG33-HEWX)

Norman Nielsen Group (1 July 2014) Selecting an online tool for unmoderated remote user testing. www.nngroup.com/articles/unmoderated-user-testing-tools/ (archived at https://perma.cc/7QKC-XS2X)

Reichelt, L (16 September 2014) Sample size and confidence: how to get your team to trust qualitative research. gov.UK User Research Blog. https://userresearch.blog.gov.uk/2014/09/16/sample-size-and-confidence/ (archived at https://perma.cc/2T26-YNNF)

Richardson, C (17 December 2014) Using unmoderated research with eye-tracking. gov.UK User Research Blog. https://userresearch.blog.gov.uk/2014/12/17/using-unmoderated-research-with-eye-tracking/ (archived at https://perma.cc/A2H3-PNQ5)

Satmetrix Systems, Inc. (2017) What is Net Promoter? Net Promoter Network. www.netpromoter.com/know/ (archived at https://perma.cc/9EV8-Q57P)

Thomas, N (13 July 2015) How to use the System Usability Scale (SUS) to evaluate the usability of your website. Usability Geek. https://usabilitygeek.com/how-to-use-the-system-usability-scale-sus-to-evaluate-the-usability-of-your-website/ (archived at https://perma.cc/U6XE-VZQF)

Usability.gov (2017) System Usability Scale (SUS). US Department of Health &
    Human Services. www.usability.gov/how-to-and-tools/methods/system-usability-
    scale.html (archived at https://perma.cc/5N7M-JU5J)
Zurb (2017) Unmoderated user testing. Zurb Word. http://zurb.com/word/
    unmoderated-user-testing (archived at https://perma.cc/V9VT-ALG6)

08

Content testing

What do people think your content means?

Content testing is a specific type of usability testing that focuses on how suitable and understandable your content is for the intended audience(s). It can be done as part of usability testing or separately.

What is good content?

I learnt what I know about content testing from reading Government Digital Service blogs. Good digital content is clear, actionable and readers can find what they're looking for. We know good content when we see it, and we're frustrated when we don't. Good content takes a lot of hard work to create, but if you get it right it can help build trust and confidence in users and can reduce the risk of errors being made by your organization and by your users.

What content testing is good for

There are many forms of content – imagery, video, infographics, various art forms, text etc. The research methods I'm talking about here focus on written content, but can be adapted for other types of content as these methods aim to gain insight into what people understand by what they see, the language they use, and what they would do with action- and task-oriented content. Finding appropriate ways to test our content helps us improve and find best practice patterns for creating it. Content testing is also a good way to understand how accessible and inclusive it is for our user groups.

What content testing is not good for

If you want to do research on the impact of content and how emotive it is, there are more effective methods to be found in the market research toolkit.

Effort required to do this kind of research

As with usability testing it is relatively easy to practise and learn these methods. You can learn the basics of running tests and gaining insights into users' understanding and language, and start doing usability testing straight away. But it does require some time and effort to become a skilled moderator, whether you are focusing on content or looking at usability more broadly. When you want to compare several versions of digital content, you may want to do multivariate testing, which will need some support from technical people, depending on your organization's set-up.

When to use content testing

Do research on your content as soon as you can in the development cycle. Particularly in the world of digital development, content can become an afterthought, looked at once the technical build has become relatively stable. As creating good content can take a lot of time and effort, creation needs to be started early and tested iteratively. If this is not possible in your line of work, I would aim to do content testing as soon as you can after the draft content is available.

How to test the effectiveness of content

You don't have to test content *in situ,* especially at the beginning of the content creation process. However, it is useful in iterative research to test the content in the context in which it will be used, to truly understand its effectiveness. As with all kinds of user research, do the testing with the users the content is being created for. There are various methods that can be used to do this.

Before you start your research

As preparation for whatever type of content testing you are doing, you can check the assumed reading age of your written content. There are various online resources to help you do this; for instance the Hemingway App (http://www.hemingwayapp.com/) identifies lengthy, complex sentences, common errors and passive sentences to help you refine your content before you put it in front of participants.

Comprehension testing

This involves asking open-ended questions about the meaning of your words. There is a lot of content out there that uses unfamiliar legal or technical words or phrases, or asks questions that may be hard for users to understand. You don't have to wait until you have a working prototype or a nicely designed leaflet to test people's understanding. You can print out the words, phrases and questions, and ask users to read them out and tell you what they mean.

It can be useful to ask open-ended questions such as, 'What does this mean to you?' You can also use open-ended and task-oriented content questions to determine if participants have understood the content and what they expect the outcomes or next steps to be, based on what they have read. Can they take action given what they have understood? For example: 'How would you use this website to sign up for xxx?' 'Based on what you read in the document, can you explain xxx to me, without looking at or rereading what you've seen?'

This method is useful for creating content for different cognitive needs and abilities. This kind of testing can remove the 'I'm taking a test' feeling from the research, keeping the pressure and anxiety levels low, as there is no 'right' answer.

Cloze testing

Cloze testing is another method that focuses on reading comprehension. Participants look at a selection of text with certain words removed and they fill in the blanks. When creating a test, you can delete words using a formula (eg, every fifth word), or you can delete selectively (eg, key words).

You can decide to accept only exact answers, or you can accept synonyms. Sample as many readers as possible for greater accuracy. You can set rules for acceptance: 75 per cent accuracy is considered successful and no refinement is required; below this threshold iteration of content design and testing would be necessary. This kind of comprehension testing is useful for when it's difficult to avoid a certain amount of 'jargon' and technical words, even though research does show that everyone prefers plain English.

The kind of comprehension testing that is most suitable for you really depends on what you are testing and with whom you are doing the research. My best advice would be: if you are not sure which kind of comprehension testing to do, run some pilot tests and see what your participants respond to most effectively, and what gives you the most useful insight.

Let people choose their own words

When you let people tell you how they feel in their own words, you can reflect this language in your content. This technique can be used on sensitive content such as dealing with the criminal justice system or personal loss. For example, gov.uk has content on what to do after someone dies (https://www. gov.uk/after-a-death), not after someone 'passes away'.

You can also use this research method to get insight into the language your user groups use, how they differ from each other and how their usage aligns with that of your organization. This is useful for getting to know your users and for starting to work out what language can be used to support the needs of diverse user groups.

A/B (comparative) testing

This kind of testing compares two (or more) versions of content to see which performs better (we'll look at this in more depth in Chapter 16 for digital products and services). It's also a good way to test how users connect with your content. You can do this by showing participants each version (making sure you alternate which version you use first, to avoid bias), or you can test this in real life, by serving each version to different users of your digital product/service and testing which is most successful at doing the thing you need it to do.

The UK National Health Service wrote eight variations of material asking users to sign up as organ donors. The test assessed the use of plain language and ease of understanding. The sign-up rate for each piece of content was measured and the multivariate test showed which call to action was most effective, but not why (Loosemore, 2014).

Highlighting content

This technique is low-fi: all you need is a print-out of the content for each participant plus one for yourself, and highlighter pens. Ask participants to read the print-out and to highlight things that made them feel more confident in green, and things that made them feel less confident in red. Once they have finished, take your own copy of the content and copy the highlighting with a matching colour for each participant. Once this is done for all the participants, you can see how the text made people feel. Darker green shows text that made people feel confident; darker red shows text that made them feel less so.

The technique is quick and easy. It allows your team to immediately understand the impact of what they're writing. You can learn how to describe your product/service in a way that's clearer and simpler, and make content choices that will benefit your users. You can also ask users to sort the words, phrases and questions according to trust, confidence, or other concerns.

Guerrilla content testing

If you don't have easy access to participants, consider using relevant events and conferences that you may be going to as an opportunity to test content 'in the wild'. You can read more about this in Chapter 18 and in Ploughman (2015).

References and further reading

Cawthorne, C and Barnes, E (6 April 2016) Guest post: looking at the different ways to test content. Government Digital Service Blog. https://gds.blog.gov.uk/2016/04/06/guest-post-looking-at-the-different-ways-to-test-content/ (archived at https://perma.cc/5N9G-2EJZ)

Gale, P (2 September 2014) A simple technique for evaluating content. gov.uk User Research Blog. https://userresearch.blog.gov.uk/2014/09/02/a-simple-technique-for-evaluating-content/ (archived at https://perma.cc/VV9A-SEVR)

Holliday, B (30 July 2014) Reversing a circle of mistrust. gov.uk User Research Blog. https://userresearch.blog.gov.uk/2014/07/30/reversing-a-circle-of-mistrust-2/ (archived at https://perma.cc/Q9VK-HGNE)

Loosemore, T (18 March 2014) One link on gov.uk – 350,000 more organ donors, Government Digital Service Blog. https://gds.blog.gov.uk/2014/03/18/organ-donorregister/ (archived at https://perma.cc/X85G-RGAU)

Ploughman, J (16 November 2015) Guerrilla testing content – it makes it better. Inside gov.uk Blog. https://insidegovuk.blog.gov.uk/2015/11/16/guerrilla-testing-content-it-makes-it-better/ (archived at https://perma.cc/VM6C-6EZT)

Waterworth, J (1 July 2015) What does this mean? Tips for testing your words. gov.uk User Research Blog. https://userresearch.blog.gov.uk/2015/07/01/what-does-this-mean-tips-for-testing-your-words/ (archived at https://perma.cc/GB6F-NTWB)

09

Card sorting

Understanding how people group and relate things

What is card sorting?

Card sorting is a method used to understand how people think about and associate things, grouping items that are related to each other.

What card sorting is good for

This is a useful method when designing or refining the structure of a website; for example what pieces of information are closely related and therefore should be grouped together and given a label. The structure of a website, also known as the 'information architecture', gives you to ability to make things easy to find: not only where they are placed in the navigation but also what they are called.

Card sorting doesn't necessarily need to focus on content and website items. It can also give you insight into people's mental models (as we'll discuss in parts Three and Four on analysing and presenting your data) and how they think about and associate anything. Card sorting can provide a good foundation for structuring of content and iteratively improving that structure, whether you know something within the structure isn't working or you are adding new things to it.

What card sorting is not good for

Card sorting focuses on content. If it is used in isolation without considering tasks and journeys, it may produce an information architecture that is unusable when users are attempting real tasks. To meet user needs, card sorting should be used in combination with other methodologies such as prototype or paper usability testing.

It can be time-consuming, depending on the amount of content being sorted and the number of participants. The analysis of the data can also be difficult and time-consuming, but there are tools that can help you with this.

When to use card sorting

Card sorting can be used at any time in the lifecycle of a product, service or experience. Depending where you are in that lifecycle and what your objectives are, different card sorting methods will be appropriate at different times. There are four methods to consider:

1 Open card sorting: the participants group the items and name the groups however they want.

2 Closed card sorting: the researcher predefines the names of the groups and asks the participants to put items in the groups they think each item is most related to.

3 Hybrid card sorting: this is a combination of open and closed sorting. You may have a few predefined groupings but participants can add additional groups.

4 Iterative card sorting: this can be used in both open and closed card sorting, where participants iteratively refine the previous participants' grouping.

When to do open sorting

Open card sorting is very exploratory. If you have no fixed ideas about how the items you are interested in should be grouped, do open card sorting. It will be useful, for example, if:

- you are building something new from scratch;
- analytics and other insights show that the current groups are fundamentally not working;
- there has been a significant change of some sort that means the current structure is no longer appropriate.

When to do closed sorting

Closed sorting is used to confirm that a pre-existing structure works across all your user groups. You may have a good idea of how things should be structured (as you have analytics and insight or you've already done an open card sort to explore what the groups should be).

When to do hybrid testing

If you are looking at the structure of a website, the analytics may show that certain parts are working effectively and others are not. You may choose to focus only on what's not working, but you may want to take a holistic view and include everything. You could include the predefined categories you are confident about and let the participants name the categories that you are not confident about. Another scenario is if you are adding new content, products or services: you can have the existing structure predefined and the new items can be added by the participants to the different categories.

When to do iterative card sorting

There are two types of iterative testing to think about. The first is multiple iterative card sorting projects: this is when you do more than one round of research, perhaps breaking it down into manageable chunks or if you have multiple user groups, doing separate research projects with each group. This kind of iterative testing is always recommended: it is rare that a single card sorting project will tell you everything that you need to know and you'll usually use a combination of open and closed card sorting.

The second is single iterative card sorting projects: this should only be used if your timescales are very tight. Having participants refine what earlier participants have done is almost like doing analysis on the fly. You won't have to merge each individual card sort to see the patterns, but you should be aware that you will probably get different results if the participants were to do it individually rather than use the iterative method where they already have a structure to work with. This is not to say that it's better or worse, but just to keep in mind it's different.

Effort required to do this kind of research

Card sorting is accessible to all levels of researcher: straightforward card sorts can be relatively easy to organize and run. However, it does require some time and effort to become a skilled moderator for particularly complex sorts. Equipment is inexpensive, whether opting for the low-tech (cards/paper) or hi-tech (online tools) options.

The time and effort required to do a card sorting project depends on the kind of sorting you are doing. Moderated face-to-face card sorting is time and resource heavy, whereas a remote unmoderated card sort is quick to set up and administer if you have participants ready to go.

How to do card sorting

Moderated card sorting

Face-to-face: the researcher and the participants are in the same room at the same time interacting with each other. Items are written on cards and the participants group the items physically on a table, while talking to the researcher about their thinking and understanding of items and groups. *Remote:* the researcher and the participants are in different places but are interacting with each other. They could be using screen sharing technology and tools such as OptimalSort (www.optimalworkshop.com) to do a 'virtual' card sort. You can also use spreadsheets for virtual/remote sorting.

Unmoderated card sorting

Face-to-face: the researcher and the user are in the same room at the same, but the researcher would not intervene and converse while the participants are grouping the items. *Remote:* the researcher would not be involved while the participants do the sorting, at a time and place of their choosing, again using tools such as OptimalSort.

Preparing your cards

There are two options for face-to-face moderated card sorting:

Option 1. Write the name of the item on the front of the card. If you aren't including the descriptions on the cards themselves, it's worth having them written separately for you (as moderator) to refer to, if the participants have questions. Not sharing the descriptions upfront means it is more of a conversation about the meaning of items on the cards.

Option 2. Write the item name on the front and a description on the back. Having the description on the card means that the participants can check for themselves that what they thought the item name meant is the same as your understanding. This will allow you to avoid inconsistent sorting based on misunderstanding of items. You can use probing questions on why the participants checked the description. Why did they hesitate? Were they unsure? Did they think it meant something different? This will help you understand in more depth which labels need to be refined.

There is no right or wrong method; it is more about preparation time required and how comfortable you feel moderating. Whether you are using option 1 or 2, it's important to have a shared organizational understanding of what each item is, so that it can be compared against the participants' understanding to identify where it converges and diverges.

To rename or not rename

Should you allow participants to rename cards/items or groups if they don't make sense, or the participants feel they have a better way to describe it? This is something you need to consider in face-to-face testing as you can have extra stationery resources available to do this. In remote testing, you can note down comments on changing names of groups, but the software used for remote card sorting often doesn't allow renaming, unless you are using a spreadsheet.

How to select your cards

CHOOSING WHAT TO TEST

The first thing to do is decide on a list of topics. This can come from a wide variety of sources such as existing or potential online content, descriptions of processes, applications and functions. Including what's planned allows you to create structures that work now and in to the near future (to a certain extent).

MAKE SURE THE GRANULARITY IS CONSISTENT

Whatever topics you decide to test, you need to make sure that they are all at the same level. For example, if the majority of your cards are individual pages, do not include other cards that are whole sections of the site; make all the cards individual pages. Other levels of the site (eg, sections) will have to be done in a different card sort, otherwise participants will find it difficult to group content at different levels of granularity.

What you select for the card sort should be representative of what you're doing research on, whether it's a whole thing or a section of something. There needs to be enough similar content to allow groups to form, but variation across the item you are focusing on, otherwise patterns and trends can't be identified.

HOW MANY CARDS SHOULD YOU INCLUDE?

The general consensus is between 30 and 100 cards. If you have fewer than 30, there are not enough items to form groups; more than 100 cards can be time-consuming and tiring for participants. I would suggest that you take into consideration the complexity of the content that you are sorting: the more complex the topic, the fewer cards should be used, as this kind of card sorting has a high cognitive load.

How many participants should you include?

Rarely will you have a group of users that are interested in all aspects of what you provide. Usually they will be very interested in one or two specific things and perhaps (if we're lucky) vaguely interested in another couple of areas. You could get everyone to sort everything, but asking participants to sort things they have no knowledge of or interest in is going to introduce inaccuracies and inconsistency.

> Quick note on participant numbers: as with usability testing, you should really be doing card sorting with five people from each defined user group.

CASE STUDY

Example of card sorting

I learnt through experience that it is not necessarily a good idea to get everyone to sort everything, for example when I did a qualitative face-to-face moderated open card sort for the UK Houses of Parliament intranet. There are three very high-level groups of people who work for the UK Parliament:

Group 1: Commons-focused (the business of Members of Parliament in the Commons).

Group 2: Lords-focused (the business of Members of the House of Lords).

Group 3: Bicameral (work that happens across both Houses).

Participants in group 1 will concentrate on Commons-related content and will not be interested in Lords' content; they may have some interest in bicameral content. Participants in group 2 will be the opposite; to be effective you would only ask them to sort Lords-related content and content that concerns the whole of Parliament. Those in group 3 will have a lot of knowledge of the bicameral work of Parliament, but it cannot necessarily be assumed that they have interest in the individual work of the House of Lords and House of Commons; some will, some won't. You will only be able to determine this by talking to them and ascertaining their areas of interest.

For quantitative testing I would work out the number of participants you need for statistical significance. This would be for unmoderated remote testing, unless you have a lot of time and resource available.

Moderated face-to-face and remote card sorting

Moderated face-to-face sorting gives you the most flexibility in the kind of (qualitative) card sort that you want to do: open, closed, iterative or hybrid. Whatever card sorting method you select, you'll need to have a short protocol written up on the things you need to say and the topics and questions you want to cover. It won't be as extensive as a usability testing protocol (see Chapter 7), but it's extremely handy as a guide to keep each of the research sessions relatively consistent. The protocol should contain:

1 Introduction and the ethical/legal issues that we talked about in Part One (5 minutes).

2 Short pre-task interview questions (5 minutes).

3 Probes and prompt reminders for the card sort.

4 Short post-task interview questions (5 minutes).

1 INTRODUCTION

In Part One I gave advice on starting your research session by explaining to the participants what the research is about, what's going to happen, how the session is being recorded if at all and how you will use and store the data. Giving some context is generally the best way to start a research session.

If you want to take photographs of the participants doing the sort (some 'action shots') you need to ask their permission to do so and permission if you are going to use them in a report. It's worth including these clauses in the consent form you'll ask the participants to sign.

The introduction of a moderated remote card sorting protocol will be very similar to the face-to-face moderated sort, with some variations. For a remote card sort, you need to make participants aware of the following:

- If anyone else is observing the session apart from you.
- The different tools you'll be using during the session.
- If you will record the session, and how you'll use and store the data.

You need to either read a consent statement for them to verbally agree to, or send them a document to sign or a short online survey to collect the consent and NDA statements that you require. If any of the software being used needs to be downloaded for the session, you may need to tell the participants to do so beforehand, otherwise you'll have to allow for plenty of time within the session to set everything up, meaning you'll have to extend the session length or limit the number of cards they are sorting.

2 SHORT PRE-TASK INTERVIEW QUESTIONS

When writing the interview questions and research tasks, refer back to Part One on asking the right kind of questions. These questions will help you understand some of the observations you make during the session on how the participants think about and group items and they will start to make the participants feel more comfortable before the sort.

3 PROBES AND QUESTIONS FOR MODERATING THE CARD SORT

Before you ask the participants to start the hard work of sorting and grouping the cards, explain what's going to happen. You can adapt the suggested explanation in the box below, depending on what is appropriate for your card sorting.

EXPLAINING A FACE-TO-FACE CARD SORT

I'm going to tell you how it's going to work – please let me know if you have any questions before we get started.

In front of you is a stack of cards. Those cards represent the (content/ functionality) for this (product/service). You should try and sort the cards into groups that make sense to you.

Don't worry about trying to design the navigation for a website; we'll take care of that.

It's not a memory test, and you don't need to try and organize the information as it is currently organized on the (product/service). I'm more interested in seeing how you would organize it into the groups you would expect to find things in.

(Open sort.) Once your groups are established, I'd like you to give each group a name that makes sense to you. You are allowed to make sub-groups if you feel that's appropriate. If you feel something is missing, you can use a blank index card to add it. Additionally, if a label is unclear, feel free to write a new label on the card.

(Closed sort.) You'll notice that there are some cards already on the table. These are the groups we'd like you to sort the cards into. If a label is unclear, feel free to write a better label on the card.

(Hybrid sort.) You'll notice that there are some cards already on the table. These are the groups we'd like you to sort the cards into. If you feel something is missing, you can use a blank index card to add it, whether it's a group or an important item. If a label is unclear, feel free to write a better label on the card.

(Iterative sort.)* You'll notice that the cards have already been sorted; this was done by the previous participants. I'd like you to have a look at the groupings they have created to see if they make sense to you. If there are changes that you want to make to the groupings, feel free to make them. You can make as many or as few changes as you want, depending on what does and doesn't make sense to you.

(All sorts.) Finally, if you think something doesn't belong, you can make a 'not sure' group. We'll look at them again at the end but there may not be a place for these cards, and that's ok.

Please feel free to ask questions during the sort if you feel the need. I may not answer them during the exercise, but I'll do my best to answer them when you've finished.

*Note that the instructions will be different for the first participants in an iterative card sort as they won't be refining a predefined set of groups. For the first participants, use whatever instructions are appropriate, whether for open, closed or hybrid sorting.

Variations for explaining a virtual card sort

These instructions assume you are using an online tool specifically for card sorting. If you are using a spreadsheet or something else, you'll need adapt these instructions to suit your tool of choice.

I'm going to tell you how it's going to work – please let me know if you have any questions before we get started.

To the side of the screen you will see a list of items. Those cards represent the content and functionality for this (product/service). You should try and sort the cards into groups that make sense to you. You can place the mouse over each item and drag it into the main area. When you start making groups, you can easily change which group an item is in by dragging it elsewhere in the main area.

(Open sort.) Once your groups are established, we'd like you to give each group a name that makes sense to you. You make a group by placing cards in the same area of the screen and the tool will automatically create the group for you. Once you have more than one card in a group, you will be able to type in the group name at the top. You cannot make sub-groups with the tool that we are using. If think sub-groups are appropriate at any point, please tell me and I will note down where you expect them to be. If you feel something is missing or if a label is unclear, please tell me and I will also note this down.

(Closed sort.) You'll notice that there are some labels already on screen. These are the groups we'd like you to sort the items into. You cannot make sub-groups with the tool that we are using. If you think sub-groups are appropriate at any point, please tell me and I will note down where you expect them to be. If you feel something is missing or if a label is unclear for an item or a group, please tell me and I will also note this down.

During the sorting phase you'll want to make some notes of the participants' comments and questions, giving you insight into what labels are or aren't working, their understanding and thought processes. As card sorting has a high cognitive load and participants will be concentrating on what they're doing, you may have to encourage them to think aloud. It can be a difficult balance to strike at first: trying to get insight into their thought processes but not interrupting these thought processes too much. As with usability testing, participants generally get used to talking to you while sorting the cards and will start to freely talk about what they are doing.

At the beginning of a sort give participants a few minutes of silence, and leave them alone with their own thoughts while they get into the flow. It may feel slightly uncomfortable but it is worth it. Once they have roughly established a few groups, you can start talking to them. If they are clearly struggling during these first few minutes, asking some open-ended, neutral questions could help them get started. Here are some example questions:

- What does this item mean to you? How would you describe it?
- What is it about the item name that makes you uncertain?
- What is it about these couple of items that makes them related for you?
- Based on the description of the card that I have just given you, does the item name work for you, or would you call it something different?
- Do you think some cards in this group are more closely related than others?
- Do you think this card could fit better in a different group or could it belong in both groups? Why is that, do you think?

It's difficult to anticipate exactly what the participants are going to say, but the questions above will cover most situations that you will find yourself in. Ultimately it's about avoiding bias and not giving the participants ideas on how to do the sorting.

4 SHORT POST-TASK INTERVIEW QUESTIONS

Wrapping up the session gives you a chance to get an overview from the participants:

- Please talk me through each of the groups you have created.
- What is it about the items in this group that makes them related?
- Why have you given the group this title?
- Are there any cards you think could belong to more than one group?
- Which group, if any, are you most confident about? Why is that, do you think?
- Which group, if any, are you least confident about? Why is that, do you think?
- Any final thoughts?

It's nice to finish on a statement of thanks such as: 'Thank you very much for your participation; it will help us in the process of improving this xxx to make it easier to use.'

Unmoderated face-to-face and remote card sorting

For remote and unmoderated card sorting the researcher would not be involved while the participants do the card sort at a time and place of their choosing, again using tools such as OptimalSort or UserZoom. Unmoderated testing is most useful for quantitative testing, when you are aiming for large numbers of people to complete the research. What we've learnt about card sorting and the fundamentals of user research so far can be used to set up your remote unmoderated card sort. To do so you'll need to include:

- an explanation;
- initial survey questions;
- sort instructions;
- post-sort questions;
- thank you statement and what happens next (Mayfield, 2011).

Face-to-face unmoderated card sorting is a more unusual way of doing a card sort: it's not a particularly good use of a moderator's time. However, it does have benefits: the participants will complete the task without any outside influence and there can be an in-depth discussion after the sort to understand what the participants have done, what was easy and what was difficult. You can read through the other types of card sorting and decide on the kind of interview you want to do.

Tools for card sorting

For face-to-face card sorting the following are essential:

1 Notecards (plain or lined). Enough notecards for the number of items you are sorting (pre-written); spare notecards if participants want to rename items; a set of notecards (perhaps a different colour or size) for group titles (blank for open sorting and pre-written for closed sorting) with spares available.

2 Pens: ideally something like Sharpies for writing on the cards. It is useful to have multiple colours for items, group titles, and participant annotation. Using felt tip pens allows for clear writing that is easily photographed.

3 Camera or smartphone: to photograph the groups created by each participant.

4 Consent form for the participants to sign to demonstrate understanding.

5 Protocol to guide you through the session, what you want to say and do, topics you want to cover. If you don't write notes on your protocol, you'll need a notepad.

Optional items:

- Video camera: it can be difficult to record card sorting in a way that allows you to capture the detail of the cards and not be too intrusive for the participants.

- Audio recorder: if you want to listen back to the conversation you have with each of the participants. (Along with the video camera – consider what you will use the recordings for.)

- Clipboard: something to rest your protocol on for taking notes. In my experience, you usually stand up a lot during card sorting as people create and refine groups on a table, but it's obviously not a requirement to stand!

For remote card sorting the following are essential:

1 An online card sorting tool such as OptimalSort or UserZoom.

2 An online conferencing and screen sharing tool (as described in Chapter 7 on usability testing).

3 If the tool does not have recording capabilities, you may want to use a screen recording, or you could use a phone instead of video conferencing.

Summary

As with usability testing, card sorting should be iterative. One card sort isn't going to tell you everything you need to know, especially if you have a large, complex content set or you have several different user groups. Don't try and do everything all in one go: this will make things difficult and complicated, not only to set up and run but particularly during analysis, where things could get unwieldy.

References and further reading

Croft, P (20 October 2014) Card sorting beginner's guide – improving your information architecture. www.smashingmagazine.com/2014/10/improving-information-architecture-card-sorting-beginners-guide/ (archived at https://perma.cc/9WHN-EHP8)

Mayfield, A (12 December 2011) Online or offline card sorting? Optimal Workshop. https://blog.optimalworkshop.com/moderated-card-sorting-with-optimalsort (archived at https://perma.cc/5MH3-N57M) (last accessed: 21 May 2017)

Spencer, D (7 April 2004) Card sorting: a definitive guide. Optimal Workshop. http://boxesandarrows.com/card-sorting-a-definitive-guide/ (archived at https://perma.cc/L829-4RPE)

Spencer, D (2009) *Card Sorting: Designing usable categories*, Rosenfeld Media, New York

10

Surveys

How to gauge a widespread user response

What are surveys?

Surveys are used frequently in both market and user research. They have limitations, but they are inexpensive to run and can potentially reach a lot of people. In Part One, we discussed using surveys for recruiting the right participants. In this chapter, we'll focus on surveys as a way of reaching a lot of people for user research, and gathering quantitative and structured data. The best practice discussed here can be applied to surveys/questionnaires you may want to conduct face-to-face or over the phone. However, in some cases, if you are able to do face-to-face research, other methods could gain more in-depth data on user experience issues; the choice depends on your objectives and who your users are.

What surveys are good for

Surveys allow you to count or quantify concepts, and you can apply what you learnt from a sample to the broader population. For example, you might have 100,000 unique users/visitors in a given year. If you collect information from 2,000 of them, you can confidently apply the information to the full 100,000 (Gray, 2014). Statistically significant data (needing about 1,000 responses) can provide stakeholders with confidence that a design or decision is effective. You may not need to aim for statistical significance, but surveys are still a useful way to gather quantitative and structured data on attitudes and opinions for analysis.

•

What surveys are not good for

It's not a good idea to ask participants to recall past behaviour you will not get an accurate reflection of the participants' actions. It's much easier to remember how you felt than what you did.

When to do a survey

You can do a survey at any stage of the development process or lifecycle (Usability.gov, 2017):

- Before a redesign you can learn about users, what they are trying to accomplish and their levels of satisfaction with the current experience.
- After launching a new or refined product/service you can learn if your new design meets the needs of users and identify areas for improvement.
- When you want to have content or features rated or ranked.
- You can conduct ongoing surveys to gain ideas for future improvements.
- You can explore the reasons people visit or use a product/service and assess how they feel about their experience.
- You can quantify results from qualitative research activities such as contextual inquiry or interviews.
- You can evaluate usability (System Usability Scale).

Effort required to do this kind of research

At a glance, it looks relatively quick and easy to put together and run a simple online survey. The effort is in getting the questions right, which isn't as easy as it looks. However, they can quickly become very complex if you need to include routing and logic to show the right questions to the right people. I don't cover this kind of survey; if you're interested in it, look at the further reading section for sources.

A NOTE ON BEING INCLUSIVE

The guidance here can be used for any kind of survey – online, face-to-face, over the phone – and the type you use should be the most appropriate for your user groups. Yes, online surveys will reach a lot of people quickly. Phone and face-to-face surveys will require a lot more time and effort but may be the most inclusive way to find the right people. This is particularly the case if the people you are interested in do not have easy access to a computer and the internet or they have low digital capability.

How to do surveys

As with any user research, before designing your survey you need to identify:

- your purpose;
- where you will find participants;
- the tool you will be using; and
- the limitations to information collection.

Get the fundamentals right (Gray, 2014; Usability.gov, 2017):

- Keep your surveys as brief as possible.
- Provide the participants with an estimate of completion time upfront.
- If possible show participants their progress while completing the survey.
- Include a mix of open-ended and closed questions.

Keep open text field questions to a minimum; multiple choice and rating scale questions are useful to represent how participants feel about a topic.

- Rating scale questions should have an equal number of positive and negative options; include neutral and don't know options – don't force them into an answer if they don't have an opinion.
- Group similar questions together and order them logically.
- Questions need to be appropriate for the audience. Ask them questions about themselves upfront; self-selection will help you serve them the right questions. Get to know how to use the logic rules of the survey tool you select.

Ask if respondents are willing to answer more in-depth questions in a follow-up survey or interview (and collect their contact details).

What you can ask about in a survey

Surveys are most useful when asking about an experience that participants have just had, so memories are relatively fresh. According to Gray (2014),

Turner (2011) and Usability.gov (2017), surveys can be used for gathering information on preferences, opinions and attitudes by asking about:

- Who your users are.
- What your users want.
- What they purchase.
- Where they shop.
- What they own.
- What they think of your product/service.
- Whether they are able to find what they're looking for.
- How satisfied they are with the product/service.
- What they like and dislike about it.
- What frustrations or issues they have had most recently.
- If they would recommend the product/service to others.
- If they have any ideas or suggestions for improvements.
- How they would describe the product/service in one or more words.
- If they could change one thing about the product/service what it would be and why.
- What features they could not live without.
- What features they could live without.
- Anything else they care to share (a good one to end with as a free text field.)

What to avoid asking about in a survey

- Don't make it mandatory to share contact and personal details (unless you are offering an incentive).
- Don't use double negatives and technical language. We looked at plain English in Part One asking the right kind of questions. Getting used to writing in this way is extremely important when using surveys to do your research.
- Don't use multiple concepts in one question: each question should be focused on one thing.

Who should fill in your survey?

If you have a target audience/user group in mind, you'll need to consider how you're going to recruit these people to respond to your survey. If anyone and everyone is to fill it in, that's obviously a lot easier, but will the results be useful? As always, it really depends on your objectives.

When to use recruitment agencies

If you want to reach new user groups/audiences, those who aren't already known to you, lapsed customers/users, or those you are aware of but are not associated with you, you'll need to engage an agency to find them. Go back to Part One and the section on who should be involved in your research to remind yourself of how to write a good recruitment brief.

You will have to be mindful of the costs of targeting a lot of specific people to complete your survey. Shop around for different quotes from the agencies to find a balance between good quality work and a good price.

When to do the recruitment yourself

If you are interested in the attitudes and preferences of existing user groups and you have available a database of customer details, get colleagues who are expert in using the database to identify suitable groups of people to contact, if you have permission to contact people in this way. If your digital product/service allows, you can deliver the survey to users while they are using it. There are various methods for having the survey appear or pop up at a certain point in a journey or experience, or after a certain time (you'll need to talk to the technical folk about that) or you can have it available on specific pages or at all times somewhere on every page. If you are doing a face-to-face survey, you may be able to stand somewhere where there is regular footfall of the relevant people.

Ask upfront about who the users are, to make sure you're getting the right people to complete the survey. Don't feel bad about kicking people out of the survey with a polite message, if they aren't the kind of person you want to hear from right now. Better for them to find out early on rather than needlessly filling in a survey. You'll also avoid having to take out the data they've input.

Do a pilot test

It is a good idea to test the survey before launching it to your full audience. Run a pilot of the survey with a subset of the audience to help refine the questions, if necessary. Initially you could ask a colleague or someone from your organization to pilot the survey. Don't give them too much information on background; only provide what any potential participants would have. Give them clear direction in terms of the type of feedback you are looking for along the lines of, are there any questions that didn't make sense to you? Are there any questions you couldn't answer or (in the case of multiple choice) were any missing the answer you wanted to provide?

When to give incentives

Whether or not you include an incentive can affect the kind of person that completes your survey. For basic five-minute surveys you don't necessarily have to offer any kind of incentive. For more detailed and complex surveys you will need to offer some kind of incentive, whether it is vouchers or cash. As is common with surveys, you can have a prize draw with three winners.

Survey tools

There are many online survey tools available. Some are free, many you'll need to pay for to get access to the right functions and allow for the number of responses you need. Research what's best within the budget you have.

For face-to-face and phone surveys, you may want to go as low-tech as paper and pen. You may want to have a spreadsheet set up to input answers when talking to people. Another option would be to have an online survey on a mobile device (tablet or smartphone). There are many tools available and the choice will depend on what is easiest for your users and what is the best way for you to gather a lot of data within your budget.

This chapter provides a brief overview and if you think you'll be conducting a lot of surveys in the future or you need a complex survey, I would recommend doing some further reading.

References and further reading

Farrell, S (25 September 2016) 28 tips for creating great qualitative surveys.
Nielsen Norman Group. www.nngroup.com/articles/qualitative-surveys/
(archived at https://perma.cc/NA6Q-6JTD) (last accessed: 18 August 2017)

Gray, C (20 November 2014) Better user research through surveys. UX Mastery.
http://uxmastery.com/better-user-research-through-surveys/ (archived at https://
perma.cc/UZV9-NQMP) (last accessed: 21 May 2017)

Jarrett C (due 2021) *surveys that work*, Rosenfeld Media, New York. http://
rosenfeldmedia.com/books/surveys-that-work/ (archived at https://perma.cc/
VQD5-C5BK)

Prelicz-Zawadzka, A (9 August 2016) How to create an effective customer
experience survey. UX Booth. www.uxbooth.com/articles/how-to-create-a-
customer-experience-survey/ (archived at https://perma.cc/MF4Q-2Q6S) last
accessed: 18 August 2017)

Survey Monkey (2017) Help center. https://help.surveymonkey.com/?l=en_US/
(archived at https://perma.cc/3NJ9-XT7T) (last accessed: 18 August 2017)

Survey Monkey (2017) Skip logic. www.surveymonkey.com/mp/tour/skiplogic/
(archived at https://perma.cc/GH85-7KJK) (last accessed: 18 August 2017)

Turner, N (7 April 2011) 15 useful user feedback questions for online surveys. UX
for the Masses. www.uxforthemasses.com/online-survey-questions/ (archived at
https://perma.cc/6CTM-GCCV) (last accessed: 21 May 2017)

Usability.gov (2017) Online surveys. www.usability.gov/how-to-and-tools/methods/
online-surveys.html (archived at https://perma.cc/Z2CT-5EN8) (last accessed:
21 May 2017)

11

User interviews

Understanding people's experience
through talking to them

.

What are user interviews?

We are all familiar with interviews in some form or another, usually job interviews. They are also a common and well-established technique used in social science, market research, user research and human–computer interaction (Preece et al, 2002), conducted face-to-face, over the phone or via video call.

What user interviews are good for

Interviews will often be one of many techniques used in iterative research. For the purposes of user research, interviews are useful for understanding attitudes and preferences (and how they change over time), common behaviours and the context in which the users live and operate, and how they think and associate certain things.

Interviews (especially when done face-to-face) are a good way to connect with those users who don't have easy access to technology, and those who have low literacy and digital skills. You can interview to gain an understanding of their experience and context without asking them to do anything they may have difficulty with and therefore feel embarrassed.

What user interviews are not good for

We have to keep in mind the fact that what users say and what they do can be two different things. Also, as we all have memory issues (it's just a part of being human), it's not necessarily a good idea to ask people to recall precise details of specific journeys and experiences.

In many cases your users won't be designers (although some of you will be designing for them), and interviews are not a good format for asking for details on creating an ideal solution or suggesting specific improvements. It's better to examine what is happening, how the user feels and what the goal is/was, and what outcome they wanted to achieve.

When to do user interviews

User interviews can be considered a quick and dirty method, when time and budget are constrained – you need insight but you don't have the resources to set up more complex research. Interviews are a good place to start project scoping. Talking to users can give you a preliminary understanding of the context you'll be working in and the issues being experienced; this will help define the scope and objectives of the project.

It is an excellent complementary technique to observation (used immediately after an activity, such as ethnography; see Chapter 14). You get a certain amount of insight from each individual method, but you will get a much more holistic insight if you use them in combination.

Effort required to do this kind of research

User interviews are one of the easiest methods to practise and learn. If you have an awareness of the fundamentals of good practice, you can start doing user interviews straight away, but it does require some time and effort to become a skilled moderator. Some sensitive topics will require skill to navigate the participants through, while maintaining their sense of wellbeing. If your research is dealing with a highly emotive subject, you need to be very sensitive to people's state of mind and wellbeing, as shown in the short case study below.

CASE STUDY
Knowing when to stop a research session early

In 2014, I spent five months helping a charity that cares for and supports people living with terminal illness and their carers. Part of my research included over 20 phone interviews that ranged from understanding people's information needs when dealing with terminal illness to looking for volunteering, money raising and donation opportunities. Many of the interviews were with people who were terminally ill or carers and family members. At the beginning of each interview I would remind people that they could take a break or stop at any time, should they feel uncomfortable or upset. Whatever circumstances people find themselves in, they still want to be helpful; even in an emotional state they may try to continue. Most of the time when the interviewees became emotional, I was the one to stop the interview.

You need to call a halt in a gentle and reassuring way. Tell them that they have been very helpful and you really appreciate their time but it is best that you stop for their own wellbeing. Also, make sure you have the number of someone or a helpline that they can call to talk about how they are feeling, should they need to. You could ask their permission for you to have someone (a professional) call them to make sure they're all right.

For this particular project I did some extra interviews to make up the numbers for the interviews that had been stopped early, but it was worth the extra time, effort and cost. *The participant's wellbeing and your own wellbeing are more important than getting research data.*

Interviews can be structured, semi-structured or an open discussion, depending on the purpose (Preece et al, 2002). Each will require a certain amount of preparation, with predefined questions.

How to do user interviews

We will go through how to prepare for interviews and then how to moderate individual and paired interviews.

Question design

We've talked a lot about questions design, particularly in Chapter 3 on asking the right kind of questions. To briefly recap:

- Avoid jargon and technical words. Use plain English as much as possible. If you do need to use technical words, explain what they mean.
- Use neutral open-ended questions that don't force the participant to answer in a certain way.
- Avoid long questions as they are difficult to answer.

- Avoid compound sentences; always split into individual questions.
- Consider words with loaded meanings in the context of your work, and whether they should be included or avoided in your questions. For example, the word 'welfare' has negative connotations in some situations.

Interview structure

If you have read the usability testing section you'll be familiar with the concept of a script or protocol and how it is structured.

1 INTRODUCTION

In Chapter 4 (Getting the legal and ethical stuff right) and Chapter 7 (Usability testing), I gave examples of how you can start your research session. Giving some context is a good way to start and is the participants' opportunity to ask for any clarification they may need before the session starts, and gives them a chance to get comfortable.

2 WARM-UP QUESTIONS

Asking some preliminary questions is a chance to get to know the participants a little better, before diving into the main focus of your interview. The questions you ask should be geared towards gaining some insight into the participants' experience related to the tasks or area that you are researching. Keep the questions quite neutral and relatively easy to answer. Keep to just a couple of questions, spending about five minutes on this.

3 MAIN QUESTIONS/FOCUS OF THE INTERVIEW

Open and unstructured interviews have an agenda but not necessarily a specific set of questions to be answered. Open and unstructured interviews have an initial opening question to get things started, but after that the moderator will let the conversation dictate the questions asked. This kind of interview can yield a lot of rich data and is particular useful when you are just starting to explore an area, but it also requires more skill to conduct such an interview (Preece et al, 2002).

TOP TIPS

- All the rules that we've already considered in terms of asking the right kinds of questions apply; it's just that they are spontaneous and responding to the situation rather than being pre-prepared.

- Be ready to follow new lines of questioning that you hadn't initially considered but that are related to your agenda.
- It is worth including some warm-up and wrap-up questions to indicate the beginning and end of the interview.

For structured and semi-structured interviews you'll need to create an interview guide to ensure that you cover the same topics with each participant. The difference between the two is the kind of questions that you include. Group related questions together to help the flow and the participants' thought processes. If you are covering sensitive subjects in the interview, try to start with easier questions and work up to the more 'difficult' questions (see the case study above).

4 WRAP-UP QUESTIONS

These, like the warm-up questions, should be relatively easy to answer. They could be a summary/review of what you've talked about or participants' overall impression of something. It's generally good to end on a light note if you can: people won't remember what you said or did, but they will remember how you made them feel.

5 CLOSING AND THANK YOU

This is the time to make the participants aware of what will happen next with your research/project, if there is any possibility of follow-up, etc. This is also the time to pay them, if you are personally sorting out the incentives. If the incentives are being paid in a different way, remind the participants how and when. You may want to give them some contact details, should they want to follow up with anything; it is up to you.

It's always nice to finish on a statement of thanks such as: 'Thank you very much for your participation; it will help us (to do xxx).'

Moderating an interview: individual participants

USING PROMPTS

Prompts are anticipated clarification and follow-up questions; they are additional to the main question (related to your research focus). They can help you delve a bit deeper into participants' answers or can give them an example if they are struggling. Examples can be useful but should be used sparingly as they are leading by nature and could skew the participants' answers.

You won't always be able to anticipate when you need a prompt, but you'll get used to using them the more research you do. It's worth noting down the unanticipated prompts during a research session as you may need to use them again. Here are some examples that will give you a sense of what prompt questions are.

SOME GENERIC PROMPT QUESTIONS

- Can you tell me a bit about why that is?
- Why do you think that is?
- Can you describe how you did this?
- Tell me more about xxx.
- How did this experience make you feel?

AWKWARD SILENCES AND NOT ANSWERING QUESTIONS

When you first start interviewing, it is tempting to fill any gaps when the participant stops talking with probing questions. In trying to fill the silence you run the risk of going off the topic of the research, asking leading and biased questions and potentially preventing the participants from saying things they had intended to before you leapt in.

It can be useful to occasionally leave an awkward silence; most participants will endeavour to fill it. You'll also get used to using 'mmm' and 'uh-ha' a lot to encourage participants to keep talking, to show you are listening, without leading them astray. With experience you will get a feel for when it's right to talk because the participants need encouragement to verbalize their thoughts, and when to remain silent.

The participants may ask you questions; it's natural to ask for assistance. It will feel like a dilemma at first: do you answer their question? It's common to want to ease participants' frustration/anxiety/stress. Whether or not you answer depends on the question. Here are a few tips on how to handle these situations:

- If it is clear that the participant is having difficulty understanding the question you have asked, try to ask it in a different way, while keeping the essence of the question and avoiding the bad question pitfalls (hello bias). Note down the question and your response, as you may need to refine how the question is phrased for subsequent participants.

- Sometimes participants will ask what you think, either to make it more of a conversation or to try to identify the answer they think you are looking for. This kind of situation needs to be politely defused without making them feel awkward, while not answering the question. This can often be done by telling them that you are interested in their experience and what they think, that this is what is important and you'd be happy to share your views after the interview is finished.

- If participants cannot answer the question, don't force them to give an answer, as it's likely to be made up. Simply note this and move on to the next question/topic.

Moderating an interview: two participants (paired interviewing)

Up until now the preparation for an individual or paired interview has been the same. However, when it comes to moderating individual and paired interviews, it is quite different.

CASE STUDY
Using paired interviewing

I first used paired interviewing during my doctoral research, in the form of paired retrospective think aloud. It sounds fancy, but essentially this means that I interviewed two people at the same time about an exercise they had just completed. This was to ensure that I did not disturb what they were doing, but it was soon enough afterwards that the activity was fresh in their minds. This kind of technique allows participants to prompt each other, discuss and seek clarification from each other. I found this a useful technique in a pedagogic environment, where you don't want to interrupt the learning process that you're observing, and the interview can almost be seen as an extension of the interaction that's already been happening to achieve the task that's been set.

Obviously not all topics of research are appropriate to be discussed in pairs, but it can certainly be used advantageously in particular settings, for instance:

- Any situation where collaboration is key to the topic you are researching. For example, when trying to understand collaborative workflows, consider speaking to several people who regularly work together (Barker, 2005).

- When trying to identify differences in working practices between teams or offices, consider speaking to several people who perform the same tasks but are based in different teams or offices (Barker, 2005).

- Friendship pairs are often interviewed in depth where the subject matter is sensitive or the respondents are likely to be more open and articulate in the presence of a friend; it is often recommended for interviewing children and teenagers (AQR, nd).

Paired interviews allow you to be more in-depth about each person's experience as well as using any similarities and differences in experience to explore the subject more deeply (AQR, nd). The paired interview is not two interviews being conducted simultaneously; rather it aims to create a dynamic in which the participants interact with each other (Barker, 2005). It can work to reduce the discomfort felt by some in the interview situation, provide more space for thinking, allow respondents to build more comprehensive responses through their discussions and enable them to augment each other's stories (Lohm, 2011).

GETTING THE MOST OUT OF A PAIRED INTERVIEW

To get the greatest benefit from a paired interview the moderator must ensure that both participants contribute to the session. Consider the following guidelines for the interviews (Barker, 2005):

- The important thing to keep in mind is that the pairing has to be right; generally the two participants know each other in some way, professionally or personally.

- Silence is not a sign of agreement.

- Alternate which participant speaks first after a question has been asked.

- All forms of multi-person research run the risk of being dominated by one of the participants. This is especially likely if the participants have a dominant-subservient working relationship (other examples include parent-child and older-younger sibling relationships).

- If one of participants starts to dominate, you can direct questions specifically to the quieter participant.

- If interviewing children (teenagers), be mindful that different techniques may be required for boys and girls or a mixed pairing (Naranjo-Bock, 2013).

RECORDING THE DATA

Recording devices will obviously capture what has been said word for word, but this is not always appropriate. Unless you have training in dictation, it's very difficult to record the interview exactly with your written notes. It is still worth taking written notes, to help jog your memory later. There are a few techniques that will be helpful when you are getting used to recording data:

- Only note down particularly interesting quotes; don't try to write absolutely everything.

- Have someone else make notes. This takes the pressure off you having to listen, talk and write at the same time, and allows you to concentrate on moderation.

- Use voice-to-text dictation software that will save you a lot of time.

I've never had access to dictation software and I have always preferred to scribble my notes on paper (and I do mean scribble, unfortunately). Some prefer to take notes directly on a device like a laptop or tablet, which certainly speeds up the analysis and sharing process, but having a device in between you and the participant could create a barrier in face-to-face interviews. There are no hard and fast rules, just aspects to be aware of.

Interview length

This very much depends on the scope of your research and the number of questions/topics you want to cover. This is where the importance of pilot testing your interview guide comes in:

- Draft your interview guide.

- Recruit a colleague to role-play or real participant(s) to interview.

- Conduct the research with the draft guide as if it were a real research session.

- Time the full session to see how long it takes you and at what point the participant becomes fatigued or agitated by the length of the interview.

- Phone interviews are generally better kept short – 30 or 45 minutes; sustaining a 'formal' conversation over the phone requires more effort compared to face-to-face and is therefore more fatiguing to both the moderator and participant. However, if they need to be longer, then they need to be longer.

- Face-to-face interviews generally can last 30–90 minutes; after an hour it's usually good to stop, before it becomes too taxing for both the participant and the moderator, but often it does depend on the subject you are focusing on.

- Paired interviews will generally need more time; 30 minutes will probably be too short but, again, it depends on the scope of your research.

- If interviewing children (and teenagers) always keep the session length short; 30 minutes generally works well, definitely no more than 45 minutes otherwise they will lose concentration and patience.

Interview tools

- Your interview guide.
- Something to take notes on.
- Consent forms.
- NDA if required.
- Recording equipment, if appropriate.

References and further reading

AQR (nd) Paired depth interview. The Association for Qualitative Research. www.aqr.org.uk/glossary/paired-depth-interview (archived at https://perma.cc/3J5G-FM9F) (last accessed: 21 May 2017)

Barker, I (4 April 2005) Fast-tracking research with paired interviews. www.steptwo.com.au/papers/cmb_pairedinterviews/ (archived at https://perma.cc/V3JQ-MV53) (last accessed: 21 May 2017)

Lohm, D (May, 2011) Sometimes is can take two – paired interviews. Monash University. www.tasa.org.au/wp-content/uploads/2011/05/Lohm-Davina-Session-70-PDF.pdf (archived at https://perma.cc/4DBD-4VGG) (last accessed: 21 May 2017)

Naranjo-Bock, C (3 June 2013) Using paired interviews to understand the current and future perspectives of teenagers. UX Matters. www.uxmatters.com/mt/archives/2013/06/using-paired-interviews-to-understand-the-current-and-future-perspectives-of-teenagers.php (archived at https://perma.cc/WM6G-7KTM) (last accessed: 21 May 2017)

Portigal, S (2013) *Interviewing Users: How to uncover compelling insights*, Rosenfeld Media, New York

Preece, J, Rogers, Y and Sharp, H (2002) *Interaction Design: Beyond human-computer interaction*, Wiley, New York

12

Diary studies

How to capture user research data over time

What are diary studies?

Diary studies can be used to record qualitative data over a set period of time, where participants will complete the diary on their own. Participants are given a framework to record their observations and data at specified times, about particular things.

What diary studies are good for

Diary studies are useful for gaining contextual understanding of experience, behaviour and attitudes over time. It can be very difficult to create scenarios in a 'lab setting' to gather these kinds of insights, and it is also high cost in terms of time for data collection and potentially data analysis too.

What diary studies are not good for

As with most methods, you need to look at the pros and cons of designing a diary study. The main disadvantage is time. There are certain contexts for which diary studies are not appropriate, such as emotive or productivity-intensive environments: you're probably not going to ask paramedics to fill in a diary about their work day, for example. Ethnography (Chapter 14) would be a more appropriate in that instance. Taking the contextual point further and thinking about the full range of human capability, there are certain user groups (along the capability spectrum) where methods other than keeping a diary would be more appropriate.

Diary studies are focused on change over time. If your research isn't about change over time, they may not be suitable.

When to do a diary study

Diary studies are useful when you want to understand long-term behaviours such as:

- *Habits:* what time of day do users engage?
- *Usage scenarios:* in what capacity do users engage? This data can be used for scenarios in usability testing in subsequent research.
- *Attitudes and motivations:* what motivates people to do some specific thing? How are they feeling and thinking?
- *Changes in behaviours and perceptions:* how learnable is a system? How loyal are people over time?
- *Customer journeys:* what is the typical customer journey and cross-channel user experience as participants interact with your organization using different devices and channels? What is the cumulative effect of multiple service touchpoints?

Diary studies are also useful for:

- Tracking how users complete a long process that is likely to take several days or more, such as shopping for a large/expensive item (eg, a house).
- Discovering what motivates users to initiate certain actions.
- Determining how your product/service fits into regular habits.
- Assessing retention.

The focus of a diary study can range from very broad to extremely targeted, depending on the topic being studied. Diary studies are often structured to focus on one of the following:

- *A specific thing:* understanding all interactions over a particular time.
- *General behaviour:* gathering general information about user behaviour.
- *A specific activity:* understanding how people complete specific activities.
- *General activity:* understanding how people complete general activities.

- *Expectations, mind-sets, moods and social or physical contexts:* a diary study can capture these influences, shedding light onto how the user experience in each time span has formed; nothing is done in a vacuum.

Diary studies are often used in combination with contextual inquiry (Chapter 15) or user interviews (Chapter 11). They are used to delve more deeply into the habits and behaviours of your users. Diary studies are longitudinal and timeframes might range from two weeks to two months. It depends on what you are investigating and how long you think it may take to observe patterns of behaviour that reflect common, or less common, habits or routines (see Bryant, 2014; Flaherty, 2016; Lallemand, 2012; Moule, 2016).

Effort required to do this kind of research

Diary studies need time and effort to develop the skills required to run them, to analyse the data captured and understand what insights it provides. If you want to start using diary studies in your work, it may be best to start small and simple.

Depending on the scope of your diary it also takes more of the participants' time and dedication compared to, say, a 30-minute interview. This has all kinds of connotations. Who are you recruiting? Is this method the best for both you and the participants? It's not a method to be taken lightly, given the commitment in time and effort.

To ensure you get the level of involvement you need from participants, provide an incentive that will keep them engaged. This compensation is typically more than you would offer for a 60-minute usability test. Consider offering the incentive in instalments as participants reach specific milestones to keep them motivated throughout the duration of the study.

How to do a diary study

1 Planning and preparation

As with all research, first you need to scope the objectives of the project, and define the focus of the study and the long-term behaviours that you want to understand. You need to:

- Specify a timeline for the study to run.
- Select data collection tools for participants to use.

- Identify who you need to participate in the research and recruit them. You'll probably need between four and six of the right participants per user group.
- Prepare instructions or support materials.

HOW LONG SHOULD THE STUDY BE?

The period of time can either be set (eg, four weeks) or you can monitor the collected data until you have what you need. In practice, a set period of time often works better as it may be difficult to find participants to sign up to an open-ended study.

RECRUITING PARTICIPANTS

Since diary studies require more involvement over a longer period of time, be extra prudent in the recruiting process. Let participants know what is involved and expected of them upfront. Ask screening questions that will help you gauge the level of commitment you will get from them during the study, and be sure to confirm they will be available for the entire study period. Aim to recruit more participants than you need: a 15–20 per cent drop-out rate is normal as diary studies last longer than other types of research and need more involvement.

CONDUCT A PILOT STUDY

Diary studies can take quite a bit of time to plan and conduct, so it's helpful to conduct a short pilot study first. The pilot study does not need to be as long as the real study, but it's worth testing your study design and related materials (Flaherty, 2016; Webcredible, 2011).

2 The pre-study briefing

Take time to get participants ready to record their data. You can do this by scheduling a meeting or phone call with each participant to discuss the details of the study:

- Introduce the project aims and reasons for this research.
- Walk through the recording schedule and discuss expectations.
- Provide key dates for contact and follow-up and the contact details of the main researchers involved for any questions.
- Discuss the tools they will be using and be sure all participants have familiarized themselves with the technology.

- Give data capture instructions, including when to record data (you can set minimum entry expectations, for example at least two entries per week) and a list of questions that each diary entry should cover.

- You could give the participants an example diary entry depending on the complexity of the data you are capturing (be aware this can skew the data: all the participants' data could look like the example you give).

LOGGING PERIOD

To make data reporting effective, it helps to be as specific as possible about what information you need the participants to record. At the same time, reassure them that they can use the style and method to record that works for them within the framework you have set. There is going to be natural variation and you need the participants to find a comfortable way to record the data, otherwise they are not going to do it. Also, uncovering the unexpected in these variations is what user research is all about!

There are various collection techniques and low- and hi-tech tools to support them. The format and technique you want to use will depend on the type of data and insight you want to capture and the time you have to analyse it. To choose the most effective technique consider the context and the type of participants you are working with: what are they going to be able to use most easily in their situation?

In *in-situ logging*, when participants engage in a relevant activity, they report important details about it immediately (or as soon as possible). As such, it is best used in situations where you don't think there will be a large volume of diary entries occurring or large amounts of data to be captured on a regular basis (Lallemand, 2012).

A less intrusive way of logging activities is the *snippet technique*, where participants only record short snippets of information about activities as they occur. Then, at the end of each day, or when participants have time, they elaborate on each snippet by providing additional details about the activity. You can consider asking participants to fill in a questionnaire to expand on their snippets, so you get specific and consistent insights about each snippet. You may want to use a more open and fluid format that allows the participants to reflect on their snippets (Lallemand, 2012).

Diaries may be open format or highly structured:

- In *open diaries* participants record activities and events in their own words, which can encourage reflection and contemplation.

- Highly *structured diaries* have closed questions and are pre-categorized to capture precise information.

- A mixed approach is often adopted to collect both qualitative and quantitative data.

You may want to consider using non-verbal cues in your data capture. There are a few different ways to do this. Participants can take photos to explain their activities and highlight things that stood out for them across the course of their day. You can gain better insight into the users' mindset than words alone offer. You can capture emotional responses on a non-verbal scale, such as that shown in Figure 12.1.

CHECK IN WITH PARTICIPANTS

Getting the insight you need will take some involvement with participants throughout the study. Plan to check in with them or give periodic reminders as needed (each day or every few days). Let participants know upfront that you will be reaching out throughout the study and agree a method of communication, so you can give encouragement or ask for clarification without being overly intrusive.

3 Post-study interview

After the study, evaluate all the information provided by each participant. Plan a follow-up interview to discuss logs in detail. Ask probing questions to uncover specific details needed to complete the story and clarify as needed. Ask for feedback from the participants about their experience of taking part in the study, so you can adjust your processes for the next time (see Flaherty, 2016; Lallemand, 2012; Moule, 2016; Webcredible, 2011; Weston, 2017).

FIGURE 12.1   The self-assessment manikin is a non-verbal scale to measure emotions, Lallemand, 2012

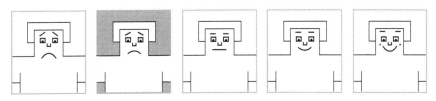

SOURCE Bradley and Lang, 1994

Diary study tools

We've had a look at the different collection techniques, and there are various and low- and hi-tech tools to support them, depending on what you are capturing and who your participants are. Is your tool of choice a comfortable way of communicating for all participants?

Paper diaries

These are the traditional type of diary recording method. They are good because they can be used by participants with all levels of technical ability; they can be used at the same time as digital devices; they're very portable and can be used to capture events as soon as they happen. However, they do have some limitations:

- Having to wait for the diary to be returned by the participant before starting analysis.
- Written accounts don't necessarily capture rich experiences in the same way that audio or video do.
- Handwritten notes aren't always easy to read, and transcribing, if required, can be time-consuming.

TOP TIP

Paper diaries should include the participant's name, instructions for capturing entries and details of when and where to return the diary so they are continually reminded of it during the process.

Digital diaries

You can ask participants to submit diary entries digitally, usually at the end of each day. There are many different digital tools that you can use to run your diary study. There are specific digital diary study tools and you can make use of survey tools, private social media groups etc, depending on your budget and what tools you have available.

FIGURE 12.2 AttrakDiff scores illustrating how the UX of a mobile application changed over a period of ten days

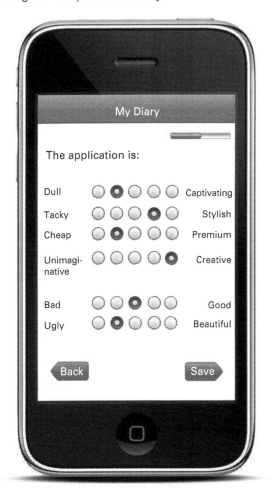

SOURCE Lallemand, 2012

Figure 12.2 is an example of a digital customer-insight tool used in a diary study that involved *in situ* logging. Figure 12.3 is another example of a digital customer-insight tool, this time one employed in a diary study that used the snippet technique.

TOP TIP

You will sometimes need to ask follow-up questions and prompt for additional detail, but with online collaborative tools it's good to be wary of interacting too much with participants, as it may alter their thoughts and actions (Flaherty, 2016; Webcredible, 2011).

FIGURE 12.3   Snippets captured during the day serve as memory aides for full diary entries in the evening

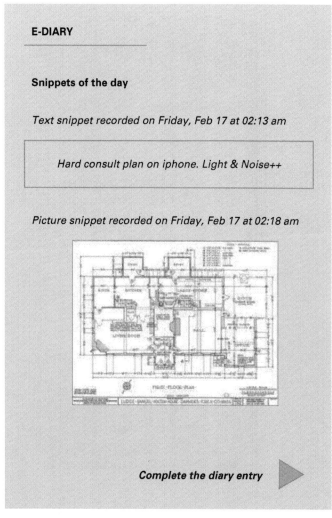

SOURCE Lallemand, 2012

References and further reading

Bradley, M and Lang, P (1994) Measuring emotion: the self-assessment manikin and the semantic differential, *Journal of Behavioral Therapy & Experimental Psychiatry*, 1, pp 49–59

Bryant, A (25 June 2014) How to get feedback over time with diary studies. User Testing Blog. www.usertesting.com/blog/2014/06/25/how-to-get-feedback-over-time-with-diary-studies/ (archived at https://perma.cc/L7U5-993Y) (last accessed: 21 May 2017)

Flaherty, K (5 June 2016) Diary studies: understanding long-term user behavior and experiences. Nielsen Norman Group. www.nngroup.com/articles/diary-studies/ (archived at https://perma.cc/PJ6W-QGFR) (last accessed: 21 May 2017)

Lallemand, C (August 2012) Dear diary: using diaries to study user experience, © UXPA, 2012. Reprinted from *User Experience Magazine*, 11, 3. http://uxpamagazine.org/dear-diary-using-diaries-to-study-user-experience/ (archived at https://perma.cc/XBQ7-6YPP) (last accessed: 21 May 2017)

Moule, J (19 May 2016) Use a diary study to extend your UX research. UX Mastery. http://uxmastery.com/diary-study-extending-ux-research/ (last accessed: 21 May 2017)

Webcredible (2011) Diary study guide: how to get the best results. Webcredible. www.webcredible.com/blog/diary-study-guide-how-get-best-results-diary-study-research/ (archived at https://perma.cc/M9U2-56WF) (last accessed: 21 May 2017)

Weston, D (2017) 6 things to consider when setting up a UX diary study. Spotless. www.spotless.co.uk/insights/6-things-for-ux-diary-study/ (archived at https://perma.cc/64CP-W55X) (last accessed: 21 May 2017)

13

Information architecture validation through tree testing

Does the structure of your information work for your users?

What is information architecture?

Information architectures (IA) are structures of information. The most common example we will be using is the organizing and labelling of website (and intranet) content and functionality. IA covers both the very broad (overall site structure and navigation) and the very detailed (labelling and content).

What tree testing is good for

A tree testing exercise (also known as an IA validation exercise) can be used to test existing structures that you have identified through insight and analytics as not being effective. Tree testing can be used to assess the draft structure created after a card sorting exercise with a large group of users. These draft structures may be adding, removing or amending existing content in some way, or they could be an entirely new structure. If you suspect the issues being experienced are related to poor labelling and poor content structure, a tree test allows you to focus on this, without consideration of design elements.

What tree testing is not good for

If you suspect that interaction or visual design has something to do with the problems being experienced, then usability testing is the way to go. Tree testing isn't a research method to use in isolation; generally it's used in combination with card sorting, usability testing or content audits, for example.

When to do tree testing

Tree testing is usually done after card sorting (see Chapter 9). Card sorting is often done with a small number of users and the results will give you a better idea of how something could be structured. A tree test will allow you to validate or invalidate the draft structure with a larger group of users. This kind of exercise can be used early and often: it's quick and easy to set up, run and analyse. You don't have to wait for a prototype to be created, or you can do this in parallel with the design process. In an ideal world IA work will start before interaction and visual design work, but this is often not the case. When it's done properly, IA doesn't just happen at the beginning of the project: it progresses from beginning through middle to end (O'Brien, 2016e).

  If your analytics aren't showing the customer journeys you expected or wanted, doing a tree test can help you understand how people are navigating through the site; this is an alternative to remote unmoderated usability testing. A draft IA can be created and tested immediately after a content audit, when it has been decided which content will be added, updated or deleted (O'Brien, 2016f).

Effort required to do this kind of research

It takes a fair amount of time and effort to become familiar with IA, if it's a new subject for you. When starting out, you may want to find someone to collaborate with who knows more about it so that you can learn from them.

  Online tools are required to do this kind of research. Do some reading on how much it is likely to cost you to do this, particularly as it's the kind of research that's best done iteratively and in conjunction with other research methods.

How to do a tree test

Preparing your tree test

As with all user research methods, good preparation is the key to gathering useful data.

RECRUITING PARTICIPANTS

Depending on what you are testing, this exercise might be relevant to all your users and potential users, or only a subset. It's worth targeting the right participants, as discussed in Chapter 10 on surveys and Chapter 3 on who should be involved in your research.

TEST MATERIALS

- An introduction to the exercise to send to participants as well as any preliminary survey questions you want to ask them.
- An information architecture, whatever stage of development it's in. You can always put content/items in more than one place if you are unsure where they belong.
- A text version of your IA: either in a text field or on a spreadsheet (a simplified version of the structure). This is the format that tools tend to use to create a clickable navigation of your structure without visual design (as shown in Figure 13.1).
- A representative task list for participants to complete. There is no right number of tasks, but the tasks should be representative of the area that is the focus of your research. Optimal Workshop, an expert in this area, recommends no more than 10 tasks per exercise (McKay, 2016). You'll need to know the correct answers to each of your tasks so that you can analyse various success metrics.
- Post-exercise survey and closing statement: you may want to get some qualitative data on the participants' experience of the exercise, thank them and share what's going to happen next.

Deciding what to test

You may not want to test the whole of your IA. If you have multiple user groups with specific interests you may want to provide separate exercises for each group, rather than have everyone test everything. If you have a very

FIGURE 13.1 Information architecture created in a spreadsheet

8	BikeSite		
9		For commuters	
0			Bike routes
1			Skills training
2			Cycling and the law
3			Tips for commuting
4		For families	
5			Places to cycle
6			Learning to ride
7			Safety tips
8		For roadies	
9			etc.
0		For mountain bikers	
1			etc.
2		For cycle tourers	
3		News & events	
4			

SOURCE O'Brien, 2016a

large structure, it could be too much information in one go for participants. The main problem with tree-testing very large structures is not technical; it's about the participants' experience of the test (O'Brien, 2016d).

How big should the IA be?

Optimal Workshop's advice on the size of structure to test (O'Brien, 2016d) is as follows. If testing a small or medium-sized structure (typically less than 500 items), you can normally test the whole tree; it's not big enough to cause any unwanted test effects. If the tree is large (500–1,000 items) you can:

- Test the whole structure, but degrade the participants' experience.
- Test a 'cut-down' version of the structure, for example focus on how well the top three or four levels work. Participants should then have time to do a larger number of tasks in a shorter total time.
- Cut the structure down to size by removing sections that are not important to the test.
- Opt to test only a particular subset of the whole structure, for example the culture section of a newspaper site.

HOW TO CUT DOWN YOUR IA

The simplest way to reduce a large structure to a more manageable size is to cut everything below a certain level, as shown Figure 13.2. Bear in mind that when reducing the size of the IA in this way, you'll only find out if participants were able to get to the right general area, rather than a specific place (O'Brien, 2016d).

If there's a section that you don't intend to test, you can chop it while leaving other sections (the ones we really want to test) at their full depth of topics (O'Brien, 2016d) as shown in Figure 13.3. Alternatively, you can select a subset of the structure, if you are particularly interested in one area (O'Brien, 2016d). In this case, you should recruit participants who have an interest or expertise in this particular area, as seen in Figure 13.4.

WHAT LABELS TO INCLUDE AND EXCLUDE?

Optimal Workshop's advice is to include global navigation items, unless they're very minor and exclude links or shortcuts that are not in the global navigation (eg, overview). You should also exclude 'escape' headings like search, contact us, help, etc (O'Brien, 2016c).

FIGURE 13.2 Cutting down your IA option 1

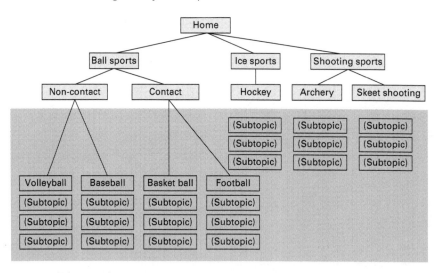

SOURCE O'Brien, 2016d

FIGURE 13.3   Cutting down your IA option 2

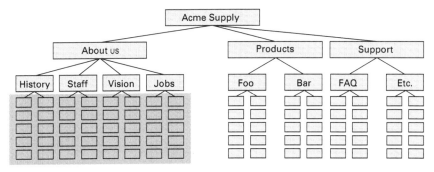

SOURCE O'Brien, 2016d

FIGURE 13.4   Cutting down your IA option 3

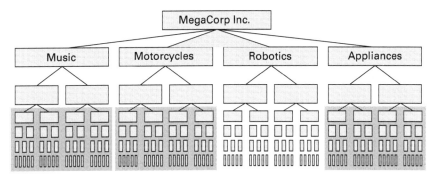

SOURCE O'Brien, 2016d

Running the test

It is worth piloting the exercise to make sure it's working or whether it needs refining before it's sent out to a large number of participants. Participants are normally contacted by email with the link to the exercise; it's worth specifying a timeframe for the exercise and stating this clearly to the participants. Keep an eye on the rate of response. It may be worth sending a reminder email halfway in the time period to encourage those who haven't completed the exercise to do so (O'Brien, 2016b).

Tree testing tools

This is an exercise that is done online remotely using tools such as Treejack (https://www.optimalworkshop.com/treejack) or C-inspector (http://www.c-inspector.com/).

References and further reading

McKay, A (18 May 2016) Treejack takes a trip with American Airlines. Optimal Workshop. https://blog.optimalworkshop.com/treejack-takes-trip-american-airlines (archived at https://perma.cc/D92Q-VVFR) (last accessed: 21 May 2017)

Nodder, C (7 July 2013) UX foundations: information architecture. Lynda.com from LinkedIn. www.lynda.com/Web-User-Experience-tutorials/Foundations-UX-Information-Architecture/122427-2.html (archived at https://perma.cc/26R6-CB8J) (last accessed: 21 May 2017)

O'Brien, D (19 May 2016a) 5 – Creating trees. Tree Testing for Websites. https://treetesting.atlassian.net/wiki/display/TTFW/5+-+Creating+trees (archived at https://perma.cc/DCB7-TBUB) (last accessed: 21 May 2017)

O'Brien, D (19 May 2016b) 8 – Setting up a test. Tree Testing for Websites. https://treetesting.atlassian.net/wiki/display/TTFW/8+-+Setting+up+a+test (archived at https://perma.cc/F844-SE3R) (last accessed: 21 May 2017)

O'Brien, D (19 May 2016c) Which headings to include/exclude? Tree Testing for Websites. https://treetesting.atlassian.net/wiki/pages/viewpage.action?pageId=164177 (archived at https://perma.cc/HM6U-LXMP) (last accessed: 21 May 2017)

O'Brien, D (19 May 2016d) Which part of the tree? Tree Testing for Websites. https://treetesting.atlassian.net/wiki/pages/viewpage.action?pageId=164168 (archived at https://perma.cc/C59Q-4HVL) (last accessed: 21 May 2017)

O'Brien, D (21 July 2016e) Tree testing in the design process — Part One: The research phase. Optimal Workshop. https://blog.optimalworkshop.com/tree-testing-design-process-part-1-research-phase/ (archived at https://perma.cc/WN8P-DE25) (last accessed: 21 May 2017)

O'Brien, D (17 October 2016f) Tree testing in the design process — Part 2: The design phase. Optimal Workshop. https://blog.optimalworkshop.com/tree-testing-design-process-part-2-design-phase (archived at https://perma.cc/WN8P-DE25) (last accessed: 21 May 2017)

O'Brien, D (4 May 2017g) Tree Testing for Websites. https://treetesting.atlassian.net/wiki (archived at https://perma.cc/9J64-ZBAB) (last accessed: 21 May 2017)

Resmini, A (2011) *Pervasive Information Architecture: Designing cross-channel user experiences,* Morgan Kaufmann, Burlington

Rosenfeld, L, Morville, P and Arango, J (2015) *Information Architecture: For the web and beyond,* 4th edn, O'Reilly Media, Sebastopol

Spencer, D (13 April 2011) *A Practical Guide to Information Architecture,* 2nd edn. UX Mastery. http://uxmastery.com/practical-ia/ (archived at https://perma.cc/2UZQ-R25G) (last accessed: 21 May 2017)

UX Booth (22 December 2015) Complete beginner's guide to information architecture. www.uxbooth.com/articles/complete-beginners-guide-to-information-architecture/ (archived at https://perma.cc/QG5P-BJUP) (last accessed: 21 May 2017)

14

Ethnography

Observing how people behave in the real world

What is traditional ethnography?

Ethnography is a field of science that studies people and culture. It is also used in user research to study people and groups as they go about their everyday lives, capturing natural and nonverbal reactions and unanticipated scenarios.

What ethnography is good for

Ethnography is designed to uncover things that you're unaware of, collecting real-world data in real-world circumstances. It is observing, documenting and analysing behaviour and is a valuable tool for discovering and understanding user needs. Ethnography can be used to understand:

- how people incorporate things into their daily life;
- authentic behaviour;
- how your and other organizations' products/services interact in people's lives.

If your work is focusing on how a particular team works, ethnographic observation will allow you to understand its interactions with other teams across the organization. Your research may include their interactions with friends and family, customers and the public, depending on the scope of your research.

What ethnography is not good for

Ethnography is not designed for quick turnaround projects. Ethnography studies are expensive in terms of time, resources and skills. They require a lot of planning and coordination to conduct even a few meetings with participants. It takes time for participants to get used to the presence of an observer, so short ethnographic projects won't necessarily yield authentic results, making them unsuitable for working in agile sprints.

CASE STUDY
Ethnography in airport design

Ethnographic research has been extremely useful in designing airports in several aspects: where to put the electrical sockets and USB charging ports, near seating areas or built into the seating itself, so people don't have to sit on the floor to charge their devices. Ethnography has also been important in airport wayfinding: where to place signage in busy areas, with many people carrying lots of luggage and trying to keep a group of people together (Larsen, 2016).

When to use ethnography

Observing people in the real world is particularly useful in the early stages of a project, as you can gain deep insight into the scope of the problem and the context in which it exists. Learning about what is really going on can help you create realistic rather than idealized products/services. It also helps in understanding the emotional values people connect to in your product or service.

Effort required to do this kind of research

Ethnography is labour-intensive; it requires complete immersion in real-world situations and social dynamics. Information and results are highly dependent on observations and interpretations so the data quality will be affected by your skill level. If you are involved in complex projects from the problem-scoping stage, working with users who have specialized needs, it's worth investing time in honing your ethnography skills. If you've used other research methods the skills you have gained will help you when starting on your ethnographic journey.

How to do ethnography

As with all research techniques, you need to clearly define your objectives so as to understand what to observe and note; ethnographic research objectives tend to be relatively broad. Emerson et al (2011) give some suggestions on information that can be captured: *descriptions of the scene*: the physical environment; the layout of workstations, desk space, clutter, break areas; and *key events and incidents*: What happened? Who did what? What are your impressions? What are team members' thoughts about and interpretations of these events? How do they feel about them?

Try to make it clear in your notes what your thoughts are and what your evidence is. You should be asking questions at appropriate times to clarify your understanding of the situation, context and interactions that are taking place. There is a balance to be struck that comes with practice: interrupting just enough to get the insight you need but not disrupting the dynamics you are observing.

Analysis of the data is also labour-intensive as a large volume of data is collected during ethnographic research. Colville Hyde (2009) suggests doing analysis throughout the data collection process, not just at the end, allowing you to react and adapt to events so you don't miss opportunities to gain insights into user behaviour.

Extending your ethnographic reach with mobile devices

What is mobile ethnography?

I like to think of mobile ethnography as a combination of ethnographic observation and diary study. Mobile ethnography makes use of communication and recording technology to capture ethnographic data.

Developments in technology allow for new research techniques: the emphasis switches from the researcher actively observing in real time to the participant recording the data. Participants are asked to record their thoughts, feelings and decisions on a regular basis through guided journal entries, shooting video, responding to prompts and capturing sound bites as they're happening, all on their smartphone or by wearing a clip camera that takes a photo every 30 seconds (Cribbett, 2015; Korostoff, 2014).

When to use mobile ethnography

Traditional ethnography requires you to be present with your subjects to observe behaviour. Mobile ethnography can be used to enhance your ethnographic observation and extend your reach by having the participants record data and observations when you are not there. You can ask them to answer contextual questions during these tasks to increase your understanding of the impact of time, environment, social pressure, motivation and previous experience. You can use interviews to gain contextual understanding and feedback using the data captured from different events and moments (Hudson, 2016).

How to do mobile ethnography

There are two main approaches to mobile ethnography. The *passive approach* to capturing the participants' experiences without any conscious action on their part will provide information on their natural behaviour, but may miss out on some detail. The *active approach* gives participants the ability to document their experiences as they see fit or on prompt (as in a diary study). It captures detail but suffers from forcing the participants to actively break their flow and decide what to document. You can take a mixed approach, combining active and passive techniques.

Ethnography tools

Traditionally, all you need is pen and paper. However, there are specific mobile ethnography tools you can use to help capture data.

References and further reading

Bailey, J (7 November 2014) Mobile ethnography. Bunnyfoot. www.bunnyfoot. com/blog/2014/11/mobile-ethnography/ (archived at https://perma.cc/B46L-3XY8) (last accessed: 21 May 2017)

Boehm, N (21 June 2010) Ethnography in UX. UX Matters. www.uxmatters.com/mt/archives/2010/06/ethnography-in-ux.php (archived at https://perma.cc/7DBK-S56W) (last accessed: 21 May 2017)

Challenger, H and Man, D (2020) Life under lockdown: studying uses of media and technology. BBC Research and Development. www.bbc.co.uk/rd/blog/2020-12-covid-lockdown-media-technology-study (archived at https://perma.cc/7DBK-S56W) (last accessed: 21 May 2017)

Colville Hyde, B (4 November 2009) Using ethnography to improve user experience. CX Partners. www.cxpartners.co.uk/our-thinking/using_ethnography_to_improve_user_experience/ (archived at https://perma.cc/Q9Q3-SZ8S) (last accessed: 21 May 2017)

Cribbett, S (16 June 2015) Using mobile ethnography to understand what people do, think and feel. Dub. www.dubishere.com/using-mobile-ethnography-to-understand-what-people-do-think-and-feel/ (archived at https://perma.cc/SQW3-NQZ6) (last accessed: 21 May 2017)

Emerson, R M, Fretz, R I and Shaw, L L (2011) *Writing Ethnographic Fieldnotes*, 2nd edn, The University of Chicago Press, Chicago, IL

Herzon, C, Skrobe, R, Wilson, C and Battle, L (2009) Ethnography. The Usability Body of Knowledge. www.usabilitybok.org/ethnography (archived at https://perma.cc/E6JW-3WRK) (last accessed: 21 May 2017)

Hudson, P (31 May 2016) Mobile ethnography in market research: fact and fiction. FlexMR. www.flexmr.net/blog/qualitative-research/2016/5/mobile-ethnograhy.aspx (archived at https://perma.cc/75PN-8VAB) (last accessed: 21 May 2017)

Korostoff, K (4 February 2014) Mobile ethnography: the new 'organic' market research tool to try in 2014. Research Rockstar. www.researchrockstar.com/mobile-ethnography-the-new-organic-market-research-tool-to-try-in-2014/ (archived at https://perma.cc/RK86-WXAW) (last accessed: 21 May 2017)

Larsen, B (1 June 2016) Building better CX through ethnography. UX Magazine. http://uxmag.com/articles/building-better-cx-through-ethnography (archived at https://perma.cc/QHH7-EYF7) (last accessed: 21 May 2017)

Weston, D (2017) When and how to use ethnographic research. Spotless. www.spotless.co.uk/insights/ethnography-when-and-how/ (archived at https://perma.cc/5FNQ-74GB)

15

Contextual inquiry

Interviewing people in their own environment

What is contextual inquiry?

Contextual inquiry (also known as contextual interviewing) can be described as a hybrid of user interviews and ethnography; it consists of a semi-structured interview method to obtain information about the context of use, with the participants then being observed and questioned while they work in their own environments. This makes the data for analysis more realistic (Herzon et al, 2010). A contextual inquiry requires participants to take the role of an expert; they are more active than in other research methods as they lead the session by demonstrating and talking about their tasks (Ross, 2012).

What contextual inquiry is good for

Contextual interviewing can help you to reveal information and understanding that users may not be aware of, and capture realistic and detailed data by observing users in their natural environment (Interaction Design Foundation, 2016). It combines the benefits of observation and in-depth conversation.

When planning for research with users of assistive technology and those with various access and skills needs, it is extremely useful to visit them. This is not only for their convenience and comfort but also for observing how they arrange their environment to meet their needs, including the technology they are using to access your product/service and what challenges they face in this environment.

What contextual inquiry is not good for

If you are interested in researching change over time, diary studies and ethnography are more appropriate and sustainable. Contextual inquiry requires more time and effort than usability testing in an artificial setting or using interviews in isolation so, if your timescales are particularly tight, it may be more practical and pragmatic to do research remotely or in an artificial setting convenient to you.

When to use contextual inquiry

Contextual inquiry is used to discover parameters, criteria, features, or process flows for design or redesign (Webcredible, 2011). Contextual inquiry is useful when it's important for you to understand the context of use for your product or service. If your participants can't travel to you and you are able to travel to them it's worth considering using contextual inquiry as your research method. Rather than meeting participants in an artificial setting close to their location, visit them in their actual location to see the reality of their environment and what they are trying to do in it.

CASE STUDY
Example of contextual inquiry

I have fond memories of a particular contextual inquiry research project that I worked on, probably because I got to wear a white lab coat and safety specs. 'Props' aside, this case shows how observing the environment (the context) reveals insights that I would not have uncovered in an artificial setting.

A pharmaceutical company wanted to look at the usability of its online index and guidelines. This was an index of procedural guidance on how to make compounds and solutions, which had to be made in a specific way to meet industry standards. The company was aware that its index wasn't optimal but couldn't articulate in more detail what was 'wrong'. As this online index was being used in a very particular setting, for a specific set of people, it made sense to choose contextual inquiry to understand how it was being used and what the issues being experienced were.

This research uncovered many interesting issues with the online index. Yes, there were usability issues with the design, structure and search function, but it also turned out that there weren't any computers in the lab where the compounds and solutions were created. The online index was accessed in a separate office, so the lab-based workers were printing out the step-by-step instructions they needed and were laminating the printouts in case acid (or something else) was accidentally dripped on them.

We are all busy people and we all have shortcuts and workarounds to help us be more efficient in our work. This kind of workaround had not been anticipated by the company management or the people who had created the index. This set-up ran the risk of people not checking when a method had been updated and therefore not following the correct procedures. As this was a serious issue it led to a rethink of the office/lab set up as well as iteratively improving the online index so it could be better utilized.

I should say that this project was undertaken before tablet devices were so ubiquitous, in case you are thinking it sounds quite old fashioned!

Effort required to do this kind of research

The learning curve involves developing similar skills to those used in interviewing and observation and, potentially, usability testing, depending on the scope and objectives of your research. As with every method, there are drawbacks. Contextual research is time- and resource-intensive: you are visiting users in their own environment and conducting in-depth observations, which takes time and planning, plus budget for travel (Interaction Design Foundation, 2016).

You may want to consider having another person with you, so that you can discuss what you observed and the possible implications. It also means that you have two sets of notes (ideally) and are less likely to miss things. However, this may not always be appropriate, so you need to be prepared to do it on your own.

You'll need to factor in travel time to the participant's location. Try to limit visits to two per day. This may sound like a light workload, but it's really important to have time to write up your notes and to consider and discuss what you've learnt after each visit.

How to do contextual inquiry

This technique is generally used at the beginning of the design process and is good for getting rich information about work practices and tools, and the social, technical and physical environments. According to Herzon et al (2010), the four principles of contextual inquiry are:

1 *Focus:* your plan for the inquiry, based on a clear understanding of your purpose.

2 *Context:* go to the participants' location and watch them do their activities, eg working.

3 *Partnership:* talk to participants about their work and engage them in uncovering any unarticulated aspects.

4 *Interpretation:* develop a shared understanding with the participants about the aspects of work that matter.

Planning a contextual inquiry

Planning a contextual inquiry involves identifying, locating and getting consent from the appropriate users and stakeholders you want to interview.

PARTICIPANTS

Include at least two people from each user group. Each contextual inquiry session is done on an individual basis, but only including one person from each group means you won't be able to identify what is or isn't common behaviour.

TIME REQUIRED AND SCHEDULING SESSIONS

An important aspect of scheduling is that you probably want to see people on a typical or busy day, whereas participants will want to see you on a quiet (and perhaps unrepresentative) day. You'll need about two hours for one session, but during the session it may become evident that this isn't enough. You may need to schedule extra sessions to avoid fatiguing the participant and to observe tasks when they normally occur.

Running a contextual inquiry session

There are different parts to a contextual inquiry:

• *Know you research questions and goals:* you don't want to just show up and watch. You'll make the most of the time available by having a standard set of questions that you can use to get to know participants' background and their typical challenges and goals.

- *Introduction:* introduce yourself, the purpose of the research and any other relevant information. You can ask if the interview can be recorded and when recording should stop/start. Offer assurances on confidentiality of the participants' data and ask for permission to use the data anonymously as part of sharing research findings, and any other consents you may need (see Part One).

- *Semi-structured interview:* used to get an overview of the participants' work. The relatively loose structure allows you to follow interesting lines of inquiry as they come up. The important thing is to go with the participants' flow, stay focused on the tasks the users are carrying out, and discuss any queries as you go along (without interrupting natural behaviour too much).

- *Active observation:* it is important to tell the participants that you want to learn from them by watching and occasionally interrupting. Make sure that you have agreed with them when you can interrupt to ask about what's happening, and when you will not disturb their work, for example during interaction with customers. When observing the users, remember your focus. You may need to ask the participants to do certain tasks that are important to your objectives, but are irregular. Note down as much as possible, even if you are not entirely convinced at the time that it's relevant to your objectives; it's all part of the bigger picture.

- *The wrap-up:* during interviews summarize what you have learnt. Be attentive to participants' reactions to your summary; they will not always tell you that you are wrong, so you have to figure it out yourself. If you didn't get it right, ask them questions and build the story with them.

Here are some important tips:

- Try to avoid interpreting as you listen. Spend time analysing and coming up with implications after the interview and observation session. This can be difficult as it is normal human behaviour to process and analyse while taking notes. A good tactic is to separate facts from any assumptions or interpretations in your notes by using a different colour or using quotation marks to indicate the words used by your participants.

- If customers are part of the participants' interaction, make sure that you get their consent; if that is not possible, do not record.

- Contextual inquiries must take place where participants normally perform their tasks. If participants won't do a session in their usual context, politely cancel their session.

- Try to offer people the highest degree of anonymity. For example, I avoid using people's names in reports or documents. However, I also have to alert people in some cases that it may be possible for others to deduce who made particular comments. It's also the case that some people specifically don't want anonymity, and want their voices to be heard clearly, and perhaps acknowledged. You'll need to make your own decisions on how to deal with these factors.

It's worth reading through the interview and ethnography chapters – 11 and 14; see also C̆engija, 2014; Gaffney, 2015; Interaction Design Foundation, 2016; Ross, 2012; Sauro, 2016, UsabilityNet, 2006; Webcredible, 2011.

Tools

Before you go on site visits, there are a few things you need to prepare. If you are audio or video recording, you will need to make sure your equipment is fully functional. Be prepared to abandon recording if your interviewee is uncomfortable or reluctant.

References and further reading

C̆engija, D (25 April 2014) Usability: what is contextual inquiry? UX Passion. www.uxpassion.com/blog/usability-contextual-inquiry/ (archived at https://perma.cc/93VD-VKNP)

Gaffney, G (11 August 2015) Conducting contextual enquiry (or site visits). UX Mastery. http://uxmastery.com/conducting-contextual-enquiry-or-site-visits/ (archived at https://perma.cc/N3PN-GS4E)

Herzon, C, DeBoard, D, Wilson, C and Bevan, N (2010) Contextual inquiry. Usability Body of Knowledge. www.usabilitybok.org/contextual-inquiry (archived at https://perma.cc/RW6Z-QWFP)

Interaction Design Foundation (September 2016) Contextual interviews and how to handle them. www.interaction-design.org/literature/article/contextual-interviews-and-how-to-handle-them (archived at https://perma.cc/LEZ5-KWS5)

Ross, J (4 June 2012) Why are contextual inquiries so difficult? UX Matters. www.uxmatters.com/mt/archives/2012/06/why-are-contextual-inquiries-so-difficult.php (archived at https://perma.cc/F9XK-XS24)

Sauro, J (16 August 2016) The essentials of a contextual inquiry. Measuring U. https://measuringu.com/contextual-inquiry/ (archived at https://perma.cc/6JRQ-W3G6)

UsabilityNet (2006) Contextual inquiry. www.usabilitynet.org/tools/
contextualinquiry.htm (archived at https://perma.cc/6YPJ-UCDE)
Webcredible (1 September 2011) Contextual inquiry research: a guide.
Webcredible. www.webcredible.com/blog/guide-conducting-contextual-inquiry-
user-research/ (archived at https://perma.cc/4R6H-DXF5)

16

A/B testing

A technique to compare options

What is A/B testing?

A/B testing is a method used to test product improvement hypotheses to see whether they will deliver the expected results or not (Rissen, 2021). You can compare two web pages by splitting your website traffic in half, showing the normal version to one half, and a newer version to the other, helping you choose between different design and content options (Rissen, 2021). Rather than deciding based solely on opinion, you can use direct evidence from your users' behaviour, at scale, to make decisions (Rissen, 2021). In an A/B test, it's important to change one thing at a time when creating your variation, otherwise you won't be able to identify which design change made a difference (for better or for worse). Half of your visitors are shown the original version of the page (known as the control) and half are shown the modified version (the variation).

What A/B testing is good for

A/B testing is used to investigate gut feelings when deciding between two potential solutions. The results in A/B tests are often surprising or unintuitive. Your goal with each test is to find out whether there's enough reliable evidence to move away from what you have now and implement your design changes fully (Rissen, 2021).

In an online setting, the types of change people test are extremely varied. Some of the many testing examples include:

- calls to action;
- headlines;
- images;
- display ads;
- layout;
- content structure;
- forms;
- email copy;
- landing pages.

Your focus will depend on the goals of your product/service. For instance, a media company may want to increase readership and the amount of time readers spend on its site, and to amplify its articles with social sharing. To achieve these goals, it may test variations on email sign-up models, recommended content and social sharing buttons. A travel company may want to increase the number of successful bookings completed on its website or mobile app or may want to increase revenue from add-on purchases. To improve these metrics, it may test variations of clickable homepage hero images, search results page, and add-on feature design.

As further examples, an e-commerce company may want to increase the number of completed checkouts, the average order value or the number of sales, so it could test homepage promotions, navigation elements and checkout funnel components, while a technology company may want to increase the number of high-quality leads for its sales team, increase the number of free trial users or attract a specific type of buyer. It may test lead-form components, free trial sign-up flow, homepage messaging and call-to-action.

What A/B testing is not good for

A/B testing can identify which of two options performs better in some way, but it cannot tell you why. If you are interested in understanding why something performs better, you can use a combination of research methods to figure this out. A classic example would be combining A/B testing with moderated usability testing, so you can watch participants use your product or service and talk to them about what does or doesn't work for them in a certain context.

When to use A/B testing

A/B testing is useful when you need to check your biases (someone is certain that a design change will work, and someone else is not so certain) or if there is no clear route to go down (Rissen, 2021). As visitors are served either the control or the variation, their engagement with each experience is measured, collected and analysed through statistical techniques to test validity. You can then determine which experience had a positive, negative, or no effect on visitor behaviour.

Effort required to do this kind of research

The effort required to do A/B testing is not just about learning the method; it's also understanding what's possible to measure and how to make sure the data you gather is reliable enough to drive your decision making, and selecting useful things for the A/B test (we are back to problem scoping again).

This is a specific skill set, with certain terminology and nuances, but at the root are many common and understandable concepts, especially if you're already thinking about research and evidence. If you aren't a performance analyst or in a similar analyst's role, it's worth trying to learn from whoever does this in your organization. There are also a lot of online resources available. There are consultancies that provide training to organizations. Also, if you aren't the designer who is creating the variations to be tested, you will need to factor in coordinating and collaborating with whoever is undertaking that task.

In summary, if you aren't already familiar with the concepts and your organization doesn't have A/B testing processes in place, setting up and running useful A/B testing won't necessarily be quick or easy. However, it is an iterative process and you will learn over time.

How to do A/B testing

The test process

It's a good idea to conduct A/B testing on a regular basis, as part of your usual design validation process. It's a tool to investigate ideas. In fact, it's a cyclical process: you redesign, test, redesign, and test again. As with any research method, there is a process to be followed:

1 **Review existing data:** you can use analytics for insight, you can also use prior research to shape questions and hypotheses. You may need to investigate new content, design or concepts, or adding a new feature, etc.

2 **Agree and capture the goals:** your goals are the metrics that you are using to determine whether or not the variation is more successful than the original. Goals can be anything from clicking a button or link to product purchases and email sign-ups.

3 **Generate the hypothesis:** once you've identified a goal you can begin generating ideas and assumptions. From those, you can create hypotheses to test (Rissen, 2021). What do you think will happen at the conclusion of your test? Once you have a list of hypotheses, prioritize them in terms of expected impact and difficulty of implementation.

4 **Create the variations:** this can be done directly by developers, or you can use your A/B testing software to make the changes to an element of your product/service. Many leading A/B testing tools have a visual editor that will make these changes easy. Ensure you note down the changes you make for each variant.

5 **Conduct the test:** when will you do your test? Do you have known peaks and troughs in visitor volumes to consider? How long will you run it? There's no hard and fast rule for the amount of time a test should run for. There are some who advocate running two-week tests no matter what; there are concepts you can use to account for seasonal variations – and even then you can always run tests again (Rissen, 2021). Depending on the amount of traffic you get, you may want to run tests for a few days or a couple of weeks, and you'll only want to run one test at a time for the most accurate results on a particular page template or user journey. Giving a test insufficient time can mean skewed results, as you don't get a large enough group of visitors to be statistically accurate. Be aware of anything that may affect your test results, so that you can account for any statistical anomalies when reviewing your results. If you're in doubt, it's

perfectly reasonable to retest. Considering the impact A/B testing can have on your bottom line, it's worth taking a few weeks to properly conduct tests. Visitors to your site or app will be randomly assigned to either the control or variation of your experience. Their interaction with each experience is measured, counted and compared to determine how each performs.

6 **Interpret the results:** once your test has concluded, it's time to analyse your results. If your variation is a clear winner, go ahead and switch to that version. If not, start the process all over again. Your A/B testing software will present the data from the experiment and show you the difference between the two versions and whether the results are valid and reliable.

Most tools will guide you through the process of setting up your test. Best practice in A/B testing includes the following:

- Show repeat visitors the same variations. Your tool of choice should have a mechanism for remembering which variation a visitor has seen. This prevents confusion, such as showing a user a different price or a different promotional offer.

- Make your A/B test consistent across the whole website. If you are testing a sign-up button that appears in multiple locations, a visitor should see the same variation everywhere.

Tools for A/B testing

A number of tools are available for A/B testing, with different focuses, price points and feature sets.

References and further reading

Armour, H (22 September 2015) What is A/B testing? Digital Marketing Magazine. http://digitalmarketingmagazine.co.uk/articles/what-is-a-b-testing/2597 (archived at https://perma.cc/RYG2-SALN) (last accessed: 27 May 2017)

Chopra, P (2010) The ultimate guide To A/B testing. Smashing Magazine. www.smashingmagazine.com/2010/06/the-ultimate-guide-to-a-b-testing/ (archived at https://perma.cc/LF3P-9KCK) (last accessed: 27 May 2017)

Constine, J (29 June 2014) The morality of A/B testing. Tech Crunch. https://
  techcrunch.com/2014/06/29/ethics-in-a-data-driven-world/ (archived at
  https://perma.cc/A8PT-ZYB2) (last accessed: 27 May 2017)

Fung, K (10 December 2014) Yes, A/B testing is still necessary. Harvard Business
  Review. https://hbr.org/2014/12/yes-ab-testing-is-still-necessary (archived at
  https://perma.cc/X3LQ-G9PW) (last accessed: 27 May 2017)

Kissmetrics (2011) A beginner's guide to A/B testing: an introduction. https://blog.
  kissmetrics.com/ab-testing-introduction/ (archived at https://perma.cc/F83G-
  G9JV) (last accessed: 27 May 2017)

Koh, M (4 May 2016) How to do an A/B test. Optimal Workshop. https://blog.
  optimalworkshop.com/how-to-do-an-ab-test (archived at https://perma.cc/
  G3QN-SGAU) (last accessed: 27 May 2017)

Kreimer, I (23 March 2017) A/B testing ideas. Optimizely Blog. https://blog.
  optimizely.com/tag/ab-testing-ideas/ (archived at https://perma.cc/D2L4-HPHW)
  (last accessed: 27 May 2017)

Miller, E (18 April 2010) How not to run an A/B test. www.evanmiller.org/
  how-not-to-run-an-ab-test.html (archived at https://perma.cc/VX6J-H4GM)

Rissen, P (2019) *Experiment-Driven Product Development: How to use a data-
  informed approach to learn, iterate, and succeed faster*, Apress, New York

Rissen, P (2021) Information referenced as Rissen 2021 was shared with me by
  Paul Rissen, author of *Experiment-Driven Product Development*, (see previous
  reference).

Rosenfeld, L (2011) *Search Analytics for Your Site: Conversations with your
  customers*, Rosenfeld Media, New York

Smith, G (2015) 10 A/B testing tools to help improve conversions. Mashable. http://
  mashable.com/2015/01/30/ab-testing-tools/#c950K6q4taqt (archived at https://
  perma.cc/UM4X-ADKN) (last accessed: 27 May 2017)

Visual Website Optimizer (2017) The complete guide to A/B testing. Wingify.
  https://vwo.com/ab-testing/ (archived at https://perma.cc/6BWJ-UFV9) (last
  accessed: 27 May 2017)

17

Getting the best
out of stakeholder workshops

What is a stakeholder workshop?

Stakeholder workshops are a way of engaging those who have an interest in the project you are working on. 'Stakeholders' are people in the organization(s) who are key to getting your project done and includes people with expertise and in-depth knowledge of the domain you are working in. The term also includes your users: they want you to get things right, so they can do what they want and need to do.

What stakeholder workshops are good for

There are several different kinds of stakeholder workshops you can run, but they all have the same aim and benefits, such as building consensus amongst various parties within your organization who have potentially opposing views and objectives. They can be used to establish a shared understanding of what certain things mean. They can create a sense of ownership of the outcomes of the project (as well as the process that will get you there).

Workshops are often important milestones in projects that kick-off certain stages or become the decision-making points. Stakeholder alignment and avoiding conflicts and misunderstandings are key at these points. Workshops are an investment of time and effort for many people, but have the benefit of collecting information in a single day that can otherwise take weeks or months to accomplish. Workshops allow stakeholders to collaborate; generate ideas, gather requirements, draft designs and solutions, agree on priorities, and identify risks and constraints. Group dynamics can generate better discussions than you would have when talking with people individually. Stakeholders react to each other and bring up questions and issues that would never occur to you, whether they have similar or different types of roles.

What stakeholder workshops are not good for

Stakeholder workshops are not designed for gathering raw data about opinions and preferences; they are not focus groups. It's best to avoid treating workshops as group usability testing as it's difficult to get useful insights from this, but it is worth demonstrating prototypes and other things that have been created during the development lifecycle. Workshops aren't about everyone agreeing in a committee meeting style; participants need to be willing to engage in activities to move thinking along and gain consensus (Pickering, 2015).

When to use workshops

If you read the 'what workshops are good for' section above, you may have formed the impression that workshops can be utilized at multiple points in a project, because of the diversity of things that can be achieved:

- At the beginning of project to agree the scope and objectives.
- When strategic direction is needed; used to identify priorities and timelines. This should be done early in the project.
- Reporting when key milestones have been reached and shaping the next stage in the project.
- You need multidisciplinary input, this can be internal with different expertise or it could be external with your users.

There are a few factors to consider when deciding when and where you can use workshops during your development lifecycle:

- *Project schedule and budget.* On smaller projects you may have time to conduct only one workshop with everyone who is involved; on larger projects you may have enough time to conduct multiple workshops.
- *Size and complexity.* On larger, more complicated projects, you may have too many stakeholders and too much to discuss for a single session.

Twelve is an ideal number of people to include in a single session: with more than that, the discussion can become unmanageable, and some people can get left out of the discussion. Having said that, I have run workshops with 60 people but that size needs different activities and helpers to help you facilitate the workshop.

- Depending on the kind of thing you are working on, you can run different kinds of workshop at different stages.

Effort required to do this kind of research

Workshops can be hugely valuable but they also require a lot of time and investment. Facilitating a workshop and moderating group discussion requires skills that take time to develop. While it can be learnt and practised on the job, in the beginning it's likely to require a lot more preparation and consideration. If you are running workshops with a large number of people, be mindful of keeping things on track and encouraging everyone to contribute and engage. Whoever is in the room, try to make it a level playing field.

You will have to factor in the time it takes to organize and prepare, especially if you are trying to get several busy people in the same room at the same time. As the researcher, you will invest time and effort in organizing, preparing, running and analysing the output of the workshop. To be effective, the participants also need to engage in the activities you include. Workshops are not talking shops; they are focused on encouraging creativity through sharing and creating tangible outputs.

How to run a workshop

During your workshop preparation, it can be worth:

- Reviewing existing research and documentation (you may want to share an overview of this in your workshop).
- Getting an in-depth understanding of what you are working with (get to know the bits that you don't normally work on).
- Interviewing some stakeholders beforehand (or after), especially if they can't attend the workshop. Doing interviews *before* could give you a feel for attitudes and expectations; doing interviews *afterwards* may allow you to explore certain topics and issues in more detail.

Planning and practicalities

Preparation is key. Get everything ready for each activity you will run before the workshop starts. Workshops need to be interactive; it's not just about you talking or having a group discussion. What activities will you use to achieve your goals? Here is a checklist for smooth running workshops:

- Have a clear agenda. Establish the workshop goals: why you are having the workshop and what the agenda will include. Share this with participants before the workshop starts (ideally with the invitation), to set their expectations. If you want people to prepare something beforehand make sure you give them enough time to do so.

- Decide on the timing of each activity and try to stick to it. It's quite easy to overrun when creativity and discussion are flowing.

- Try to keep workshops to about three hours. They will be three hours of hard work, so include breaks. Having said this, I have run all-day workshops, it's tough (on everyone) but doable. Try to do the workshop before or after lunch: a long break of 30–60 minutes can kill momentum.

- If the workshop is face to face, make sure you can access the venue before the workshop starts so that you can set up everything in advance.

- It is difficult to run a workshop on your own – facilitating and moderating, capturing information, setting up exercises, etc. It takes two or three people to run a good workshop.

- Have a 'no phones' policy, to help people focus on the task at hand.

- Keep instructions and output visible for all in the workshop.

- Check people's understanding by inviting questions.

- Include individual, small and large group exercises if possible. This will cater for how different people like to interact and think.

- When doing group activities try to have a representative range in each group, so people interact with those they don't necessarily work with every day.

- Capture everything: if the workshop is face to face, photograph everything that has been produced and ask someone to make notes of the discussions that happen. If the workshop is digital, artefacts can be captured directly in the tool you are using, but you may still need someone to take notes on discussions that happen.

- It can be useful to include photos or screenshots in any reports you may be writing about the workshop.

- Focus on the users: when people are disagreeing due to their differing opinions or priorities, bring the focus back to the users. There needs to be a balance between organization and user needs; but user needs can often break an organizational stalemate.

What kind of workshop can you run?

The workshop research format can be used in a multitude of situations. Generally, any kind of workshop can be used to diverge and converge: get all the ideas and assumptions (diverge) out there and synthesize them into something achievable and agreed (converge).

KICK-OFF WORKSHOPS

At the beginning of a project or a new, distinct stage of a project, workshops can be used to agree the scope and objectives. In a few hours, you can start building consensus among various parties with potentially opposing views and objectives. This is a good time to identify where there are disparities in people's thinking, understanding and assumptions; get these on the table and then establish a shared understanding for this particular project or milestone.

ENGAGEMENT (MILESTONE) WORKSHOPS

When a milestone has been reached, it's good to share the progress that has been made (whether this is positive or negative). This can create a sense of ownership of the outcomes and the work done to achieve them, even for those who aren't directly involved in the work but have a stake in the outcome. This is a good time to check the strategic direction and to validate the priorities and timelines.

REQUIREMENTS GATHERING

This kind of workshop is another to run early on in the development lifecycle. These workshops are about gathering assumptions, identifying what your organization thinks is required to achieve the objectives through sharing expertise and knowledge from relevant areas of the business. If your organization doesn't already have insight into the users this work is focused on, this is a good time to sketch out who you think the users are (personas), their attitudes, behaviours, motivations and needs. Any requirements and personas created during the workshop should be validated by subsequent user research.

DESIGN WORKSHOPS

Gather the internal expertise in the room to sketch out initial designs for your project. This kind of workshop is not just for designers or the technical people: there will be others who have insights into how things can be developed.

CO-DESIGN WORKSHOPS

Also known as 'participatory design', co-design workshops are where you are designing with your users, who can be included at any stage of the design process. You can include the users to gain insight and ideas on attitudes, motivations, context, preferences, needs and issues. You can create or refine outputs such as experience and journey maps, scenarios and storyboards, and discuss designs not only in the visual sense, but anything that needs to be created to achieve the outcomes, such as content, process and experience. These workshops can highlight any disconnect between your organization and your users (Anić, 2015).

CONTENT WORKSHOPS

If you are a content designer or strategist you may already be using content workshops; if not it's definitely something you can start doing. Content workshops can be used to:

- Review and challenge content styles, strategies, workflows and governance.
- Agree what needs to be done to improve existing content and what content types are needed.
- Train people in content best practice and organization style guides.
- Draft governance documents, style guides, workflows for content creation and improvement.

To learn more about running workshop activities to achieve your objectives, see the References and Further Reading section at the end of the chapter.

Who needs to be there?

The kind of workshop you are running will determine the appropriate group. Who is important to achieving the desired outputs and what kind of activities are you doing? Don't invite everyone; that won't be productive. Who actually needs to be there? You will need those who:

- make decisions;
- have information you need;

- have 'clout', ie those you need to keep on side to ensure the project gets backing, continuous funding, etc;
- are involved in making the thing happen.

Basic structure of a workshop

- The introduction should set the tone of the day. It should be welcoming and make people feel comfortable. It should set out who you are, the agenda, the objectives and who is present.
- What you know so far (audience, current situation, design, research you and others have done, issues); this is optional.
- Warm up activities.
- Core activities.
- Summing up. Try to make your summary uplifting and positive, so that people go away from the workshop feeling energized and productive.

Face-to-face workshop tools

The tools you need will depend on the kind of workshop you are running. The workshops I have covered usually require all or some of the items in this checklist (Pickering, 2015; Sharma, 2012):

- Post-its. Lots and lots of Post-its, of different colours and maybe different sizes.
- Pens. Different colours and sizes. Board markers and Sharpies generally work well.
- Paper. For sketching, noting down what's been said and agreed (or not).
- Blue-Tac. To stick things on the wall, so it's easy to share what has been generated.
- Flipcharts. Again, a good way to capture ideas and share with others.
- Sticky dots. Used for voting and prioritizing.
- Camera. Photographs are extremely useful for documenting what's happened in a workshop. Optional: video camera to capture workshops.

- An appropriate space to hold the workshop. Definitely big enough for the number of participants to sit and move around in. Ideally, away from the office and somewhere you are allowed to use Blue-Tac on the walls.

- Refreshments.

ODE TO POST-ITS

An easy way to capture ideas.

Having one idea per Post-it forces people to be concise and focused.

They are easy to move around and group.

Post-its are your friend in user research.

Digital workshop tools

If you are running your workshop remotely, which in my experience works very well, the tools you'll need can include video conference software. If you are going to have breakout groups at some point in your workshop, you may need a couple of accounts available, unless your tool has breakout room functionality. You may need a tool to record the things that have been discussed or worked on; it really depends on the purpose of your workshop as to what that tool will be. It could be a document or spreadsheet, something like Trello or Miro.

References and further reading

Anic´, I (5 November 2015) Participatory design: what is it, and what makes it so great? UX Passion. www.uxpassion.com/blog/participatory-design-what-makes-it-great/ (archived at https://perma.cc/G3LM-9ABE)

Boag, P (4 August 2015) 10 ways get more from your UX workshop. Boag World. https://boagworld.com/usability/10-ways-to-get-more-from-your-ux-workshop/ (archived at https://perma.cc/XK59-WH43) (last accessed: 27 May 2017)

Buley, L (18 November 2013) UX method of the week: strategy workshop. Rosenfeld Media. http://rosenfeldmedia.com/ux-team-of-one/ux-method-of-the-week-strategy-workshop/ (archived at https://perma.cc/ZT8B-PHVG) (last accessed: 27 May 2017)

Cao, J (2017) The practical guide to empathy maps: 10-minute user personas. UX Pin Studio. www.tadpull.com/how-to-use-empathy-map-for-user-experience-mapping/ (last accessed: 27 May 2017)

Flowerdew-Clarke, M (15 September 2014) How to run successful stakeholder, user and content workshops. Building Blocks. http://blog.building-blocks.com/insights/how-to-run-successful-client-user-content-workshops (last accessed: 27 May 2017)

Gamestorming (2017) http://gamestorming.com/ (archived at https://perma.cc/J5XV-TTEA)

Gilbert, K (30 November 2016) The co-design workshop: the facilitator's pocket guide. Connections. https://connection.domain7.com/the-co-design-workshop-the-pocket-facilitators-guide-e36a6c9e08d4 (archived at https://perma.cc/B7Y5-R33F)

Government Digital Service (2016) Analyse a research session. Service Manual. www.gov.uk/service-manual/user-research/analyse-a-research-session (archived at https://perma.cc/836T-6FUA)

Gray, D, Brown, S and Macanufo, J (2010) *Gamestorming: A playbook for innovators, rulebreakers, and changemakers,* O'Reilly Media, Sebastopol

Hohmann, L (2007) *Innovation: Creating breakthrough products through collaborative play,* Addison-Wesley, Boston

Kaner, S (2014) *Facilitator's Guide to Participatory Decision-making,* 3rd edn, Jossey-Bass, Hoboken, NJ

Knox, N (27 June 2014) How to use persona empathy mapping. UX Magazine. http://uxmag.com/articles/how-to-use-persona-empathy-mapping (archived at https://perma.cc/LAW5-9FBP) (last accessed: 27 May 2017)

Leavy, P (2017) *Research Design: Quantitative, qualitative, mixed methods, arts-based, and community-based participatory research approaches,* Guilford Press, New York

Mazur, M (26 July 2016) The power of workshops in the UX process. User Testing Blog. www.usertesting.com/blog/2016/07/26/workshops/ (archived at https://perma.cc/9RBX-SC6M) (last accessed: 27 May 2017)

Myhill, C (20 August 2014) Running a kick-ass kick-off workshop. Just UX Design. http://justuxdesign.com/blog/running-a-kick-ass-kick-off-workshop (archived at https://perma.cc/SVZ3-EAYN) (last accessed: 27 May 2017)

O'Keefe, B (26 February 2015) How to facilitate a design workshop for stakeholders. Effective UI. www.effectiveui.com/blog/2015/02/26/how-to-facilitate-a-design-workshop-for-stakeholders/ (archived at https://perma.cc/6XZW-88WM) (last accessed: 27 May 2017)

Pedalo Web Design (2017) Stakeholders engagement workshops. www.pedalo.co.
uk/services/user-experience-ux/stakeholder-engagement-workshops/ (archived at
https://perma.cc/8LYP-FZHY) (last accessed: 27 May 2017)

Pickering, K (20 May 2015) What is the value in stakeholder workshops? Numiko.
http://numiko.com/blog/what-value-stakeholder-workshops (archived at https://
perma.cc/HR9Y-4DGV)

Ross, J (4 May 2015) Understanding stakeholders through research. UX Matters.
www.uxmatters.com/mt/archives/2015/05/understanding-stakeholders-through-
research.php (archived at https://perma.cc/R8N7-MNAM) (last accessed:
27 May 2017)

Sauro, J (9 September 2014) 7 techniques for prioritizing customer requirements.
Measuring U. https://measuringu.com/prioritize-requirements/ (archived at
https://perma.cc/P6KN-CGPS) (last accessed: 27 May 2017)

Sharma, A (24 April 2012) Creativity-based research: the process of co-designing
with users. UX Magazine. https://uxmag.com/articles/creativity-based-research-
the-process-of-co-designing-with-users (archived at https://perma.
cc/85K5-PQX5)

Sharma, A (30 August 2016) Participatory design as a research method. https://
medium.com/the-making-of-appear-in/participatory-design-as-a-research-
method-bc42c01943b1 (archived at https://perma.cc/GY83-38WK)

Sharon, T (2012) *It's Our Research: Getting stakeholder buy-in for user experience
research projects*, Morgan Kaufmann, Burlington

Tadpull (2017) Empathy maps for UX. www.tadpull.com/how-to-use-empathy-
map-for-user-experience-mapping/ (last accessed: 27 May 2017)

Turner, N (11 December 2014) How to plan and run the perfect UX workshop. UX
for the Masses. www.uxforthemasses.com/ux-workshops/ (archived at https://
perma.cc/5G6P-SMGG) (last accessed: 27 May 2017)

Turner, N (16 May 2016) 5 techniques for prioritising features (or user stories) to
try out. UX for the Masses. www.uxforthemasses.com/5-techniques-prioritising-
features/ (archived at https://perma.cc/96H6-GW2S) (last accessed:
27 May 2017)

18

Guerrilla research

Running fast-paced research in the real world

What is guerrilla research?

Guerrilla research is a quick, flexible and low-cost method of conducting research; the 'just do it' approach (Foolproof, 2014). It is 'the art of pouncing on lone people in cafés and public spaces, [then] quickly filming them whilst they use a website for a couple of minutes' (Belam, 2010).

What guerrilla research is good for

Guerrilla research is useful for a variety of reasons:

- It's low cost.
- It's quick to get results.
- It answers small-scale design questions quickly.
- You can involve your wider team in doing research.
- It can help you understand the real-world context of use, especially when testing on mobile devices outside.
- Unexpected research encourages people to be open and honest.

What guerrilla research is not good for

Because guerrilla research is a quick and dirty method it can often only provide high-level insight and it can be difficult to get the right cross-section of participants. You also need to consider:

- Environmental challenges such as the weather.

- Competing for people's attention as they go about their day.
- The potential to experience technical issues during the research.

When to use guerrilla research

Guerrilla research is not detailed and rigorous enough to be the sole source of data. It can give just enough insight to make informed decisions, in the early stages, when exploring problems and opportunities. It can also increase your understanding and build initial hypotheses for more in-depth research and design (Foolproof, 2014).

Effort required to do this kind of research

If you feel comfortable with the fundamentals of user research, guerrilla research can be done very quickly. Some preparation should be carried out so that you have a focus, but you need to be prepared to be flexible and react to unexpected situations as this kind of research is less structured and controlled than others. It is therefore useful to be familiar with what you are testing and the format you are using (whether it's on a digital device, on paper, etc).

To be honest, for me the biggest barrier to using guerrilla research techniques is having the confidence to stop people on the street, at an event, etc. I don't find it easy asking strangers for help. You may want to do this research in pairs, with one person doing the recruiting and the other doing the research. I know which one of the two I'd rather be!

How to do guerrilla research

Below are some of the ways you can use guerrilla research.

Guerrilla usability testing

The essence of guerrilla research is that you go to your users, rather than making them come to you. You can take your product or service out on a laptop, phone or sketchpad to wherever your users may be and approach them.

Contextual user interviews

These are short interviews with people in their own environment: their home, place of work, etc. Doing the interview this way can yield insight into how users' environments affect how they use your product or service.

Cut-down ethnography

Ethnographic observation is a good way to capture how things are used in real life. You don't need to get too hung up about formalized notes. Most of the time your scribbles will work just fine: it's about triggering memories that you can turn into insight and actions.

Tips for recruiting and conducting effective guerrilla research

Success lies in the planning. Have an agreed list of questions or tasks to focus on for achieving your research objectives. Prioritize your tasks/questions; it's difficult to know how much you can get through and how long people are willing to spend with you, when you have just approached them. Agree beforehand the kind of data you aim to capture; there will always be things you didn't expect, so it helps to be focused in your short research sessions. Establish the top issues, task completion (if you are usability testing), etc.

Prepare a short introduction that quickly communicates what you are doing and why you want them to take part. You'll need a cut-down version of the ethical and legal points you have to cover (see Part One) and an explanation of how the research is going to run.

Choose your locations carefully, based on the target groups you are recruiting and, before approaching participants, assess their body language and behaviour. Hailing people in the street, café or conference hall is challenging. At times it can be demoralizing, but you just need to keep on keeping on.

Be flexible in your approach: scale, refocus and modify your tactics according to how it's going. It can be more iterative than doing research in the lab. Also, keep sessions short – they shouldn't really be more than 15 minutes – and keep it casual: offer food and/or a coffee in exchange for people's time, if appropriate to the setting.

Tools for guerrilla research

The tools required really depend on what you are testing. You may need a digital device or just a paper notebook. It's generally best not to have too much equipment to carry round and present to participants. Keep it relatively low key. You could use video, audio and photography (but this is optional). Guerrilla research can produce compelling stories about real users. However, it's not always appropriate to capture data in this way, and it can sometimes put people off participating.

References and further reading

Belam, M (3 June 2010) 10 tips for ambush guerrilla user testing. Currybet. www. currybet.net/cbet_blog/2010/06/10-tips-for-ambush-guerilla-us.php (archived at https://perma.cc/MPM5-MLU5) (last accessed: 27 May 2017)

Foolproof (18 March 2014) The hidden value of guerrilla research. www. foolproof.co.uk/thinking/the-hidden-value-of-guerrilla-research/ (archived at https://perma.cc/4M4H-D42E) (last accessed: 27 May 2017)

Interaction Design Foundation (May 2017) The pros and cons of guerrilla research for your UX project. www.interaction-design.org/literature/article/the-pros-and-cons-of-guerrilla-research-for-your-ux-project (archived at https://perma. cc/4BYX-KS57) (last accessed: 27 May 2017)

Myhill, C (30 September 2014) Guerrilla research tactics and tools. UX Booth. www.uxbooth.com/articles/guerrilla-research-tactics-tools/ (archived at https:// perma.cc/AE4Q-KU2C) (last accessed: 27 May 2017)

Pirker, M (24 March 2016) 7 step guide to guerrilla usability testing: DIY usability testing method. User Brain Blog. https://userbrain.net/blog/7-step-guide-guerrilla-usability-testing-diy-usability-testing-method (archived at https:// perma.cc/KH8Z-PJVG) (last accessed: 27 May 2017)

Simon, D P (2 July 2013) The art of guerrilla usability testing. UX Booth. www. uxbooth.com/articles/the-art-of-guerrilla-usability-testing/ (archived at https:// perma.cc/F56A-KCQW) (last accessed: 27 May 2017)

Webcredible (2017) Guerrilla research. www.webcredible.com/services/investigate/ guerrilla-research/ (archived at https://perma.cc/A5GJ-3UR3) (last accessed: 27 May 2017)

19

How to combine user research methodologies

As I have mentioned before, user research is an iterative and continuous process. Throughout the development lifecycle, whatever you are working on, there will be different methodologies that are appropriate at different times. There isn't one correct way to combine methods, but there are some common ways of working that I will outline here to give you an idea of how you could combine methods yourself.

Where to start when advocating user research

If carrying out user research is not usual in your organization, it's possible that you'll be experiencing difficulty getting time, resource and budget signed off to do some. I have been in this situation myself and I know it can be difficult to get buy-in for something when it's at the theoretical stage, ie the research will in theory benefit the organization/project. Also, people may not want to admit there's a problem with your product or service. In my experience, the best way to get across the benefits of user research is to show people the evidence of what it can do – but you can't do that until you've done some actual research, right? It's a tricky situation to be in.

Use guerrilla research to kick start the process

This is a good time to do some guerrilla research (Chapter 18). You can quickly and cheaply gather some initial evidence and insight to demonstrate:

- The issues being experienced by users.
- How users think and feel about a topic, which may be at odds with the organization's position.

- How people behave and do things in the real world.
- Some insight into how things could be progressed and improved.

SHOW DON'T TELL

In my experience, evidence is the most powerful way to advocate user research.

Showing colleagues the insight you can get from a quick and dirty piece of research is a great way to build support for more in-depth and structured research. You can use guerrilla research as a small glimpse into the potential of user research as a business tool.

CASE STUDY
Example of guerrilla research

I was working on a website redevelopment project, for a site that had not changed for many years. The organization in question had little awareness of agile and user-centric ways of working, and I was a lone user-centric warrior.

There was enough budget available to work with an outside agency to do most of the initial (discovery) research to understand who the users were, what they needed and what had to be done. However, there wasn't enough budget to do research with all of the presumed primary user groups. How were we going to choose who we would include in the research?

It was assumed that the large internal audience and their needs was the most important group for this public website. I had a hunch but no evidence that this wasn't a valid assumption: we didn't really know anything about what they needed, how they went about doing their tasks, or the issues they might experience, nor what their mental models were. I took it upon myself to do some guerrilla user research with this audience. In the space of two weeks I visited three different locations in the UK and carried out a combination of interviews, usability testing and card sorting with 15 people. By the end of the two weeks I had gained these insights into the internal users:

- What tasks they performed.
- How they did those tasks.
- The issues they experienced.
- Their mental models and how they associated and grouped information.

All these things would be a useful grounding to start the main project work. The most critical thing that I learnt was that most of this group of users weren't using the website! Only a small sub-section were using it and even then they did so irregularly in a specific time-sensitive context. They had other means of doing the things they needed to do, and could therefore be considered a secondary rather than a primary audience.

This guerrilla research helped to make decisions on which audiences to include and exclude. All it cost was my time and effort, plus some travel expenses.

What to do when guerrilla research isn't appropriate

There are always going to be situations and environments where guerrilla research isn't appropriate; a prime example would be doing research with patients in a hospital. In such cases, you can do some desktop research: has anyone published work about a similar organization or situation that shows how user research was used and the results that were achieved?

It can be useful to show that equivalent organizations in your field/industry have experienced similar issues and successfully done some user research and benefited from it. Not only does it show that it's possible, it also shows that others have a competitive edge.

Combining guerrilla research and desktop research

What is better than one piece of evidence? Multiple pieces of evidence! If you can, do some guerrilla research to show what you can do yourself and combine this with evidence others have published in related areas. I hope this will help you on the road to getting support for doing more user research.

Common research scenarios and combining methodologies

Developing and/or improving a product or service

Whether you are building something entirely new or improving an existing item that is suboptimal, a similar iterative approach can be used. Table 19.1 shows which methods could be used in this scenario.

TABLE 19.1 Developing or improving a product or service – combining methodologies

Steps	Method	Scenario and explanation
1	Stakeholder workshop (Chapter 17)	Start your project by getting all the relevant people in the same room at the same time to share the understanding of the current situation, agree the scope of the project and gather initial requirements.
2	Interviews (Chapter 11) or contextual inquiry (Chapter 15)	Once you have internal agreement of the scope, it's time to get feedback and insight from the actual users. I have given interviews and contextual inquiry as methods here, but it really depends on the work you're doing. Ultimately you are validating (or overturning) stakeholder assumptions from the workshop and gaining insight into users' behaviour and their barriers.
3	Design a prototype	Combining the outcomes of steps 1 and 2, it's time to do an initial draft of the new product/service or draft several potential options.
4	Usability testing (Chapter 7)	You don't want to invest too much time in designing and building anything before you test it with users to see what is and isn't working.
5	Iterate	The insight gained from usability testing should be used to improve the prototype, which can be tested again to validate the changes made. Once a new or improved product or service has been launched, the insight, improve, validate cycle should continue.

Reorganizing content and structure

Table 19.2 gives an example of which methods could be used in an iterative approach to content and information architecture development (and improvement).

As I mentioned above, there are no strict rules for how to combine methodologies in iterative research; it really depends on the situation and the work you are doing. So, I have included another example (Table 19.3) of a content and structure improvement project.

TABLE 19.2 Reorganizing content and structure – combining methodologies, example 1

Steps	Method	Scenario and explanation
1	Usability testing (Chapter 7)	For existing products or services, if a problem has been identified through analytics or feedback, you may want to gain insight into why there is a problem before going any further. Whether you are working on a digital or non-digital item, you could do some usability testing, setting people tasks to work through so you can observe them and the issues they are experiencing.
2	Closed card sorting (Chapter 9)	Imagine that you have established that certain parts of your product have labels and a structure that don't match how the users think. You've gained enough insight that you have a good idea how to resolve these problems. You can do some closed card sorting (with your predefined groups) to see if your new structure and labelling work with a small sample of your user groups.
3	Draft information architecture	Insight from the closed card sort will allow you to fix any initial issues and create a draft information architecture.
4	Tree test (Chapter 13)	The draft information architecture can then be tested with a much larger sample of relevant users (with something like Treejack from Optimal Workshop).
5	Content testing (Chapter 8)	You can also test content for users' understanding. This is particularly useful if the work done up to this point has shown that there is a mismatch of language used between users and your organization.

Figuring out if a new concept is worth investing in

Whether you don't really know what the problem is or you are trying to figure out if something new is worth investing in, it is likely that you will start with broad research and progressively become more focused (as visualized in Figure 19.1). Table 19.4 shows an example of moving from asking broad to specific questions in your research.

Summary

We have worked through just a couple of scenarios of how you might combine different methodologies during the lifecycle of a project. Choosing

TABLE 19.3 Reorganizing content and structure – combining methodologies, example 2

Steps	Method	Scenario and explanation
1	Content testing (Chapter 8)	You have anecdotal feedback (from frontline staff/call centre staff/survey/etc) that some of your content is confusing. You do some content testing, gathering evidence to demonstrate that users can't complete certain tasks because critical content is missing.
2	Open card sorting (Chapter 9)	Your team has identified what new content needs to be written and agreed some initial names for this content. While this content is being drafted, you can do an open card sort to understand how users would group new content items and if they comprehend the draft labelling.
3	Content testing (Chapter 8)	The draft content can be tested with users. Is it understandable? Can they take appropriate action based on what they have understood?
4	Closed card sorting (Chapter 9)	You can do some closed card sorting with a small sample of your defined groups, based on insights from the open card sort and content testing, to see if your new structure and labelling work for them.
5	Tree test (Chapter 13)	The draft information architecture based on closed card sort results can then be tested with a much larger sample of relevant users (using something like Treejack from Optimal Workshop).
6	Content testing (Chapter 8) and/or usability testing (Chapter 7)	The new content can be iteratively tested, and research (such as usability testing) can be done, combining the new structure and the new content together (with existing content) to understand if it all works holistically in real-life form with realistic tasks.

the right methodology or combination will depend on what you're trying to achieve at each stage.

The main thing to keep in mind is that there isn't one method to rule them all. There isn't one method that is suitable in every circumstance. This also means that if you're going to be taking on the responsibility of iterative user research, you will be learning how to use multiple methods. This may sound scary, but we humans are good at the learning thing; the experience you have gained from one piece of research can be taken into another with a different methodology. There will still be a learning curve associated with

FIGURE 19.1 A visualization of broad to focused research and some example research methods that may be appropriate

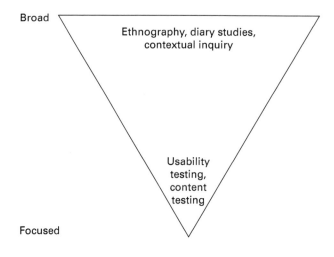

TABLE 19.4 Developing a new concept – combining methodologies scenario

Steps	Method	Scenario and explanation
1	Stakeholder workshop (Chapter 17)	You can kick off with a workshop to share examples of similar concepts in other industries, generate ideas and agree the scope of the initial work to be done on the new concept.
2	Ethnography (Chapter 14), diary study (Chapter 12), contextual inquiry (Chapter 15)	Depending on the time you have available you can choose a user research method suited to asking broad questions, finding out how things work in the real world, in a particular context.
3	Stakeholder workshop (Chapter 17)	You may want to check with the stakeholders to share the insights gained from the broad research and agree the direction you will move in.
4	Prototyping	Assuming that the research has indicated it's worth pursuing this new idea, you can start to sketch out some thoughts.
5	Usability testing (Chapter 7)	You may want to start getting feedback on your ideas from users very early on, for example doing usability testing on a paper prototype and sketch storyboards.
6	Iterate	As work progresses, and prototyping becomes more high fidelity, you can continue to do iterative research. At some point you may want to include a co-design workshop (designing with end users) and the process will include regular checks with stakeholders at workshops, retrospectives or show and tells.

the new methodology, but it'll be less steep. Every time you do some user research you'll learn something new about the methodology itself, as well as the topic of your research. This is just one of the many reasons I love doing user research.

Part Two summary

I assume you have now read through a method or two that may be relevant to your research needs. You may have already decided what kind of research you're going to do and started preparing for it. Even if you haven't started your preparation or decided exactly what kind of research you need to do, hopefully it's been a useful trip through how to do the research part of user research. We've looked at:

- usability testing;
- content testing;
- card sorting;
- surveys;
- interviews;
- diary studies;
- information architecture validation;
- ethnography and mobile ethnography;
- contextual inquiry;
- A/B testing;
- stakeholder workshops;
- guerrilla research; and
- combining methodologies.

Just as the methodologies themselves weren't the beginning of the story, they are not the end either. Now that we have a better idea of how to do the research with people, in Part Three we'll learn what to do with the data that you have.

PART THREE

Analysing user research data

Now that you have done the research you're likely to have a huge amount of data and you need to do something with it; to analyse the data and share the results in a way that has the most effective impact. What you do with it depends on several factors:

- the purpose of research;
- the kind of research you've done;
- the audience for the results of the research;
- your available time and resources.

When you have more experience doing user research, you'll start deciding the type of analysis during the planning phase.

The main questions are: What is the most useful and persuasive use of this data? How can you make data into information and information into knowledge? Part Three will focus mostly on qualitative data and provide:

- an overview of the analysis methods;
- when and where they should be used.

The methods of analysis we'll go into are:

- **Content analysis:** making sense of and coding lots of qualitative data.
- **Affinity diagramming** (identifying themes): are the problems/insights you have uncovered related to each other?

-
- **Going beyond initial analysis:** how to get deeper into the themes of your data.

- **Agile analysis:** how to do analysis that fits into the agile sprint cycle.

- **Cataloguing and prioritizing issues:** once you have gathered the evidence, identifying what is a serious issue and what is not.

- **Creating a user needs backlog:** this is a neat way of summarizing who the user is, what they want to do and what they want to achieve.

- Analysing data to **create personas** to communicate user characteristics and behaviour.

- Using **mental models** to visualize how users think and identify opportunities.

Qualitative data tends to yield a wealth of information, but not all of it is meaningful or directly relevant to your current research question. As the user researcher, it's your job to sift through the raw data and find patterns, themes and stories that are significant in the context of your research question.

Doing analysis is a skill unto itself and it's an essential part of the process of turning your user research data into actionable insight. We need it to make what we've discovered during the process of doing the research useful, to have an impact on improving things, in making things that are user centric. The doing of research gets the most attention because it's the most 'visible' part of the research process; this is the actual learning from the users bit. Analysis is essential in understanding the users; without it we have a mess of raw data. If you've been doing research and analysis for a while, you probably have some good notions of what the data is telling you, but if you don't have rigorously identified insights, you don't have evidence.

It is not widely understood that it takes time and practice to develop the skill to do high-quality analysis. The biggest impact of this on the user researcher is that they often feel they don't get enough time to analyse their research, especially in an agile environment; as soon as the research sessions are finished the team are demanding results and insights. Analysis is often not well scoped when commissioning research, as analysis is harder to quantify compared with the doing of research, for example 10 30-minute interviews (this observation was shared with me by Amy Stoks of Affinity UX in New Zealand).

Our natural instinct is to believe we can remember everything we heard or saw in an interview, for example. It is unwise to make decisions based on raw notes and data; presenting unassimilated and uncategorized data does not make the decision-making process more objective, and can be very misleading. In the same vein, recommendations based on a single data point can lead a team down the path of solving the wrong problem or solving a problem in the wrong way. This is simply reacting to data, not making sense of it (Naylor, 2019).

Analysis should be repeatable, traceable, you should be able to pick up and continue someone else's work, and someone else should be able to do this with your work. Decision making becomes objective with the robust analysis of quality data.

There is no single right way to do analysis of qualitative user research data. Analysis tends to be an in-depth and detail-oriented process that takes time, and it can take several iterations of using an analysis method to get what you need. If you are working to tight immovable deadlines or in a particularly fast-paced, agile environment, you won't have time to go into such depth with your analysis, the depth to which you analyse the research and therefore the method of analysis you pick will be influenced by your own context.

Now you know what type of data you will be generating, and the context in which you will analyse the data, this will help you understand the most suitable analysis technique to use.

Preparing your data

Depending on the type of research you are doing and the context you are doing it in, you will have different types of data that you will be analysing:

- The most common type of data is notes, either written by you during moderation and/or by those observing the research.
- If you are lucky, you may have full transcripts of research sessions from audio and video recordings.
- Video recordings themselves are a common type of data.
- You may have images that support audio or text content from the sessions.

It's worth doing some processing of the data before you get started on the analysis. You need to review the data to see if any needs to be removed. Was there a participant who didn't really fit the profile you're focusing on? You should remove their data. Perhaps you only have partial data for some participants, you should remove this too. You don't need participants' personal identifying information (names, etc) to do the analysis, so it is good practice to remove these from the text. I acknowledge that it is more time consuming to edit personal identifying information from videos, but if you have the time, it's definitely worth doing. All this is good GDPR practice and data management (as discussed in Part One), which will help you in the analysis process.

If you have generated physical artefacts, ideally they should be captured digitally. This makes them easier to store, and accessible to others in your team who may be involved in the analysis. If you need to keep the physical artefacts, keep them somewhere safe and secure in line with GDPR guidelines for digital things. You need to be rigorously ethical, again discussed in Part One (Saladaña, 2016).

References

Naylor, Z (9 July 2019) A guide to user research analysis. UX Booth. www.uxbooth.com/articles/a-guide-to-user-research-analysis/ (archived at https://perma.cc/23ED-4A2G)

Saladaña, J (2016) *The Coding Manual for Qualitative Researchers*, Sage, Los Angeles

20

Content analysis

Understanding your qualitative data

TABLE 20.1 Content analysis method summary

Method summary
Suitable for data generated from: qualitative methods such as interviews, contextual inquiry, ethnography and diary studies, usability testing and open text field survey questions too. Can be used in agile and lean environments.
Use if you want to: identify patterns in qualitative data, and summarize by counting the patterns/various aspects of the content. You can make sense of large amounts of qualitative data.

We looked at content testing in Part Two Chapter 8, but content analysis is not limited to whether your written content is effective. Content analysis can offer some techniques to help you start to get a grip on large amounts of semi-structured data (such as quotes, verbatims and first-hand written accounts) and interpret what you have. Content analysis is a way of codifying and categorizing qualitative data.

Coding is not a precise science, it's an interpretative art. To code is to put things in systematic order. The data you are coding will be about human routine, rituals, rules, roles, relationships (Saladaña, 2016). Things to take into account within these are behaviours, emotions, actions, verbatim quotes (Hall, 2019), concepts, interactions, incidents, terminology or phrases used. Things grouped together won't necessarily be exactly alike, but they will have things in common.

Patterns (regular, repetitive, consistent occurrences) can be characterized by:

- similarity (things happen the same way);
- difference (they happen in predictably different ways);
- frequency (they happen often or rarely);
- sequence (things happen in a certain order);
- correspondence (they happen in relation to something else);
- causation (one appears to cause another) (Saladaña, 2016).

How to code your qualitative data

To start analysing your data, first you need to decide if you will start by having:

- predetermined codes;
- no codes;
- predetermined codes but adding new ones that come up.

You can think of codes as a way to tag your data; you are assigning a code to a piece of data to ascribe what that data means and how it relates to other data. A code is a brief description of what is occurring in the data. Each time you note something interesting in your data, you write down a code. A code is a description, not an interpretation. It's a way to start organizing your data into meaningful categories (Mortensen, 2020).

Pre-set codes

There are a few of ways to create categories upfront:

1 from the objectives and hypothesis of the research;
2 scanning through the data first;
3 from previous research on the subject.

Aim for the categories to be comprehensive and mutually exclusive. They also need to be understandable to others, for example those in your team. Your categories need to be clearly described and agreed upon by those doing the analysis with you. You may need to revise them as you go through the data and learn more. Also agree if you are going to include synonyms of certain words or if these are ruled out if you are doing analysis in a group.

No codes

This takes more time because you are exploring the data with a completely open mind. This is probably the least common way to code your data, in the field of user research anyway, but it can be useful when you are at the very beginning of the process, for example when you are in a discovery phase. You will need to go through the data multiple times, to identify and capture the themes (code categories) that come out of the data.

Pre-set codes and emergent codes

To my mind, this is the least biased but also the most methodological way to do analysis, as research data can often surprise you with unexpected findings and insights. You identify your preset codes and as you are coding the data, you allow new codes to emerge, things that you hadn't necessarily anticipated. You will still need to have meaningful labels for your emergent codes, which are related things that have come up multiple times (more than twice). You will need to keep revisiting the emergent code categories to make sure they are mutually exclusive and coherent.

Refining the codes

Ideally, you should go through the data more than once with whatever code type you are using. This will allow you to have confidence in the consistency of the coding, and now that you are more familiar with the data, there may be instances that you want to recategorize.

Avoiding bias

Ideally, more than one person will code the data, with all those involved comparing their coded data at the end. If there are disparities in your coding, then you should explore and discuss it further, to get to the bottom of where these differences have come from and why. Through this discussion aim to reach a consensus on how to code these pieces of data.

The differences will likely lie in the nuance of the way things are said and phrased by the users. The questions you should be asking yourself include:

- Are they using different words to describe the same thing?
- Are similar words being used to describe different things?

How to do content analysis

You can think of the dataset in units of analysis; a unit can be one sentence long or a segment (it's unlikely to be a whole paragraph). It's a sequence of words that relate to a single code category.

A step-by-step guide

- **First, get to know your data.** If you have time, re-read or re-listen to any content you have to become familiar with.
- **Identify what data will be coded.** You may want to take a transcript, for example, as a whole dataset. Or you may want to break down separate questions (eg from interviews) into separate datasets – it really depends on how focused or wide-ranging the objectives and topics of your research are.
- **Code the data:**
  - read through and assign relevant codes to units of analysis in the dataset;
  - if using, give the emergent categories names and identify every time they occur;
  - keep revisiting the emergent categories to ensure they are mutually exclusive and coherent;
  - identify where pre-set codes occur;
  - as you code your data you may identify subcategories of your main categories.
- **Count the instances that fall into each code category** to show the relative importance of the information. If you are doing this analysis manually, for reliability get more than one person to code the data. You may need to analyse a single dataset multiple times until the category list is stable.

- **Identify patterns and connections within and between code categories.** It is helpful to write a summary for each category that describes the key ideas being expressed. Then review the relationships between categories. Do certain categories consistently occur together? You may wish to develop a table or matrix to illustrate relationships across two or more categories.

- **Reflect on what it all means.** What have you learnt? What are the major lessons? What will those who use the results of the evaluation be most interested in knowing? (Based on the Taylor-Powell and Renner (2003) approach). Another approach shared with me by Amy Stoks of Affinity UX is to ask 'What's at stake?' 'What's the impact of the insight on the participant and on the people receiving the insight?'

You may be wondering what content analysis categories (code schema) look like. Table 20.2 is an example of a made-up research question, **'What is the benefit of the summer drama workshop programme?'** asked of fictional students in the pretend summer programme (this example was adapted from an actual example of research conducted by Taylor-Powell and Renner, 2003).

TABLE 20.2 Example of a coding schema

Category	Sub-category	Abbreviation
Improved knowledge of acting		A
	Improving performance skills	AIS
	Increasing confidence	AIC
	Getting to know self better	ASB
	Increased range of methods to use	ARM
Improved knowledge of genres		G
	Understanding storytelling options	GUS
Benefits of working with peers		P
	Learning from each other's experience	PLE
Benefits of working with experts		E
	Role modelling	ERM
	Learning from experts	ELE

Analysis is both a team and an individual sport

If possible you should do a combination of both group activity and your own analysis. The reason for this is to get the perspective of your team, build consensus and gain a shared understanding of what the data is telling you. But (often) it's difficult to do analysis to the appropriate depth in a group setting alone. There is also a certain amount of data preparation and cleaning that needs to happen before and after analysis has taken place that's best done by one or two people. For large datasets in particular, there will generally be multiple rounds of analysis to wrangle the data into an understandable state.

Things like prioritizing insights, outcomes, actions, are very much a team sport. This can be done most effectively if the team is familiar with the research in the first place, to understand what is most important. This is why it is ideal that those participating in the analysis have also observed some of the sessions. It's easy to get lost and overwhelmed at the beginning of the analysis process if all you have to go on is a transcript, for example.

> Group coding can be more democratic and time-saving but it can also be time-consuming and fraught, depending on the complexity and quantity of the data (Saladaña, 2016).

Advantages of content analysis

Content analysis is a way of quantifying qualitative data:

- Uncovering of text, identifying terminology use and frequency of occurrence.
- It is relatively cheap to do, as it can be done by hand. Although it can be labour intensive if you have a large amount of text, it can be done in a group and is therefore adaptable to agile and lean ways of working.
- It can be highly reliable if done systematically.
- It can be adapted to cover imagery, video and audio (Get Revising, 2013).

Semiotic analysis (the analysis of signs and symbols) can be used for analysing visual data (Saladaña, 2016).

Disadvantages of content analysis

As with every data collection method, there are disadvantages to each analysis method. For content analysis:

- It is possible that important code categories are missed because they were not included in your code schema.
- The reliability and effectiveness of the results are related to the quality of the categories you have created and how they have been interpreted.

Analysis tools

When I was a poor doctoral student, I did this kind of analysis physically with paper, highlighter pens and sticky notes. Using non-digital means of analysis is still useful if you and your team are together in the same place at the same time, for example.

There are many digital tools to aid your analysis process. There are dedicated analysis tools such as Reframer in Optimal Workshop, Condens and NVivo. You can make use of such tools as Spreadsheets, Trello, Miro etc. When teams are not co-located or you are doing analysis asynchronously it's essential to do it digitally.

Optimal Workshop: https://www.optimalworkshop.com

Condens: https://condens.io

NVivo: https://www.qsrinternational.com/nvivo-qualitative-data-analysis-software/home

Trello: https://trello.com/en-GB

Miro: https://miro.com/

References and further reading

Cotton, S (10 January 2016) Content analysis coding. YouTube. www.youtube.com/watch?v=wilBzZLjZ1M (archived at https://perma.cc/B6TN-ZE4Q)
Get Revising (17 May 2013) Advantages and disadvantages of content analysis. https://getrevising.co.uk/grids/advantages_and_disadvantages_of_content_analysis (archived at https://perma.cc/5SRD-65DH)

Hall, E (2019) *Just Enough Research*, 2nd edn, A Book Apart, New York
Mortensen, DH (2020) How to do a thematic analysis of user interviews.
    Interaction Design Foundation. www.interaction-design.org/literature/article/
    how-to-do-a-thematic-analysis-of-user-interviews (archived at https://perma.cc/
    N4UD-KR8U)
Saladaña, J (2016) *The Coding Manual for Qualitative Researchers*, Sage,
    Los Angeles
Silverman, D (2011) *Interpreting Qualitative Data*, 2nd edn, Sage, London
Sommer, BA (2006) Content analysis. The University of California Davis.
    http://psc.dss.ucdavis.edu/sommerb/sommerdemo/content/doing.htm
Taylor-Powell, E and Renner, M (2003). Analyzing qualitative data. University of
    Wisconsin Extension, Program Development and Evaluation. https://
    learningstore.uwex.edu/assets/pdfs/g3658-12.pdf (archived at https://perma.
    cc/8XD5-2S3K)

21

Identifying themes through affinity diagramming

TABLE 21.1 Affinity diagramming method summary

Method summary
Suitable for data generated from: usability testing, interviews, diary studies, qualitative survey results, ethnography, contextual inquiry, guerrilla research.
Use if you want to:
• Identify and group user functions as part of design
• Show the range of a problem
• Uncover similarity among problems from multiple customers
• Give boundaries to a problem (problem scope)
• Identify areas for future study
• If used correctly it can be used to create personas (discussed in Chapter 25)
• As a brainstorming tool, allowing a group to codify ideas, hypotheses, and predictions
• Allows a design team to take into account the primary pain points, concerns, and needs of users
• For information architecture ideas that haven't come from card sorting
This method is suitable for agile and lean ways of working. It's a useful way of getting a first cut of the data to show stakeholders and get them on board with research themes early (this method was shared by Amy Stoks of Affinity UX).

Affinity diagramming (also known as affinity mapping) is useful when you need to identify patterns from qualitative data. Writing ideas on sticky notes and grouping them around themes is a way to identify patterns and insights from large amounts of qualitative data (physically or digitally).

It is a participatory method (something to do collaboratively as a team, rather than in isolation). This is a method you can use as a part of your analysis across any user research method that generates qualitative data.

Thematic and content analysis might be considered more rigorous, especially if done with software, and can be done by an individual. Affinity diagramming is a visual method of analysis, done through collaboration and physically moving pieces of data around into groups.

How to do affinity diagramming

There are a few different ways to start your analysis for affinity diagramming:

Step 1: Combining individual and group work

- Go through all the data yourself, highlighting each interesting piece of data relevant to the purpose of the project.
- Write down each discrete piece of data on sticky notes.
- At this point, including slight variations on similar themes in the sticky notes, additional analysis of this can be done as a group.

Step 2: Initial sorting through group work

- The first step is to decide who you need to include in the group. Will it be your immediate team? Those working directly on the product/service? With your wider stakeholders? This really depends on the project and your organization.
- Share out all your raw data amongst the group.
- Get each person to highlight interesting discrete pieces of data relevant to the purpose of the project. **Make sure everyone is familiar with these before you start the analysis.**
- When all of the wider dataset has been reviewed once, get the workshop participants to swap and review someone else's initial analysis, highlighting anything else they think is relevant that has been missed (in a different colour, to show where the differences are – you may have time to review this and you may not).

- **Optional:** now the group is becoming familiar with the data, if time allows, have a discussion about any differences in the data that have been highlighted by different people and why some thought it was important and some did not. It's possible this will bring to the surface different assumptions or priorities that people have for the research and the results that can be addressed, discussed and clarified within the group. It may also indicate the need for some wider clarification communications.

- Get the group to swap data again and write out each of the discrete pieces of data (that have been highlighted).

- For certain types of data/research/objectives (discussed below), it may be useful to note where the data has come from on the Post-it or use different-coloured sticky notes to indicate different sources of data – colour coding can be defined ahead of time.

This kind of process with a group will take you anywhere from several hours to several sessions of several hours. The amount of time depends on how large the dataset is and whether you are extracting unique pieces of data from the larger dataset together, or whether you are doing this as preparation for the group session.

Step 3: Analyse and produce themes and insights

- You'll probably need a couple of hours for the group session (the amount of time depends on how large the dataset is and whether you are extracting unique pieces of data from the larger dataset together, or whether you are doing this as preparation for the group session).

- At the beginning of the group session, explain the purpose of the session as well as the overall project objectives, to help them understand the context of what they are doing.

- Once all the data is on sticky notes (whether this was done as a group or individually before the group session) give an equal number of sticky notes to each workshop participant (try and mix up who gets what data).

- Ask for a volunteer to start the grouping process. Get them to read out and stick each sticky note on the wall (or whatever you are using to do your grouping, eg a large table). If possible at this stage, ask them to start grouping similar things together and to explain why they consider the things they are grouping to be similar.

- Each workshop participant in turn should follow the same process, reading out each piece of data and explaining where they put it and why.

- Encourage and facilitate constructive discussion and questions regarding the groupings to gain consensus along the way.

- If there is duplication or sticky notes with subtle variations, you will need to discuss whether the sticky notes are describing the same thing or different things. If there are multiple versions of the same thing, agree on a definitive version (it may require writing out a new sticky note, combining elements of the various descriptions, or there may be one existing sticky note that articulates it best).

- Depending on the size of the overall dataset and the number of groups emerging, you may want to agree to temporary names for groups to make it easier to follow the process that is happening.

- Once all the data has been sorted into groups look at each group in turn, reading out everything that is in the group. There may be outliers that need to be discussed and moved to another group. Is each of the groups coherent? If a group seems too wide-ranging you may need to split groups up to make them more consistent.

- Once the groups are stable give them names, describing what the group consists of, agreed through moderated discussion.

- There may be a hierarchy in the groups, but this should be considered once the groups are relatively stable. Try to avoid adding this kind of complexity too early in the grouping process; it is possible that it will restrict your thinking and creativity too much in the beginning.

- If physically sorting data, take photos of each group so that you can create and share easy-to-read representations in the group (this can be done with something as simple as PowerPoint).

- Now that you've described what each group consists of, you can consider this description the theme of the group. You may want to refine the theme further, depending on your needs. You can then compare the themes that you have identified and ask yourself how the groups relate to or interact with each other.

- You can use a liberating structure exercise,* to identify what these themes and groups mean for your work. This is the start of identifying your insights. How much additional work you do on the themes and insights really depends on your timescales and the work you are doing.

* Liberating structures are a series of exercises that allow you to innovate in a structured way. There are many different kinds of exercises available, several of which are suitable for helping you gain insight into your data. For example, you could look into 'Nine Whys' or 'What? So What? Now What?' – you'll find details on liberating structures in the reference section (Lipmanowicz and McCandless, 2021).

Affinity diagramming is a relatively simple process, but it can take substantial time to break large amounts of text data into 'units of information', especially if you have data from many sources. Large affinity projects can require anything from hours to days to complete and the interpretation of the resulting groups of data can require many hours of focused effort.

Tools

Again, you can use sticky notes and a wall, but if you are taking a digital-first approach, there are many tools that you can make use of such as:

- Optimal Workshop: https://www.optimalworkshop.com
- Trello: https://trello.com/en-GB
- Miro: https://miro.com/
- Mural: https://www.mural.co/
- Spreadsheets

Large scale analysis

When you have a large amount of data, one way to handle it is to force a reduction in the data. For example, once all the data points are extracted, ask workshop participants to identify the 10 things they considered the most important highlights that relate to each research question (Green, 2017).

These kinds of methods, as you can see for yourself, are labour intensive, but this is only the start of the process. This is what you need to do to wrangle your data into a manageable form for the next step in the analysis process. I don't say this to scare you – I say this to help set your expectations and in turn your team's expectations of how much time and effort is required to analyse your data properly and to make the findings and insight as useful and usable as possible.

Advantages of affinity diagramming

- It can involve the whole team, helping everyone to feel like they own the data.
- Helps to build a collaborative team.
- Consolidates lots of data into meaningful groups and themes.

Disadvantages of affinity diagramming

- Can be time-consuming.
- Can be exhausting (Bevan et al, 2009).

References and further reading

Bevan, N, Shor, K and Wilson, C (June 2009) Affinity diagramming. Usability Book of Knowledge. www.usabilitybok.org/affinity-diagram (archived at https://perma.cc/3W28-XBXM)

Government Digital Services (August 2016) Analyse a research session. GDS Service Manual. www.gov.uk/service-manual/user-research/analyse-a-research-session (archived at https://perma.cc/VM3Z-S5K9)

Green, C (20 December 2017) How we did a large-scale group analysis of user research data. User Research in Government. https://userresearch.blog.gov.uk/2017/12/20/how-we-did-a-large-scale-group-analysis-of-user-research-data/ (archived at https://perma.cc/BFA4-PDWJ)

Lipmanowicz, H and McCandless, K (2021) Liberating structures. www.liberatingstructures.com/ (archived at https://perma.cc/ES9Z-JALB)

Spencer, B (25 March 2016) UI/UX Principle #16: Use affinity diagrams to collaboratively clarify fuzzy data. Fresh Consulting. www.freshconsulting.com/uiux-principle-16-use-affinity-diagrams-to-collaboratively-clarify-fuzzy-data/ (archived at https://perma.cc/33ZV-36AH)

22

Thematic analysis

Going beyond initial analysis

TABLE 22.1 Thematic analysis method summary

Method summary
Suitable for data generated from: qualitative methods such as interviews, contextual inquiry, ethnography and diary studies, usability testing and open text field survey questions too.
Use if you want to: identify patterns in qualitative data and summarize by counting the patterns/various aspects of the content in greater depth.

In the content analysis chapter, we saw that once you have coded all of your material you need to start abstracting themes from the codes. You go through your codes and categorize them together to represent common, salient and significant themes. The initial groups you identify when labelling these clusters of codes (and perhaps even single codes), with a more interpretative and 'basic theme'.

You may be able to group your basic themes into 'organizing themes' and these themes should link to a global theme; this should then link to the vision and values of your organization – think of 'theory of change', as shown in Figure 22.1.

If this description of thematic analysis doesn't resonate, have a look at Salma Patel's (2018) explanation which looks at it from a different lens – you can find the details in the references.

If you want to get into more complex analysis, I highly recommend reading Saladaña (2016).

FIGURE 22.1 • An example of how to structure a thematic analysis

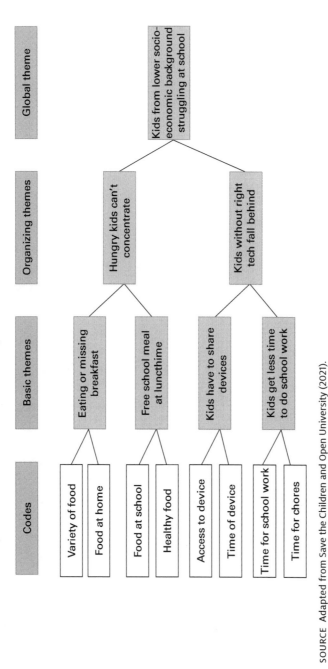

SOURCE Adapted from Save the Children and Open University (2021).

References and further reading

Patel, S (31 January 2018) Thematic analysis – how do you generate themes? https://salmapatel.co.uk/academia/thematic-analysis-how-do-you-generate-themes/ (archived at https://perma.cc/EB5C-M5CJ)

Saladaña, J (2016) *The Coding Manual for Qualitative Researchers*, Sage, Los Angeles

Save the Children and Open University (2021) Monitoring, evaluations, accountability and learning framework: 6 methods of data collection and analysis. https://resourcecentre.savethechildren.net/keyword/monitoring-evaluation-accountability-and-learning-meal (archived at https://perma.cc/8HGV-VAN2)

23

Agile analysis

TABLE 23.1 Agile analysis method summary

Method summary
Suitable for data generated from: qualitative methods such as interviews, contextual inquiry, usability testing and open text field survey questions too.
Use if you want to: identify patterns in qualitative data, and summarize by counting the patterns/various aspects of the content in an agile or lean environment.

You may be in a team environment that is using agile or lean UX ways of working and already have research included in the sprint planning process. If research isn't already included, it can be very difficult to get user research done and used in an effective way with the cadence of work. It can be at odds with the agile development process. However, the agile development process can include user research throughout, not just at the end to validate what has been done, but also during sprints to solve user problems.

During the iterative research phase in agile teams (such as alpha and beta), a common user research practice is for the team to debrief after each interview, usability test, or field study to discuss what was learnt or observed. Doing this, while also reviewing the notes and observations, helps researchers hear the same information from a new perspective. This can easily be done if everyone is in the same place at the same time; it can also be done digitally if people are remote, using different methods.

Face-to-face synchronous

Observers note things down on sticky notes during the session, then everyone adds these to predetermined themes (on the wall or whiteboards) during the break between sessions and this can be reviewed at the end of the day. You can have an 'Other' category to analyse later, for anything unexpected that comes up outside your predetermined themes, which is very common.

Before the research sessions start

Agree predetermined themes:

- based on project research questions/objectives;
- following the user journey (steps/screens);
- based on the tasks you are focusing on.

Agree on annotations for observations for tracking patterns in the data. These should be the sorts of codes that can easily be used to mark notes, for example:

- Give each participant a code, such as 'P1' for 'participant 1'.
- If task-based, give each task a code, such as 'T1' for 'task 1'.

If observers are all in the same room, you can use the sticky note and wall option:

1 Observers will write an observation on a sticky note whenever a participant says or does something interesting or relevant.

2 Make one observation per sticky note (with agreed annotation).

3 Observers are capturing raw data, not their own interpretation of what has been said or done, to avoid bias. This means observations of what has happened or direct quotes from what the participant has said.

4 Use one colour of sticky note per participant for all observation notes. This is useful when you come to affinity sorting.

Advantages of this method

This means your initial analysis is done by the end of the research. It gets those observing the research involved in the analysis, continuing to get buy-in for the research process.

Disadvantages of this method

This kind of analysis is pretty high level and to a certain extent reactionary. I would strongly advise against this being the only analysis you do – it's a useful place for the team to start but it's likely to be a relatively superficial analysis.

The rainbow spreadsheet method

The rainbow spreadsheet method uses a spreadsheet to record whether participants acted in the way your team expected. It provides a structure for note-takers to record what participants did during each session. This technique is very useful for a fast-paced agile environment.

The spreadsheet has the following columns:

- task;
- assumption;
- one column per participant (ie P1, P2);
- notes for observers to record extra detail.

In the column labelled 'the participants' you can choose different colours to fill in each cell, which represent different factors that are important to your work. The simplest version of this would be green for yes and red for no, as used by Fu (2019), making it easy to visually summarize which participants validated the team's assumptions and which did not.

Before research sessions start:

1 Get your team to write down all their assumptions on the thing you are testing.
2 Add the assumptions to the spreadsheet. Make sure they are mutually exclusive and don't repeat – one per row.

Each observer can have their own sheet, and you can compare afterwards (you as an individual, and then as a team). This can be completed after each session, with everything being digital (no write-up time). Observations can be affinity sorted or gathered together per assumption or per task. These are compared to the colour coding on the spreadsheet. Again, ideally, this should not be the only analysis you do.

FIGURE 23.1 Example of the rainbow spreadsheet

Task	Assumption	P01	P02	P03	Notes
1	Clicks on the Transaction tab	Yes	Yes	Yes	P01 said it was a 'good guess'
2	Uses 'refine start query' to change search fields	Yes	No	Yes	P01 confusion on why refining is needed to start with
2	Removes the previous search criteria	Yes	Yes	No	
3	Uses the 'to' field to filter to older than 3 weeks	No	No	No	P02 used the 'to' field as a 'from' field instead. This won't return the right results
4	Navigates to task tab	Yes	Yes	No	P02 didn't know where they had arrived at P03 didn't get how this tab differs from the transaction tab
4	Clicks on 'change filter'	Yes	Yes	No	P03 assumed that tabs were the same

SOURCE Fu (2019)

Advantages of this method

Compared to note taking followed by affinity mapping, the rainbow spreadsheet method has a number of benefits:

- it can be faster and more focused compared with sticky notes and affinity diagramming;
- there is less writing for the note-takers;
- it's obvious when the team's assumptions about how people will use the product are different to how they actually use the product;
- it focuses on user behaviour, not opinions or explanations;
- there's a clear record of your research findings that's easy to check in the future.

Disadvantages of this method

This method also has some drawbacks:

- Your note-takers may be too focused on looking for the assumptions to see what else is happening.
- You may need to check the accuracy of observations if the team is new to user research – are assumptions really being proved or disproved? This will require some facilitation on your part when discussing and comparing findings with the team (Fu, 2019).

There are other ways to use the rainbow spreadsheet in your (agile) user research. Instead of assumptions, you can record observations in the rows of the spreadsheet and use a colour per participant. Each time a thing is observed in a participant, you can colour that cell in. This will quickly show you patterns in the data, the size of observation, and the kinds of things you are observing in each participant, as discussed in Cabrera-Mieles (2019).

References and further reading

Cabrera-Mieles, Z (16 February 2019) The rainbow spreadsheet: a visual method for research analysis. UX Collective. https://uxdesign.cc/the-rainbow-sheet-a-visual-method-for-research-analysis-a7e7d2011058 (archived at https://perma.cc/M89T-NHZG)

Dimov, Z (4 May 2018) Fast UX research: an easier way to engage stakeholders and speed up the research process. Smashing Magazine. www. smashingmagazine.com/2018/05/fast-ux-research/ (archived at https://perma. cc/4U3E-RNBK)

Fu, C (13 September 2019) How a spreadsheet can make usability analysis faster and easier. User Research in Government. https://userresearch.blog.gov.uk/ 2019/09/13/how-a-spreadsheet-can-make-usability-analysis-faster-and-easier/ (archived at https://perma.cc/EP4M-ZNMT)

Furthermore (18 August 2016) 7 steps of lean user research. https://medium.com/@ furthermore_ux/7-steps-of-lean-user-research-ee1d6f2ff5f4 (archived at https:// perma.cc/9G2S-PCGP)

Government Digital Service (20 November 2017) User research tips posters. GovDesign. https://github.com/alphagov/govdesign/blob/master/Poster_ UserResearchTips.pdf (archived at https://perma.cc/QH7Y-ZJYX)

Kirkland K (16 February 2017) How a knowledge kanban board can help your user research. User Research in Government. https://userresearch.blog.gov. uk/2017/02/16/how-a-knowledge-kanban-board-can-help-your-user-research/ (archived at https://perma.cc/73CM-4DRW)

Reichelt, L (29 October 2014) Anatomy of a good sticky note. User research in government. https://userresearch.blog.gov.uk/2014/10/29/anatomy-of-a-good-sticky-note/ (archived at https://perma.cc/9H2D-ZRWD)

24

Analysing usability data and cataloguing issues and needs

If the aim of your work has been to identify, catalogue and prioritize issues with your product or service, identifying issues requires different processes depending on whether you have gathered qualitative or quantitative data – or you may be combining the two.

Cataloguing issues from qualitative data

Once you've completed each usability testing session, there are various ways to start gathering the data together to start your analysis, depending on what is useful in the context and objectives of the research you are doing.

You can organize the data points:

- by task;
- based on product or service features;
- by design categories (eg navigation, IA, images, content, layout, CTAs);
- by journey flow (steps in a journey) (You, 2019).

A step-by-step guide to identifying issues or needs

First, get to know your data. Once you have organized your data, if you have time, re-read or re-listen to any content you have to become familiar with it. You will probably have reams of written notes on things you have observed and things that the participants said. It can be useful to review data after each research session to synthesize and identify key themes. Once all the research sessions are complete, you can use a process similar to that described in the content analysis chapter.

TABLE 24.1   Cataloguing issues from qualitative data method summary

Method summary
Suitable for data generated from:
• Moderated face-to-face usability testing
• Moderated remote usability testing
• Unmoderated face-to-face usability testing
• Guerrilla research (usability testing)
Other possible sources:
• Contextual inquiry
• Ethnography
• Diary studies
• Content testing
Use if you want to: identify usability issues and user needs from your data. This methodology is suitable for agile and lean ways of working.

Identifying all the things. These things may be needs or issues or both in each transcript without categorizing or counting them at this point.

Group similar issues together. You can use tools like Optimal Workshop's Reframer or Miro to do this, or use the low-tech method of writing issues on sticky notes (one issue per post) and then create a group (read Chapter 21 on identifying themes through affinity diagramming).

Identify patterns and connections within and between groups:

• You may need to go back to the original recordings (if available) to understand if the same problems have been described in different ways (in different research sessions) or if they're subtly different issues.

• What are the similarities and differences in the issues that have been identified? What are the relationships between categories? Do certain categories consistently occur together? Is it possible there is a cause-and-effect relationship?

A step-by-step guide to analysing journeys

Whether you are remote-first, or in person, a tool like Trello (or Miro, etc) is useful to gather your data together (or you can use a spreadsheet or a wall/table in the same way):

• Each column in Trello will represent an entity you are interested in, for example, each step in a user journey.

- Take a screenshot of each screen in your journey or each feature or function, etc (depending on what you are doing). Put the screenshot and a description in the first card.
- Under each screenshot, gather each individual observation (ideally for each person who observed the sessions).
- You can label each observation card in different ways, using colour codes, for example, to represent different participants, different types of observation, severity, etc to help see any potential initial patterns within a column and between the columns.
- You can also add cards for potential fixes in each column.
- You could add an additional column for general or high-level observations.

Next step in usability analysis

Count the instances that fall into each group. This is one way to show the relative importance of an issue.

Consider the context. You may have some low-frequency issues that are important (or critical) to fix. This happens sometimes in qualitative research as there can be variations in how users complete tasks. If an issue was serious for one or two participants, it's worth considering the importance of this issue. Was this just an issue for them or will it be a much wider issue for others? You may show it to others, try to replicate it yourself or get others to replicate it. If you aren't certain, you may need to do some more research focusing on this area. You should have noted down whether the participant required your assistance during a task, as this will also help you identify the seriousness of the issue.

Prioritize your issues. Once you are confident you have a comprehensive list of issues, you can prioritize them: what is most important to fix first? You can create a table to catalogue your issues, such as Table 24.2 (you can simplify further by not including the cost of fixing the problem, initially). A more complex table may be appropriate for your needs, including issue groups, rather than just numbering the issues, highlighting how issues are related to each other.

In Part Four (UX Storytelling) we'll look at other ways to present this data to bring to life the issues for your intended (internal) audience.

TABLE 24.2   An example of how to catalogue the issues you've prioritized

Issue #	Priority	Issue description	Recommendation	Cost of fixing

User needs backlog and writing user needs

User needs describe a user and the reason why they need to use the thing you're building. User needs are written to:

- track what you need to do;
- think and talk about your work from a user's perspective;
- prioritize your work (Government Digital Services, 2016).

'User needs' are the needs that a user has of a product/service. User needs are never really 'done'; we're just better or worse at meeting them, depending on the work we do.

User needs are usually written in the following format:

> I need/want/expect to... [what does the user want to do?]
> So that... [why does the user want to do this?]
>
> If it's helpful, you can add:
>
> As a... [which type of user has this need?]
> When... [what triggers the user's need?]
> Because... [is the user constrained by any circumstances?]

User needs are written from a personal perspective using words that users would recognize and use themselves. Focus on what's most important for your users, so you don't create an unmanageable list of user needs. It can also be helpful to group them, by persona, stage in the process of using the thing, or another relevant theme.

User needs tend to be high-level, broad in scope and stable over time. Your team can use them to write user stories. User stories describe a specific feature (content, functionality, etc). Your user stories should include enough information for your product manager to decide how important the story is. They should always include:

- the person using the service (the actor);
- what the user needs the service for (the narrative);
- why the user needs it (the goal).

It is usually the responsibility of design and development people, led by the product manager, to write user stories. However, as a user researcher, it is useful to be aware of them. See Salma Patel's work (2019) for a more in-depth description of the difference between user needs and user stories.

The most important part of a user story is the goal. This helps you:

- make sure you're solving the right problem;
- decide when the story is done and a user's need is met.

If you're struggling to write the goal then you should reconsider why you think you need that feature.

User needs can be combined with a product backlog if you are working in an agile environment. A product backlog is a complete and constantly maintained list of requirements currently in development. If you aren't working in an agile environment, this is still a useful thing to create.

User needs aren't the only way to express requirements. Check out the further reading section to find useful sources on the Jobs to Be Done framework.

Advantages of cataloguing issues and user needs

These methods are a great way to keep track of what work needs to be done and the barriers that currently exist that need to be removed, which is an essential part of the development lifecycle.

TABLE 24.3   Table for cataloguing your user needs backlog

User need	Priority	Persona	Content type	Functional requirement	Acceptance criteria

Disadvantages of cataloguing issues and user needs

Although the context and the user group are considered in these methods, it's not designed to give you an in-depth understanding of who the users are and how they behave, there are other more suitable methods for this, such as personas (Chapter 25) and mental models (Chapter 26) to name but two.

Cataloguing issues from quantitative data

TABLE 24.4   Cataloguing issues from quantitative data method summary

Method summary
Suitable for data generated from:
• Unmoderated face-to-face usability testing
• Unmoderated remote usability testing
This methodology is suitable for agile and lean ways of working
Use if you want to: identify usability issues

Usability metrics

In general, usability metrics let you:

- **Track progress between releases.** It's hard to improve something if you don't know how well you're doing.
- **Assess your competition.** Are you better or worse than others? Where are you better or worse?
- **Make decisions before launch.** Is the design good enough to release to an unsuspecting world (Nielsen, 2001)?

Usability metrics include a combination of system and user performance measures:

- system response times;
- number of errors made;
- time taken to complete the task;
- task completion success rate;
- user satisfaction ratings.

These can be summarized in three points that make up the ISO usability standard ISO/IEC 9126-4 Metrics:

- **Effectiveness:** The accuracy and completeness with which users achieve specified goals.
- **Efficiency:** The resources expended in relation to the accuracy and completeness with which users achieve goals.
- **Satisfaction:** The comfort and acceptability of use (Mifsud, 2015).

MEASURING EFFECTIVENESS

$$\text{Effectiveness} = \frac{\text{number of tasks completed successful} \times 100\%}{\text{total number of tasks undertaken}}$$

Although we'd all like to achieve a 100 per cent completion rate, in 2011 a study of 1,200 usability tasks showed that the average task completion rate is 78 per cent (Sauro, 2011).

MEASURING EFFICIENCY

Measuring time efficiency, for example, can get very complicated. If this is something that you are interested in you can read more in Mifsud (2015).

Errors can be unintended actions, slips, mistakes or omissions that a user makes while attempting a task. You should ideally assign a short description, a severity rating and classify each error under the respective category (Mifsud, 2015).

$$\text{Efficiency} = \frac{\text{number of errors made}}{\text{number of steps in the task}} \times 100\%$$

MEASURING SATISFACTION

There are many ways to measure satisfaction, and there is much good advice online about this. I will highlight two examples here:

- Single Ease Question (SEQ) can be used after each task is completed, as to how easy it was to complete the task on a scale of 1–5 (1 being very hard and 5 being very easy).
- System Usability Scale (SUS) can be used after all tasks are completed as a rating of the overall experience. You can read more about this in Chapter 7.

OTHER METRICS TO CONSIDER

There are many other metrics you can consider. I've given a few examples below, but this is not an exhaustive list:

Effectiveness:

- The ratio of successes to failures.
- Percentage of tasks completed successfully on the first attempt.
- The number of persistent errors.

Efficiency:

- Time to complete a task.
- Time to learn.
- Time spent on errors.
- Frequency of help or documentation use.
- The number of repetitions or failed commands.
- Time taken on the first attempt.
- Time to achieve expert performance.
- Time spent on correcting errors.

Choosing the right metrics really depends on the product/service you are delivering, as does the meaning of success. For example, if you are delivering an online application for credit cards, time taken on a task is something very different to a site aggregating news content.

References and further reading

Albert, B and Tallis, T (2013) *Measuring the User Experience: Collecting, analyzing, and presenting usability metrics*, 2nd edn, Morgan Kaufmann. Massachusetts

Christensen, CM et al (September 2016) Know your customers' 'Jobs to Be Done'. Harvard Business Review. https://hbr.org/2016/09/know-your-customers-jobs-to-be-done (archived at https://perma.cc/D4T3-P9E4)

Government Digital Service (23 May 2016) Writing user stories. GDS Service Manual. www.gov.uk/service-manual/agile-delivery/writing-user-stories (archived at https://perma.cc/5869-KHVA)

Mifsud, J (22 June 2015) Usability metrics – a guide to quantify the usability of any system. Usability Geek. http://usabilitygeek.com/usability-metrics-a-guide-to-quantify-system-usability/ (archived at https://perma.cc/7SWA-56YB)

Nielsen, J (21 January 2001) Usability metrics. Nielsen Norman Group. www. nngroup.com/articles/usability-metrics/ (archived at https://perma.cc/NN2R-BPRV)

Patel, S (6 December 2019) User needs vs user stories in agile development. https://salmapatel.co.uk/academia/user-needs-vs-user-stories-in-agile/ (archived at https://perma.cc/6WDJ-BKWH)

Pavliscak, P (2 June 2014) Choosing the right metrics for user experience. UX Matters. www.uxmatters.com/mt/archives/2014/06/choosing-the-right-metrics-for-user-experience.php (archived at https://perma.cc/KW95-3FBT)

Sauro, J (21 March 2011) What is a good task-completion rate? Measuring U. https://measuringu.com/task-completion/ (archived at https://perma.cc/MC2N-7R4U)

Sauro, J and Lewis, JR (2016) *Quantifying the User Experience: Practical statistics for user research*, 2nd edn, Morgan Kaufmann, Massachusetts

Seeley, J (15 March 2010) Usability testing metrics. Design + Research. https://designandresearch.wordpress.com/2010/03/15/usability-testing-metrics-jeff-seeley/ (archived at https://perma.cc/E9Q9-P7AY)

Strategyn (2017). Jobs-To-Be-Done theory and methodology. Strategyn. https://strategyn.com/jobs-to-be-done/jobs-to-be-done-theory/ (archived at https://perma.cc/H9KG-VSR9) (last accessed: 11 July 2017)

Travis, D (2 May 2003) Discount usability: time to push back the pendulum? User Focus. www.userfocus.co.uk/articles/discount.html (archived at https://perma.cc/89NW-3RQ2)

You, Y (10 May 2019) Turning user interview notes into design actions — my 5 step process. UX Collective. https://uxdesign.cc/turning-user-interview-notes-into-design-actions-my-5-step-process-f12b1955f716 (archived at https://perma.cc/U9EM-ECSJ)

25

Analysing data to create personas to communicate user characteristics and behaviour

TABLE 25.1 Creating personas method summary

Method summary
Method suitability: qualitative user research where you have gathered data on the demographics, attitudes, behaviour, tasks and other characteristics. This methodology is suitable to agile and lean ways of working.
Use if you want to: bring your user groups to life, allowing your organization to engage with them on a human level to build better products and services for them.

A persona should feel like the profile of a real individual while capturing characteristics and behaviours most relevant to your design decisions (Hall, 2019).

What are personas?

Personas are fictional profiles (based on real data) to represent a group of users with shared interests, goals or characteristics. Each persona provides a specific example of a person within a segment of your audience: what they do, how they behave, their attitudes and preferences. They are a character for your teams to engage with and ensure that products and services aren't designed for your organization but for the intended users, focusing on real scenarios (unless your organization is the intended user, hello intranets).

In the process of your research, you'll learn a lot about your users, even if this wasn't the main focus of the research; it's inevitable, it's user research (Stickdorn and Schneider, 2014).

Personas (and mental models, see Chapter 26) are methods where the line between analysis and presentation of data becomes blurry. They are both ways to understand and share your insight.

As we've already discussed in Part One (who should be involved in your research), useful personas go beyond demographics and represent people's motivations, wants, needs, tasks etc.

There is no set information that has to be included in your personas – as with so much we've looked at in this book, it really depends on your product or service and the purpose of your research and results. Table 25.2 contains components that you can pick and choose from to make up what will be the most useful personas for you at the time.

ESSENTIAL TIP

Personas should not be created once and used forevermore. As with all user research, personas should be iterative and seen as living, breathing things that change over time. Each time user research is done, your personas should be revisited and re-validated. Is the information they contain still true? Or have your customers changed – in their behaviour, attitudes, tasks? Or do you have a new set of customers that you haven't really considered before? It is also possible for primary and secondary personas (depending on who your key focus is) to change over time, as people/society/technology etc change, as your business adapts to the new.

What to include in your personas

Table 25.2 is a list of components you can consider for inclusion in your personas, depending on your objectives and the data you have gathered. Components could be set as codes in your initial content analysis (see Chapter 20).

TABLE 25.2   What data to include in your personas

Persona components		
Backstory and narrative	**Project specific attributes**	**Behaviour and context**
Name	Scenarios (see Chapter 32)	Tasks or goals
Photo	Attitudes and belief (about your thing)	Current way of doing tasks (including hacks)
Quotes	Current situation (using your thing)	Triggers (what causes them to do a task)
Demographics	Level of experience (with your thing)	Motivations (emotional and rational)
Day in the life of	Frustrations/constraints	Needs
Role and responsibilities	Prior knowledge	Wants (different to needs!)

If you are going to include a picture in the persona, here are a few dos and don'ts.

Persona good practice:

- You may consider having someone draw portraits of your theoretical users or shapes with facial expressions.
- Be diverse but realistic in your representation of your users.
- You may want to consider whether or not gender is important for your personas. Do you need to include demographic characteristics to represent the users?
- Consider whether the addition of a picture will enhance your team's engagement and understanding of the persona, or bias them.

Persona bad practice:

- Don't use actual photos of your participants.
- Don't use photos of staff members.
- You may want to avoid stock photography.

Anti-personas:

Anti-personas are groups of people that you aren't designing/writing for. They are created in the same way as a persona. If you are tight on time and budget, focus on creating your personas first; over time you can invest in anti-personas.

Personas can be very useful if they:

- are developed based on sufficient research data and rigorous analysis;
- cluster people who share similar goals, motivation and behaviour/needs;
- are a useful way to gather together multiple sources of data;
- can help a team build empathy with your users.

Personas can be a waste of time if they are:

- built based on assumptions that aren't taken from user research data;
- produced without going through a rigorous process of analysis;
- clusters of superficial groupings based on demographic characteristics or job roles.

Don't base your clusterings of data to form a persona primarily on demographics or role types. The best practice is to group together similar behaviours. It is quick and easy to group by role type but look at the data again. Do different roles in fact have the same behaviours?

How to present your personas

If you search for examples of personas online, you will generally see very glossy, poster-like representations that look like they have been made by a graphic designer. This level of presentation isn't necessary, but it is worth spending some time (it really depends on how much time you have) to make the personas engaging and the information easy to digest.

Personas can be information-rich (or perhaps information-dense), synthesizing a lot of information into just a few pages, so it's important that they are in some way visually appealing, breaking down information in a coherent way. There is a common format that tends to be used to do this, which you can follow and adapt to your needs, not only to help you create your personas, but to help those you are sharing the information with, and the reader to understand the personas, as shown in Figures 25.1 and 25.2.

FIGURE 25.1   A simple example of how to present your personas.

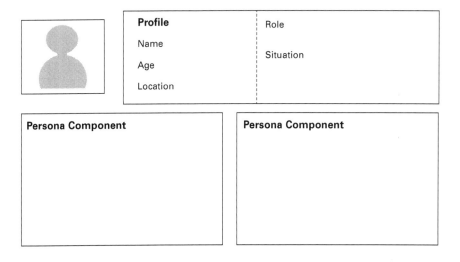

FIGURE 25.2   An example of how to present your personas with more information.

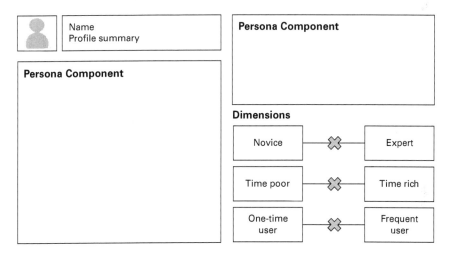

If you're still wondering what a completed persona looks like, Figure 25.3 is a very basic example to put it into context.

FIGURE 25.3   An example of a basic persona

Profile	Role: Small business owner.
Name: Jasmine	**Situation:** Owns marketing and PR company.
Age: 43	Experienced in marketing. Still learning about and getting to grips with online and social media.
Location: London	Married, no kids. Has master degree.

High-level user needs	Current solutions and frustrations.
Save time online and maximize resources.	Using multiple tools; Hootsuite, native analytics etc.
Find interesting content to share.	Have to learnt how to use multiple tools.
Schedule posts. Cross-post where relevant.	A lot to stuff still being done manually.
Evaluate impact of work.	Paying another company to measure influence, doesn't know how accurate it is.
Network with other professionals online.	Using LinkedIn for networking.

Depending on how much information you need to convey, you may not be able to include everything on one page. If this is the case I would try to limit it to two or three pages per persona, to make the content easy to digest and more memorable.

Using '**dimensions**' can be a useful and simple way of summarizing certain characteristics of each persona and these can be compared across personas.

If you have more complex characteristics or elements that you want to compare and summarize there are lots of useful graphical ways to do this. I recommend trying to summarize as much as you can visually for the personas where appropriate, rather than having large amounts of text.

A more advanced method: using activity theory to create your persona

Activity theory is a holistic approach to understanding people's behaviours and the needs they have, and how their motivations can result in different behaviours even if on the surface two people look like they are from the same user group. A high-level example would be a lawyer motivated by making money and a lawyer motivated by helping people. These differing motivations are likely to result in different behaviours and perhaps different needs. You can analyse each individual according to the framework below, pulling out the different elements on separate cards.

Persona elements – a framework

- Goals and motivations: what is the person trying to achieve, and why?
- Needs: what needs does the person have in the context of motivation and goal?
- Activities/tasks: what kind of activities does the person carry out and why?
- Environment: what is the person's physical and social context?
- Interaction/community: who are the people and communities the person is interacting with, and why?
- Tools/objects: what are the tools/objects the person uses, and why?
- Rules: are there any rules governing their decisions and actions?

It's important to arrange the framework elements vertically. This makes it easier to compare between individuals. And makes it easier to add to or move the research findings around. It will help you identify the gaps. As with other forms of analysis discussed in the book, group people with the most similar patterns to form one persona (Zhao, 2016).

How many personas?

A common question that gets asked is, how many personas are the right number of personas? As usual, it depends – who your audience is and how many groups have distinct behaviours and motivations. But keep in mind that general wisdom says having more than eight personas becomes difficult to manage. Eight is a lot of 'people' to keep track of and empathize with whilst you are designing products and services.

References and further reading

Bernstein, G (26 May 2015) How to create UX personas. UX Mastery. http://uxmastery.com/create-ux-personas/ (archived at https://perma.cc/3TLB-3N6X) (last accessed: 12 June 2017)

Browne, N and Christakopoulos, A (2019) User research and performance analysts working together for better outcomes. User Research in Government. https://userresearch.blog.gov.uk/2019/05/15/user-research-and-performance-analysts-working-together-for-better-outcomes/ (archived at https://perma.cc/6JQK-K4XY) (last accessed: 15 May 2021)

Cable, S (28 June 2017) Don't use photos in your personas. CX Partners. www.cxpartners.co.uk/our-thinking/dont-use-photos-in-your-personas/ (archived at https://perma.cc/C97M-53JH) (last accessed 11 July 2017).

Hall, E (2019) *Just Enough Research*, 2nd edn, A Book Apart, New York.

Rowley, NAA Jr (20 March 2013) Include your clients in the persona research process with affinity mapping. Iacquire. www.iacquire.com/blog/include-your-clients-in-the-persona-research-process-with-affinity-mapping (last accessed: 12 June 2017).

Stickdorn, M and Schneider, J (2014) *This is Service Design Thinking*, BIS Publishers, Amsterdam

Zhao, T (6 September 2016) Using activity theory to build effective personas. User Research in Government. https://userresearch.blog.gov.uk/2016/09/06/using-activity-theory-to-build-effective-personas/ (archived at https://perma.cc/F3XL-PRB2)

26

Analysing data to create mental models

Visualizing how user think and identify opportunities

TABLE 26.1 Creating mental models method summary

Method summary
Method suitability: mental models can be created from a variety of data. For example, usability testing observations, interview data, diary studies, contextual inquiry. This methodology is suitable for agile and lean ways of working.
Use if you want to: visualize and understand how your user groups think about your product/service and identify where the gaps and opportunities are.

A mental model is a person's intuitive understanding of how something functions based on their past encounters, exposure to information, everyday experience and judgement. Mental models are about belief rather than fact. In the context of what we're considering here, it's what the user believes about how your service/product works. Their mental model of the thing (product, service, etc) will affect how they decide to use it, the way they behave whilst using it and the decisions they'll make about it. Mental models are based on past encounters, everyday experience and judgement; they show what people believe about your thing, how it works, what it does etc and how close these beliefs are to your reality (Young, 2007).

User experience mental models are a visual representation of how people think and feel, and can be a useful model for how people would approach using your thing. Using the process of creating mental models to analyse your data can give you a deep understanding of people's motivations, thought processes, emotions and philosophy (Young, 2007). It's about creating empathy and understanding of the tasks users do to achieve an outcome, what the users think and feel whilst doing the tasks, and the questions they have along the way to achieving their outcome.

The use of mental models in your work can support both strategic direction and tactical decision making on iterating a product or service design. For example:

Tactical:

- Validating design ideas/wireframes.
- Types of content to be improved.
- What functions are required.
- Iterating existing information architectures.

Strategic:

- What you'll work on next.
- What to focus on in discovery phases.
- New information architectures.
- New content to go into production.

In reality, a user interface can never correspond to every user's mental model. However, you can create user interfaces that match the mental models users would most likely have. It is often most useful to have a mental model for each persona for a particular journey or experience. Be mindful that mental models are not static. People's mental models can change based on learning from everyday experiences.

In order to understand why mental models are so important to designing things, you need to understand conceptual models. A conceptual model is the actual model of the product or service the user experiences (ie through an interface) – the reality rather than the belief. If the conceptual model and the user's mental model don't match, the user will find the thing hard to learn and use. Thus, your conceptual model needs to take into account the user's mental model. However, we are rarely talking about a single mental model. You have multiple user groups with varying mental models and your conceptual model needs to make your product or service as easy to use as possible for all your primary user groups. That sounds like a daunting prospect – unachievable perhaps? This is a great example of why user research is so important. Analysing your data will show you where the user groups overlap in their mental models and where they diverge. You can design, refine and validate concepts through user research to meet the needs of diverging mental models, ultimately gaining a better understanding of what works for the majority of users, although it will never be perfect. It is also useful to combine them with personas for an in-depth view of who your users are and how they think.

MENTAL MODEL CASE STUDY 1
Web browser URL and search bars

Jakob Nielsen highlights potential confusion in mental modelling when users fail to recognize key differences between similar (but not identical) parts of a system.

Many users seem unable to distinguish between the search field on Google and the URL entry field in a browser. These users will use Google to search for the name of a well-known website in order to click the link rather than simply entering the name plus '.com' in the URL bar, a problem that Google Chrome tries to resolve by making the URL bar a search tool.

It appears that users know that they can type stuff into a box and get taken to where they want to go but are uncertain as to the functionality of any given box. This offers an explanation as to why browsers have evolved to treat the URL box as a search box in many cases now. The functionality of the browser had to change to meet the user's mental model as the mental model itself was too confused to easily adopt the design pattern that users encountered (Nielsen, 2010; Interaction Design Foundation, 2017).

MENTAL MODEL CASE STUDY 2
Smashing Magazine cartoon

Smashing Magazine has a great 'mental models' cartoon that explains what mental models are and why they are useful through the example of a health tracking app. Definitely worth a read, see the references at the end of this chapter for the URL (Young and Colbow, 2012).

Important note: If you are innovating, pushing the boundaries and providing people with something they haven't seen before or considered yet, you can change people's mental models. There is a certain amount of inertia to overcome, as it takes time and effort to change a mental model. This factor should be taken into account when developing something new, and should inform your underlying understanding of users' reactions during testing and after the initial launch, potentially. If the product or service is providing a valuable experience for the user they will make the effort to learn new ways. If they do not consider it valuable they will walk away and find something else.

How to create your own mental model: version one

Unsurprisingly there is more than one way to create a mental model, so I will give a couple of examples of how it can be done. The first example is simpler than the second. Which method you use really depends on your level of experience, the amount of time and effort you can put into the analysis and creation, and what your project requires.

In a mental model visualization (Figure 26.1), how people behave (think/feel) are represented as columns above the horizontal line. The functions/features/content of your product/service are represented below the horizontal line in support of the users' columns. Where there are no supportive columns, these are gaps in your offering and are now opportunities to improve what you provide to the users.

Using the scenario discussed in Part One, 'Support Charity', below is an example of questions identified from interviewing users regarding how they feel about donating to charities, as shown in Figure 26.1.

Box 1 contains the questions that the user has when they are trying to decide which charity to donate to if they don't have a strong affinity to one particular charity.

Box 2 contains the existing content on the Support Charity website that supports the questions that the user has.

Box 3 contains the content that currently doesn't exist, but is required to support the user's mental model of the donation process.

This is a simplified example of one column in a mental model. Figure 26.2 shows another simplified version of a mental model showing the column represented in Figure 26.1 in the wider context of a donation mental model. The boxes are in sequential order of the likely thought process (as shown in Figure 26.2).

FIGURE 26.1 An example of a mental model column

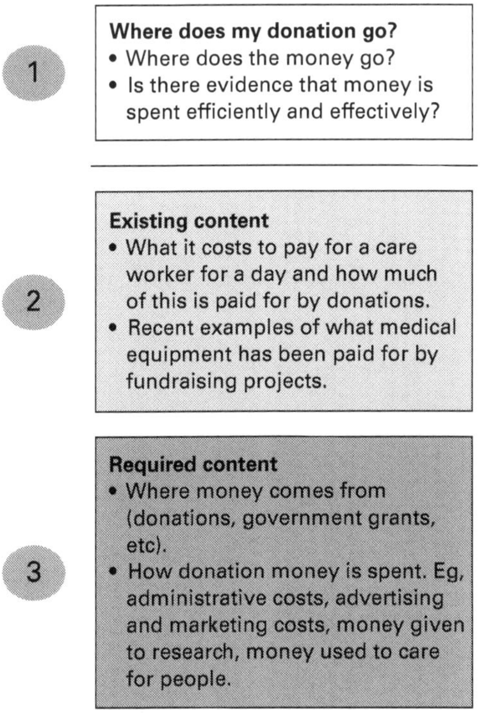

Where does my donation go?
1
- Where does the money go?
- Is there evidence that money is spent efficiently and effectively?

Existing content
2
- What it costs to pay for a care worker for a day and how much of this is paid for by donations.
- Recent examples of what medical equipment has been paid for by fundraising projects.

Required content
3
- Where money comes from (donations, government grants, etc).
- How donation money is spent. Eg, administrative costs, advertising and marketing costs, money given to research, money used to care for people.

You can use methodologies discussed in Part Three (analysing the data) to identify the users' actions and questions to make up the top row (box 1). Identifying what currently exists requires an audit of what you have in terms of content, functions and other relevant assets (box 2). Comparing box 1 and box 2 will identify the opportunities you are currently missing to complete box 3.

How to create your own mental model: version two

Version two is a more in-depth way to analyse your data to create your mental models. In this version, you code your data on the following four themes; you can visualize this as an empathy map:

- What is the user **doing?**
- What is the user **feeling?**
- What is the user **thinking?**
- **Who else is involved?**

FIGURE 26.2 A simple example of a mental model, for Support Charity

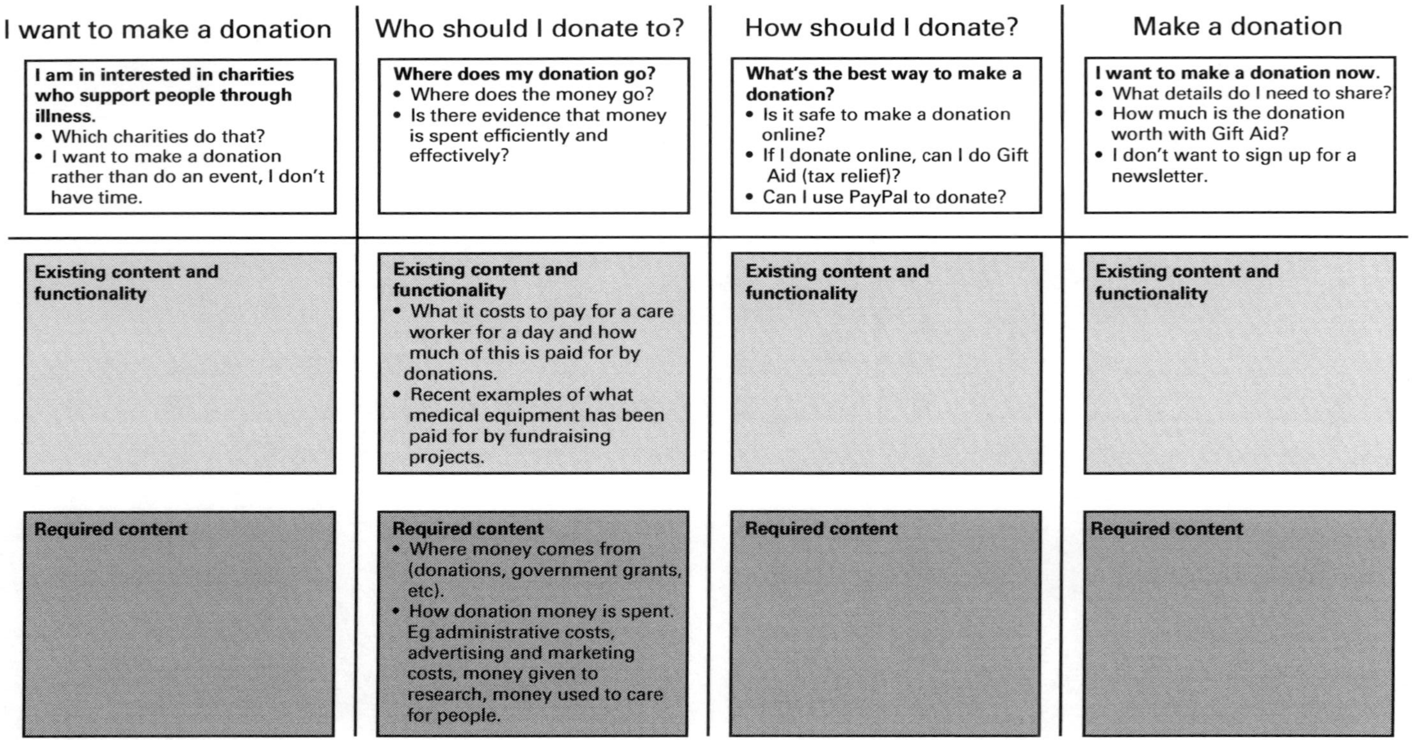

I want to make a donation

I am in interested in charities who support people through illness.
- Which charities do that?
- I want to make a donation rather than do an event, I don't have time.

Existing content and functionality

Required content

Who should I donate to?

Where does my donation go?
- Where does the money go?
- Is there evidence that money is spent efficiently and effectively?

Existing content and functionality
- What it costs to pay for a care worker for a day and how much of this is paid for by donations.
- Recent examples of what medical equipment has been paid for by fundraising projects.

Required content
- Where money comes from (donations, government grants, etc).
- How donation money is spent. Eg administrative costs, advertising and marketing costs, money given to research, money used to care for people.

How should I donate?

What's the best way to make a donation?
- Is it safe to make a donation online?
- If I donate online, can I do Gift Aid (tax relief)?
- Can I use PayPal to donate?

Existing content and functionality

Required content

Make a donation

I want to make a donation now.
- What details do I need to share?
- How much is the donation worth with Gift Aid?
- I don't want to sign up for a newsletter.

Existing content and functionality

Required content

FIGURE 26.3 An example of an empathy map, to support analysis and creation of mental models

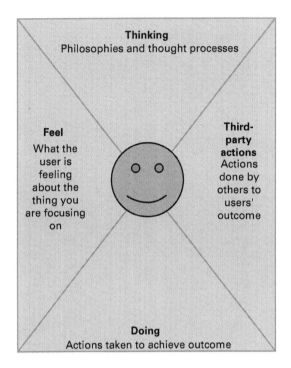

FIGURE 26.4 An example of the 'mental model version two' coding schema

Figure 26.4 shows the coding schema you can use to mark up your interview transcript, for example.

Figure 26.5 is an example of how the transcript text is marked up with your coding schema.

As you can see, each type of thing is marked up in the text. These can be used to create a more detailed 'skyline' mental model.

You can also create posters to share with stakeholders that summarize the essence of a persona in the form of a mental model. The example poster in Figure 26.7 shows how you can encapsulate each theme into the mental model poster.

FIGURE 26.5 An example of an interview transcript marked up using the four elements of the coding schema

Here is a excerpt from a fictional interview done for Support Charity, to help improve the their internal IT infrastructure.

Interviewer: So can you tell me your daily work routine?
Participant: There isn't really a routine. Each day is different depending on what is needed at the time. I could be in the office doing admin or I could be out and about, talking to stakeholders and finding out about progress of projects we are supporting.

Interviewer: Do you need internet access when you are in or out of the office?
Participant: I always need internet access wherever I am. In the office I'm on the WiFi on my laptop, it connects automatically. When I'm in the field, I take my personal tablet with me.

Interviewer: Do you ever have problems with connectivity, or is it generally reliable?
Participant: It's good in the office, most of the time. Most of the time is OK out of the office, but depending where I am , If the place doesn't WiFi I'll connect to my personal hotspot.

FIGURE 26.6 An example of a mental model column (for version two)

Examples for version two were inspired by a workshop I ran with Nick Forrester and Nick Breeze at Government Digital Service for the user research community in 2018.

FIGURE 26.7   An example of a mental model (version two) poster and how it incorporates each element of the coding schema

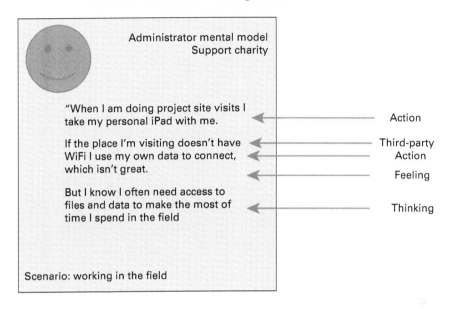

References and further reading

Ballav, A (17 May 2016) Mental models and user experience. UX Matters. www.uxmatters.com/mt/archives/2016/05/mental-models-and-user-experience.php (archived at https://perma.cc/2AVU-F97Z) (last accessed: 12 June 2017)

Interaction Design Foundation (September 2016) We think therefore it is – conceptual modelling for mobile applications. www.interaction-design.org/literature/article/we-think-therefore-it-is-conceptual-modelling-for-mobile-applications (archived at https://perma.cc/D2T2-BR7S) (last accessed: 12 June 2017)

Interaction Design Foundation (May 2017) A very useful work of fiction – mental models in design. www.interaction-design.org/literature/article/130558 (archived at https://perma.cc/4NQZ-4WWR) (last accessed: 12 June 2017)

John, K (9 September 2020) Using mental models to understand complex services: Analysing how users behave and what help they get from organisations. Caution Your Blast. www.cautionyourblast.com/journal/using-mental-models-to-understand-complex-services (archived at https://perma.cc/7W6A-PDUB)

Nielsen, J (18 October 2010) Mental models. Nielsen Norman Group. www.nngroup.com/articles/mental-models/ (archived at https://perma.cc/YCY4-2MR8) (last accessed: 12 June 2017)

Weinschenk, S (8 October 2011) The secret to designing an intuitive UX: psychological concepts underlying good user experience and usability. UX Magazine. http://uxmag.com/articles/the-secret-to-designing-an-intuitive-user-experience (archived at https://perma.cc/K43Q-D32Z) (last accessed: 12 June 2017)

Young, I (2007) *Mental Models: Aligning design strategy with human behavior*, Rosenfeld Media, New York

Young, I and Colbow, B (23 April 2012) Mental model diagram – cartoon. Smashing Magazine. www.smashingmagazine.com/2012/04/mental-model-diagrams-cartoon/ (archived at https://perma.cc/6HFZ-PMVP) (last accessed: 12 June 2017)

27

Turning findings into insights

One of the most skilled things to do within the analysis-synthesis phase of user research is turning data into information and information into knowledge. You can also describe this as turning research findings into research insights.

This is something even experienced researchers can find challenging, but that doesn't mean you should avoid it if you don't consider yourself an experienced researcher. It is something to work on throughout your user research journey, to hone these skills.

It's important to say that both findings and insights are useful; which you need depends on the context, as usual. You may also be wondering, what's the difference between a finding and an insight? It's a good question! So let's get into some definitions.

Data is the raw numbers that we capture according to some agreed-to standards and is unprocessed (you could say it's raw data). This is what you collect during the doing of research. Data doesn't tell you what actions to take from the data; you haven't learnt anything from it yet, you've just gathered it together.

Findings are a collection of data points that we can use to understand something about the thing being measured. These can include observations of behaviour, interactions, issues, perceptions, opinions and attitudes. Findings are the 'what' (you can also think of this as information). They are what you have after processing and analysis of a specific dataset; you've made some meaning out of the data, and it is true for the product/service you gathered the data on and analysed in that context.

Insight is the understanding of the motivation behind the finding – what is going on with the particular situation or phenomenon and why it is happening.

- Good insights have longevity.
- Insights are behaviour and attitudes that are true beyond a single product or service.
- Insights are backed up by multiple data points, quotes and observations from multiple research activities.

Triangulation and compelling description of the insight reduces the possibility of data being misinterpreted and teams doing the wrong work when they act on research data (Brown, 2020; Fang, 2019; Sticktail, 2019; Dalton, 2016).

What are actionable insights?

The next step in the process is to make the insights actionable. Insights by themselves are useful for contextual knowledge of the space you are working in and the people who are your users. **Actionable insight** is taking what you've learnt (your triangulated evidence/insight) and making it relevant to the specific thing you are working on right now. You can do this by combining insights, business goals and knowledge, and business constraints to allow you to identify the gaps, opportunities, and what the best next step is.

FIGURE 27.1 Actionable insight diagram

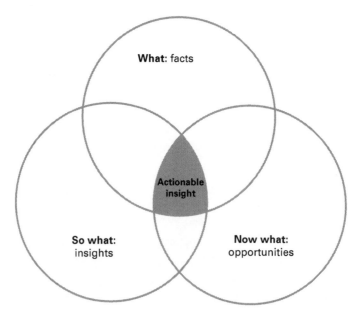

Table 27.1 shows an insight taxonomy, a framework you can use to structure your insights. This particular framework for actionable insights is adapted from the Uber insight framework. Most of the elements of the framework are important to include to have a well-established insight, which is an insight that has been triangulated and corroborated with multiple pieces of data. There are a couple of elements I've added to make it more actionable; you can consider these to be optional elements. Optional elements include business domain information and whether it is a short-, medium- or long-term action.

TOP TIP

An important step before triangulating different sources of data is to evaluate if they are compatible for triangulation. The questions to ask to understand data compatibility include:

- Are datasets focusing on similar user groups?
- Are the types of research focusing on similar research questions/objectives?
- Are the datasets focusing on a similar thing (eg product/service/business area)?
- Are the datasets of a similar granularity?
- Is the data still relevant? For example, the business direction hasn't changed since the data was collected.

TABLE 27.1   Insight taxonomy

Insight	**Who**: specific user type; it could be a segment or persona
	Where: location – the insight is based on cities, countries, regions
	What: a notable behaviour or situation
	Why: an explanation of the behaviour or situation – what is the motivation?
Facts	**Data points**: user quotes, anecdotes, observations that support the insight
	When and who: when was this insight identified, has it been revalidated over time? When does it become no longer true? Who did the work?
	Sources: what type of research do the data points come from?
Business domain	Relevant business context: goals, constraints, domain knowledge
Opportunities and recommendations	Description of recommended actions based on the insight, business goals and objectives
	Is this a short-, medium- or long-term action?

Adapted from Fang, 2019

Each time you do user research you will generate more data/facts. Ideally, you will make time to review your data and findings against your insights, asking yourself, does this new data strengthen the insight or contradict it? If it's contradicted, then this is likely to be something that needs to be explored further. As mentioned earlier, good insights have longevity, but it's wise to review insights to see if they are still accurate and relevant. Insights won't be correct forever, especially if there are big changes in your organization, market, etc.

As mentioned above, it's worth noting that turning findings into insight is one of the most advanced things you can do in your user research practice. Once you get to this stage, generally a librarian would be curating and maintaining a research insight library. The majority of practitioners and organizations aren't at this level of maturity yet.

However, you can aim to triangulate data as often as possible. And practise framing your findings:

- in the context of the business domain you are working in;
- going beyond the 'what' and identifying the 'why'. Why is this behaviour concurring? This will help you look beyond a specific product or service to a more 'universal truth'.

Atomic research

Atomic research is another method you can use for turning data generated during research into actionable insights. One method isn't better than another, it's just what makes sense to you to use at the time.

Atomic research is an approach to managing research knowledge. Check out Sharon (2017) to find more information on how WeWork has used this methodology to build a user research library. It goes beyond the user need structure to incorporate the context in which the insight was found (see Chapter 24 to learn more about users' needs) and is particularly useful for multidisciplinary teams with several groups doing different types of research.

Experiments generate data; facts are observations/useful information extracted from the data. Facts are combined together to create contextual insights. Contextual insights are used to draw out findings and make decisions.

We can imagine a scenario for Support Charity, redesigning the donation payment process. Facts have been identified from several experiments (pieces

FIGURE 27.2 The elements that make up the atomic research model

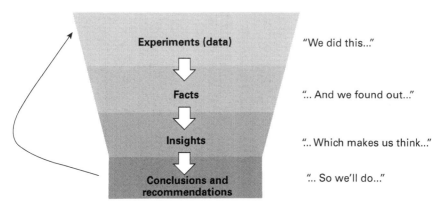

SOURCE Pidcock, 2018

of research): a survey, an A/B test, a moderated usability test and an unmoderated usability test. Combining these facts about the button language and icons gives us an insight that currently the labelling on the payment button is confusing and would benefit from the addition of an icon. This will lead to the action of adding an icon to the button and further research on the most effective icon and labelling for the button.

Triangulation in this method is described as making connections between the atomic units: facts, insights and conclusions. Combining facts and insights strengthens and validates decisions made, and using multiple sources means better decisions are made (Pidcock, 2018).

Combining and triangulating data and documenting it in this way is powerfully persuasive when tough decisions need to be made. As with the insight taxonomy previously described, it allows evidence to be reused in the future. This means that you may not need to do certain primary research in the future, or you can focus your research on a specific thing, because of the knowledge you have captured and made accessible through the stored insights. This reduces the likelihood that research will be unnecessarily repeated, although it is important to validate findings and insights from old research to test if they continue to be true or not. As you have documented where the insights have come from/what they are based on, this will allow you to assess if a specific insight is relevant to the thing you are doing right now.

FIGURE 27.3 Example atomic research in practice

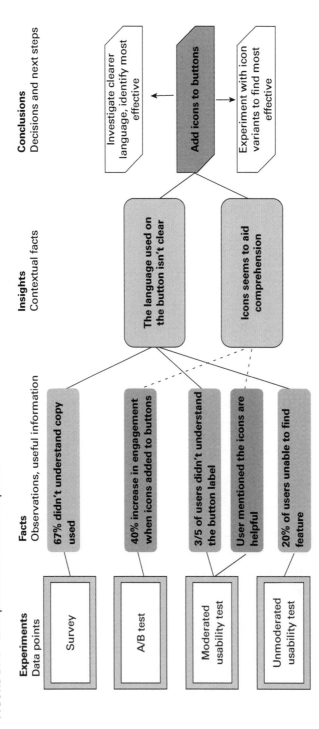

Experiments
Data points

Facts
Observations, useful information

Insights
Contextual facts

Conclusions
Decisions and next steps

Survey

A/B test

Moderated usability test

Unmoderated usability test

67% didn't understand copy used

40% increase in engagement when icons added to buttons

3/5 of users didn't understand the button label

User mentioned the icons are helpful

20% of users unable to find feature

The language used on the button isn't clear

Icons seems to aid comprehension

Investigate clearer language, identify most effective

Add icons to buttons

Experiment with icon variants to find most effective

SOURCE Adapted from Pidcock, 2018

Part Three summary

Part Three has covered multiple ways of analysing your user research data. My advice would be, whatever method you are using, to carve out time to do the analysis – give yourself as much as possible, if you can. There is often pressure to deliver results as soon as possible after the research has been done. It can help to give some initial results, heavily caveated that these are a work in progress, before communicating the final findings of the analysis. Involving your team as much as possible during the process, rather than having a big reveal at the end, can also help with the analysis and communication process.

Getting enough time to do analysis

It's not possible to give accurate timescales for how long it will take to complete a round of research. It is dependent on so many factors, such as the type of research you are doing, what kind of people your participants are, how long it takes to get internal sign-off for the various things needed for research, to name a few. How long it takes to plan, prepare, do and analyse the research is a significant factor in incorporating user research into workflows, especially in agile environments (as discussed in Chapter 23).

When building something new or working on a live product/service, there are different ways to incorporate user research into your workflows. Figure 27.4 shows what moving from building a new thing to iterating a

FIGURE 27.4 High-level steps in building a new product or service and iterating an existing product or service

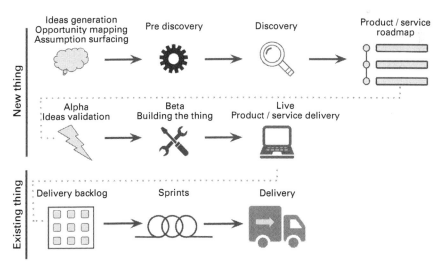

thing that is live can look like in terms of stages of research, design, development and delivery.

If you are building a new product/service in an agile way, there tends to be a significant investment in research upfront, with discovery research understanding the problem, the users and their context, for example.

The Government Digital Service Manual for building services in an agile way suggests that a **discovery phase should last 4–8 weeks** (GDS, 2019). As mentioned above, it's dependent on what you are researching and how your organization works. I've seen many discoveries that **last 12 weeks, or significantly longer**. In the discovery phase, there will be a lot of focus on doing and analysing research.

Taking the example of a 12-week discovery, time spent could be organized as such:

- 1 week planning;
- 2 weeks recruiting participants and preparing research materials;
- 3 weeks doing the research;
- 4.5 weeks analysing;
- 1 week preparing for and communicating the results;
- 0.5 weeks of wrap-up and decision making.

Discovery research methodologies can include interviewing, contextual inquiry, diary studies, ethnography and surveys, for example. Therefore, you are likely to have a large amount of semi-structured qualitative data to analyse, drawing on analysis methods such as content analysis, thematic analysis or personas, for example.

It can be very useful to have a pre-discovery phase, particularly if you and your organization are new to this sort of research. The pre-discovery phase, which I suggest doing some further digging on, is time to:

- work together to generate ideas, identify opportunity and surface assumptions before doing discovery research;
- understand the business context;
- confirm objective and expected outcomes;
- prioritize focus areas for research;
- set up processes to enable research and other relevant kinds of work;
- set up the appropriate kind of team (appropriate in terms of size and skillsets);
- agree on budgets, etc.

If the discovery phase results in the decision to continue with developing the concept/opportunity identified, then the alpha phase is next. The alpha phase is where ideas for solutions are tried and tested. The Government Digital Service Manual suggests that the **alpha stage should last 6–8 weeks** (GDS, 2019). Again, alpha phases can last much longer than this, **often beyond 12 weeks**. The alpha phase is about iterative research, design and validation of ideas. This requires a different workflow structure.

In an alpha sprint, which may last two weeks, time spent could be organized as such:

- 1.5 days planning;
- 3.5 days recruiting participants and preparing research materials;
- 2 days doing the research;
- 1 day analysing;
- 1 day preparing for and communicating the results;
- 1 day of wrap-up and decision making.

Alpha research tends to consist mostly of usability testing types of research activity. You'll be drawing on qualitative usability analysis methods, such as group affinity diagramming or the rainbow spreadsheet method.

For agile research and analysis, it is suggested that one hour of analysis is spent for every two hours of research (GDS, 2016). It could be closer to a 1:1 ratio – as always, it depends. All this is to say that in analysis terms, agile analysis is high level and rapid.

If the decision at alpha is to build the product/service, the **beta phase** will last between **at least 8–12 weeks** to deliver a minimum viable product (MVP) that you can continue to iterate on once the thing is launched and live. The beta also needs to incorporate research and design/development. Whereas the alpha phase will mostly be qualitative research, beta will ideally combine qualitative and quantitative research.

Some of the beta sprints may look similar to alpha sprints, depending on what work is being focused on and the kind of research method that is needed, which will affect how the sprint should be structured. You are more likely to draw on a wider range of research methodologies during beta compared with alpha. For example, A/B testing, quantitative and qualitative usability research and analysis methods, affinity diagramming and mental models are often useful in this phase.

FIGURE 27.5 Legend for Figures 27.6 and 27.7

| Planning | Preparing and recruiting | Doing research | Analysing | Sharing and communicating |

FIGURE 27.6 Relative time taken for each phase of the research process depending on the type of research and analysis done

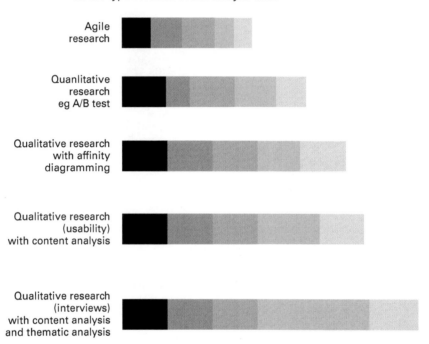

If quantitative research is properly scoped and has a well-defined hypothesis, analysis of the data will also be rapid, as often the tools you are using will calculate the statistics for you.

These research and analysis activities are more likely to be incorporated in alpha and beta phases.

Once the product/service has been launched and is live, and your team continues to iterate on the MVP, there are multiple kinds of research and analysis to do:

• You'll have a delivery backlog to develop, test, iterate and deliver. This kind of validation research consists of short discrete pieces of work for design elements and interaction components, for example.

- You will also need to do tactical research if the analytics show something isn't working. You need to do research to understand the problem, and the team will try solutions that will then need to be validated – these are medium-sized pieces of research work.

- Strategic research will be larger pieces of work, setting the strategic direction and roadmap of a product or service (Handa and Vashisht, 2016).

You'll be drawing on a wide range of research methods and therefore a range of analysis methods too. Combining these types of research and analysis will support the product/service meeting users' needs now and in the future.

For qualitative research, analysis is expected to take longer than the research itself. For example, 20 hours of research (20 one-hour interviews) will take between 40–60 hours to analyse. This may be a surprise to you, and it is often a source of contention when teams are waiting for results to be delivered. But as I mentioned in the introduction to Part Three, robust analysis takes time.

FIGURE 27.7   Relative time taken for each phase of the research process depending on the type of research and analysis done

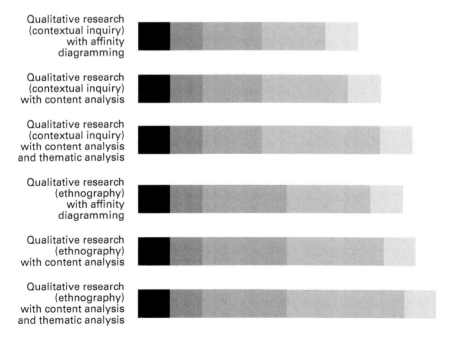

These research and analysis activities are more likely to be incorporated in the discovery and live phases.

Figure 27.8 approximates a dual-track agile way of working. I am not an agile expert – actual experts may not agree with me – but very few agile teams have successfully combined research and design in agile sprints, so what I propose here could be worth experimenting with, to see if it works for you.

The research track can take longer, allowing for time to prepare for research, and for analysis and decision making after the research sessions are completed. I have heard experienced user researchers comment that it can be useful to start the research process ahead of design and development work, particularly when recruiting external participants, to embed research in agile processes. Often there are multiple developers, and maybe multiple designers on a multidisciplinary team; at the same time there is likely to be only one user researcher. For these and other reasons, the research track could take longer than the work required for the designs/wireframes to be ready for research to happen. This is not to diminish the work of designers and developers. As always, how much effort is required for research, design and development depends on the work being done and what stage of development you are at. Once analysis has occurred and results are shared, and the team has made decisions about what they are working on next, the researcher can begin preparing for the next round of research, at the same time as the next phase of design and development starts.

FIGURE 27.8 Parallel research and design and development activities that can happen in agile multidisciplinary teams

Research

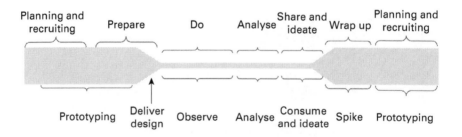

Design and development

This type of sprint planning may not work for your team. The questions that the team as a whole need to ask when planning are how you will plan multidisciplinary work to ensure research results get used, and whether design and development work decisions are based on evidence.

I wish I could give you a more precise answer on the time needed to analyse your research and how to embed this in your team's workflows. But I hope this is helpful in planning and scoping work with your team. If you and your team are fairly new to the research process, scope more time for analysis than the time taken to do the research sessions.

There can be a blurry line between analysis and presentation of results for certain methods. Now we'll look closely at some options of communicating what you have learnt gathering and analysing user research data.

References and further reading

Brown, J (2020) Data vs. information vs insight. Benedictine University. https://online.ben.edu/programs/mba/resources/data-vs-information-vs-insight (archived at https://perma.cc/CJQ3-8R2Q) (last accessed: 11 April 2021)

Cooper-Wright, M (12 September 2015) Design research from interview to insight. Design Research Methods. https://medium.com/design-research-methods/design-research-from-interview-to-insight-f6957b37c698 (archived at https://perma.cc/VU53-N8AF) (last accessed: 11 April 2021)

Crnković, E and Kvakić, I (7 December 2020) Dual-track agile – the what, the why, the pros and the cons. Bornfight. www.bornfight.com/blog/dual-track-agile-the-what-the-why-the-pros-the-cons/ (archived at https://perma.cc/5Z2R-ZJFF)

Dalton, J (28 March 2016) What is an insight? The 5 principles of insight definition. Thrive Thinking. https://thrivethinking.com/2016/03/28/what-is-insight-definition/ (archived at https://perma.cc/USR4-8WPQ) (last accessed: 11 April 2021)

Fang, E (27 August 2019) The power of insight: a behind-the-scenes look at the new insights platform at Uber. Uber. https://medium.com/uber-design/the-power-of-insights-a-behind-the-scenes-look-at-the-new-insights-platform-at-uber-26f85becc2e6 (archived at https://perma.cc/S7RN-5QUD) (last accessed: 11 April 2021)

Government Digital Service (8 May 2019) How the discovery phase works. GDS Service Manual. www.gov.uk/service-manual/agile-delivery/how-the-discovery-phase-works (archived at https://perma.cc/KZ88-84K9)

Government Digital Service (8 May 2019) How the alpha phase works. GDS

Service Manual. www.gov.uk/service-manual/agile-delivery/how-the-alpha-phase-works (archived at https://perma.cc/8S8Y-FLKP)

Government Digital Service (19 February 2021) How the beta phase works. GDS Service Manual. www.gov.uk/service-manual/agile-delivery/how-the-beta-phase-works (archived at https://perma.cc/V6HV-DNQL)

Government Digital Service (24 May 2019) Analyse a research session. GDS Service Manual. www.gov.uk/service-manual/user-research/analyse-a-research-session (archived at https://perma.cc/69M8-GAGP)

Handa, A and Vashisht, K (21 November 2016) Agile development is no excuse for shoddy UX research. UX Matters. www.uxmatters.com/mt/archives/2016/11/agile-development-is-no-excuse-for-shoddy-ux-research.php (archived at https://perma.cc/9BR7-YYAC)

Pidcock, D (16 May 2018) What is atomic UX research? Prototype.io. https://blog.prototypr.io/what-is-atomic-research-e5d9fbc1285c#e009 (archived at https://perma.cc/Z9TB-S8F3) (last accessed: 11 April 2021)

Rivas, C (8 October 2019) Doing a pre-discovery to understand the priorities and goals of an organisation. DXW. www.dxw.com/2019/10/doing-a-pre-discovery-to-understand-the-priorities-and-goals-of-an-organisation/ (archived at https://perma.cc/73ZP-FRTH)

Ross, J (5 November 2018) Scoping user research. UX Matters. www.uxmatters.com/mt/archives/2018/11/scoping-user-research.php (archived at https://perma.cc/J2LS-EMGU)

Sharon, T (12 January 2017) Democratising UX. Tomer Sharon. https://tsharon.medium.com/democratizing-ux-670b95fbc07f (archived at https://perma.cc/G9QR-QRTS)

Sharon, T (16 March 2018) Foundations of atomic research. Timer Sharon. https://tsharon.medium.com/foundations-of-atomic-research-a937d5da5fbb (archived at https://perma.cc/T6UN-5A3V) (last accessed: 11 April 2021)

Sharon, T (23 June 2018) The three most popular questions about atomic research. Tomer Sharon. https://tsharon.medium.com/the-three-most-popular-questions-about-atomic-research-56a5414d3d17 (archived at https://perma.cc/8MMG-6RD4) (last accessed: 15 May 2021)

Sticktail (14 February 2019) How to write valuable user insights. https://medium.com/@sticktail/how-to-write-valuable-user-insights-84b4290d94e8 (archived at https://perma.cc/9M4P-6783) (last accessed: 11 April 2021)

PART FOUR

UX storytelling

Communicating your findings

A common expectation is that something will come out of the research you have done, something tangible that stakeholders can read or see. What that tangible thing is really depends on the objectives of your research and the amount of time you have to complete the project. Now that you have analysed the data, we'll discuss how best to communicate what you have discovered in the most effective way for your audience in the time you have available. The most important question here is, what story do you need to tell? Because the data won't speak for itself.

It's easy to spend a long time making your findings look pretty, which may not be where your effort is best placed. It's true that good-looking data and reports can help 'naive' stakeholders take the work more seriously, but prioritize substance over style. Make sure you've done all the right analysis and know the story you want to tell before you do what seems like endless iterations of design for your output (report). An appropriate amount of effort to make your work easy to read and easily digestible is worth it, but the glossy magazine-quality graphics are often not worth your time.

The methods of storytelling we'll go through are:

- **Executive summaries and detailed reports:** different stakeholders will have differing amounts of time to understand your research. We'll look at the level of detail to provide to different audiences.

- **Video playback:** creating video on particular topics is another powerful way of communicating your findings.

- **Customer journey mapping and experience mapping:** plotting and visualizing a user experience with your product/service, from the users' point of view.

- **Scenarios and storyboards** are a way of exploring the usage of your product or service in greater detail as the presentation of a map. They are often combined with personas to describe the typical or ideal experience of a specific user group.

- **Infographics** are suitable for making your numbers and statistics accessible.

- **Refining the design:** how to go about changing information architectures, interaction designs and visual designs.

Further reading

Government Digital Service (2016) Sharing user research findings. GDS Service Manual. www.gov.uk/service-manual/user-research/sharing-user-research-findings (archived at https://perma.cc/VVQ4-4SKN) (last accessed: 12 June 2017)

Inchauste, F (29 January 2010) UX storytelling for a better user experience – part one. Smashing Magazine. www.smashingmagazine.com/2010/01/better-user-experience-using-storytelling-part-one/ (archived at https://perma.cc/VVT5-QPT8)

Inchauste, F (11 February 2010) Better user experience with storytelling – part two. Smashing Magazine. www.smashingmagazine.com/2010/02/better-user-experience-through-storytelling-part-2/ (archived at https://perma.cc/4K52-4RM9) (last accessed: 12 June 2017)

Martinez Salmeron, J (28 October 2013) Recent trends in storytelling and new business models for publishers. Smashing Magazine. www.smashingmagazine.com/2013/10/recent-trends-in-storytelling-and-new-business-models-for-publishers/ (archived at https://perma.cc/AC5G-AGT4) (last accessed: 12 June 2017)

Quesenbery, W and Brooks, K (April 2010) *Storytelling for User Experience: Crafting stories for better design*, Rosenfeld Media, New York

28

Making recommendations

How to make your research findings actionable

Part of effective communication of the findings and insights gained from user research sometimes includes making recommendations on how to act on them. It depends what type of environment you are working in; you may deliver these to stakeholders or work with your team to identify the actions. To make your 'report' as practical as possible, you'll need to make recommendations about how to fix problems and issues, or how to maximize opportunities that have been identified, how to progress the project, etc.

It's unlikely that you'll have all the solutions and recommendations yourself. To make these recommendations as realistic as possible and to get buy-in from the people who will either be signing off what happens next or doing the actual work to make the changes, consult those people before you formally share your suggestions. Who you talk to depends on what you initially think the solution/recommendation will be. If you do not know where to start with your recommendations, you could run a workshop to share your findings and brainstorm initial solutions/recommendations/next steps.

What kinds of things can you recommend?

- You may need to do more research into a specific area. This can be difficult to hear if time and money have just been spent doing research. Be very clear about why more research is needed and give a summary of the intended approach and hypothesis.
- Changes to internal processes.

- Changes to digital product front- and back-end.
- Brand realignment.
- Realignment of product/service proposition.
- Changes to communications and content.
-

This is not an exhaustive list of things that may come out of your research. Some of what you recommend could be quick fixes; others may be fundamental changes that are going to be expensive. It can be useful to identify the different types of recommendations you are making, using labels such as those shown in Table 28.1.

User research reports and recommendations can be overwhelming and sometimes people are frozen by the thought of the effort required to improve things. Labelling the types of recommendations you have made gives people something to work with. It's easy to identify what can be done now, quickly and easily, and what needs to be planned for, where additional budget will have to be found for large pieces of work.

TABLE 28.1 Categorizing your recommendations

Long term	Expensive	Hard to fix
Medium term	Medium budget	Medium fix
Short term	Cheap	Quick fix

29

Creating executive summaries and detailed reports to present results

TABLE 29.1

Method summary
Method suitability: any user research. Executive summaries are suitable for agile and lean ways of working; however, you are unlikely to do a detailed polished report in these circumstances.
Use if you want to: reports and summaries are the most common type of presentation that can be applied to any type of research you've done, to explain the objectives, the research conducted, the conclusions draw from it and what should happen next.

The length and level of detail you should go into in your report depend on your objectives, the stage you're at in your project, time available and the audience. For example, if you are doing usability testing during agile sprints you may want to do a brief write-up of the issues, recommendations and video playback (see Chapter 30). If you have the CEO, directors, business analysts and developers as your audience you'll probably want to do an executive summary for the CEO and directors, and a detailed report for the business analysts and developers, so they know what work needs to be done to progress the project.

Report structure

When I worked at Bunnyfoot as a consultant, the mantra was always to make reports as practical and useful as possible. This often meant presenting reports in graphical format, normally in PowerPoint rather than as a thesis in Word. If you are going to write a report on your research, you might want to include:

1 Title page

2 List of contents

3 Executive summary

4 Research objectives and methodology

5 Test materials

6 Participant summary (if appropriate)

7 How to read this report (ie, understanding the issues and recommendations)

8 Detail of results grouped logically into sections

9 Research limitations to consider

10 Summary: conclusions and next steps

Executive summaries

The executive summary should be written last and should work as a stand-alone document that could be shared separately with the appropriate audience. A good executive summary will cover (ideally in one page) a short context-setting piece and:

- Research purpose.
- Research and analysis methods.
- Main focus of the summary: findings and recommendations.
- Bringing it all together briefly: limitations and a positive summary sentence.

Participant details

When sharing participant details, it's important to ensure anonymity, however many people you are sharing the data with. Don't include names and contact details in your reports; this will breach the confidentiality of your participants, even if you are sharing video of them. Share just enough to show they are relevant to your organization and research. Table 29.2 shows some anonymized participant details you could include in your report.

TABLE 29.2 Anonymized participant details

Participant #	Persona / audience type	A couple of relevant demographics	Digital literacy	Other relevant characteristics or behaviours
P1	Project manager	Female 31 Married	Expert	Does research online before talking to anyone about the service

How to read the report

For those new to user research, you can include brief guidance on reading the report, aiding understanding of the information you are sharing. For example, if you are writing a report about qualitative usability testing, you may want to equip the reader with an understanding of how the report is broken down into issues and recommendations (as shown in Figure 29.1).

In your report, it's also useful to give a written description and, where appropriate, include graphics and visual mock-ups of findings and recommendations (this is considered in more detail in Chapter 28). People process information in different ways, so using both text and visuals will help most people digest your report; also, having text and graphics together is less off-putting than seemingly endless reams of text.

Ordering your findings and recommendations

If you have a lot of information to convey, give some thought to how best to structure your findings and recommendations. If your research has focused on a service/product where sequential order is important, you may want to present your report in this order. Alternatively, you could place whatever you want to have the most impact first, followed by items of decreasing importance (see Figure 29.2). Your readers are likely to run out of steam at some point, so it makes sense to include the most critical things first.

There are lots of ways to structure your reports; I can't cover them all here. The best advice I can give is to think about the story you want to tell and how to arrange your content to tell it.

FIGURE 29.1 An example of how to set out your report

Descriptive title: issues & recommendations

Good: Best practice worth highlighting, features that contribute to excellent usability or user experience.

Issue: First summarize the issue in one sentence if possible.

Then describe the issue in more detail if necessary. You may want to take a screenshot or include video of the issue.

Recommendation: Describe your suggested recommendation for improving the user experience.

Only include recommendations that have been reviewed and discussed for appropriateness.

You may want to include a sketch of the recommendation if appropriate.

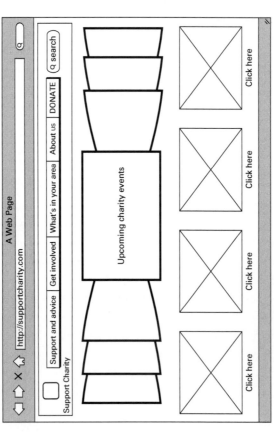

"Quote about an issue"
P1

FIGURE 29.2 An example of how to structure report content

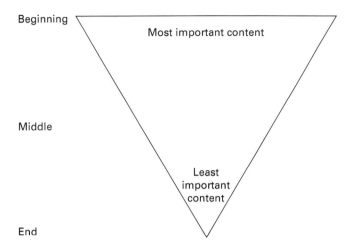

30

Using video playback to present your research results

TABLE 30.1

Method summary
Method suitability: any user research that has been video recorded. This methodology is suitable for agile and lean ways of working.
Use if you want to: a powerful way to quickly make a point about the user experience of your product/service.

Videos are a powerful way to communicate your findings, to see the participants, and to show the context of what you have recommended, especially if people haven't been able to observe the research. Videos can be used as part of a report that you are writing, in agile retrospectives at the end of a sprint, and as part of a workshop or presentation you are giving. In an ideal world, all stakeholders would watch the relevant videos, but this is wishful thinking, especially when you are likely to have hours of footage.

If you want to be hard line about it, and I hope you do, get buy-in from the project owner (if that isn't you) to require anyone with decision-making powers who didn't observe the research to watch a certain amount of video before they have a say. That could be two or three representative videos of the research in full, or whatever seems appropriate.

How to edit your user research videos

If you have chosen to go down the route of video highlights, I have a few useful tips. Before you start, be aware that making video highlights can be time-consuming. There are a few things you can do to help the process:

- First identify what you need videos of – a particular issue, interaction, attitude, etc.
- Read through your notes to identify key observations and quotes for each of the participants and then find them in the footage rather than going through all the videos.
- Try to time stamp your notes during the research, if you think you've just observed or heard something you may want to include in your video report.

What to include in your videos

- Make each snippet of video as short as possible.
- Try to include enough context to make it clear what the participant is doing or talking about. This might involve editing the video and/or including a title for each video describing the theme or what is occurring.
- If possible find more than one example of the issue, interaction, attitude, etc. It can be useful to show something that happened multiple times to emphasize its importance.
- If including a montage of lots of participants, apply a label to identify who said what (such as the participant's number).
- Only create and present videos for the most important points you are making.

31

Using journey and experience maps to visualize user research data

TABLE 31.1

Method summary
Method suitability: data for maps can be gathered from multiple sources. If you are looking at a digital product/service you may start with your analytics, looking at users' journeys and paths. You can draw on other sources you may have such as customer satisfaction and feedback data and social media data, combined with user research data using contextual inquiry, ethnography, usability testing, interviews, diary studies and workshops. These methods are suitable for agile and lean ways of working.
Use if you want to: provide visualizations of users' experience of a service/organization.

The terms 'journey map' and 'experience map' are often used interchangeably, but they do have different purposes. An experience map visualizes an end-to-end user experience for a particular user group accomplishing a particular goal. An experience map is product or tool agnostic, whereas a customer journey map visualizes how people use a particular product or service to achieve a goal. For the purpose of this book, I'll use the shorthand of 'experience map'. These maps visualize the touchpoints where users interact with the product/service and are generally used to construct the journey. The maps can also represent the users' emotions, expectations, motivations and questions at each interaction. Experience maps usually represent a certain period of time, for example from initial contact through engagement into a long-term relationship.

It is useful to have a separate map for each of your personas/user groups. These maps provide a high-level overview of factors influencing users' experience, constructed from their perspective, and they are time-based, although the time is not necessarily linear. Importantly, the touchpoints can be across multiple channels, both digital and non-digital.

As the maps synthesize the circumstances, motivations and experiences of the user/service interaction, they can be used to identify problem areas and opportunities for innovation, as well as what the service is doing well, across channels, departments, journeys and devices. Maps are particularly useful when the experience takes place over several weeks or months and involves:

- lots of separate steps or events;
- more than one location;
- different people or teams;
- several related services or touchpoints (Government Digital Service, 2017).

UX Mastery (2014) and Adaptive Path (2011) suggest that, as experience maps cover doing, thinking and feeling, the 'must have' components of a customer journey map are:

- *Personas:* the main characters that illustrate the needs, goals, thoughts, feelings, opinions, expectations, and pain points of the user.
- *Timeline:* a finite amount of time (eg, one week or one year) or variable phases (eg, awareness, decision making, purchase, renewal).
- *Emotion:* peaks and valleys illustrating frustration, anxiety, happiness, etc.
- *Touchpoints:* customer actions and interactions with the organization; ie what the customer is doing.
- *Channels:* where interaction takes place and the context of use (eg, website, native app, call centre, in-store); ie where customers are interacting.

How to create an experience map

Once you have gathered your data, the next step is to think about the layout of your experience map. There are no hard and fast rules for this, but there are two main types of visualization (Churruca, 2013): *timeline,* where touchpoints are located over a path, organized either left to right or top to bottom, which is the most common kind of experience map; or *wheel:* used where interaction phases are more relevant than touchpoints, used mainly for reflecting an overall experience.

The success and clarity of your experience map will depend largely on choosing the right layout and graphic elements. You can find out more about this in Churruca (2013), where you can also see classic examples of both wheel visualizations (Lego Experience Map) and timeline visualization (Starbucks Service Experience). Here we will focus on the timeline visualization; even within this format there are various ways to design it. Adaptive Path is an authority on experience maps; the Rail Europe visualization is an excellent example that can be seen on Adaptive Path's website (Risdon, 2011).

I have laid out the main components of an experience in Figure 31.1. It is a 'blank' map to show you what components generally go where on your visualization. Figure 31.2 is an enlarged version of the icons that can be used in the experience map.

You may not want to include all these elements in your experience map; it really depends on your product/service and what you need to visualize. Your map doesn't necessarily need to look like Figure 31.1; you can find lots of examples online, and for some thoughts on the differences see Churruca (2013).

Map variations

If you are concerned that these maps look very complicated and difficult to create, you could simplify them to meet your needs or current level of experience; see Figure 31.3 as an example. You can also create maps for competitors, as a visual way of benchmarking how you are doing against them.

Another variation is the customer lifecycle map that represents multiple journeys over time, visualizing key events in the use of the service from initial contact to when the customer leaves or no longer has use for the service provided. These kinds of maps are holistic overviews: it's important to represent change over time, rather than just taking snapshots (Interaction Design Foundation, 2017).

Experience maps are not service blueprints, but they can be a starting point for them. Service blueprints are a visual schematic that incorporates users, the provider and other relevant parties, the users' touchpoints and behind-the-scenes processes. Such work needs to be created collaboratively

FIGURE 31.1 Example of what to include in your experience map

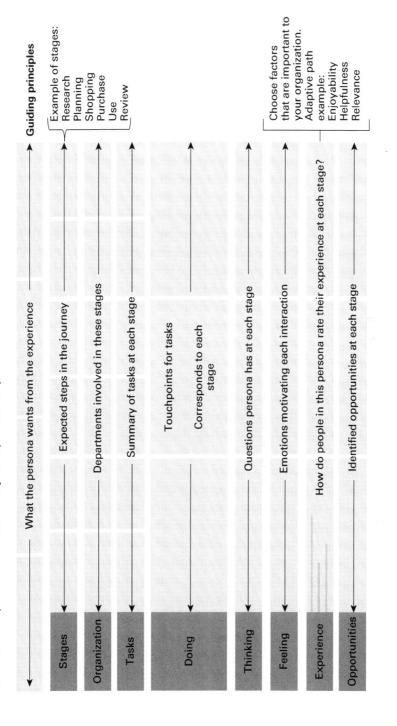

FIGURE 31.2 A close up of the 'doing' icons

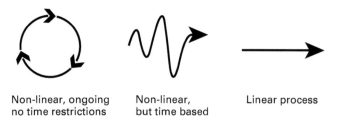

Non-linear, ongoing   Non-linear,   Linear process
no time restrictions   but time based

FIGURE 31.3 Simple experience map

Date or likely timeline	Date of interaction	Date of interaction	Date of interaction
Touchpoint	Email	Phone	Written note
Description	Description of the interaction, the intention and emotions experienced	Description of the interaction, the intention and emotions experienced	Description of the interaction, the intention and emotions experienced
Emotion	:-)	:-(	:-|
Outcome	What happened as a consequence on the interaction and potential next steps and options	What happened as a consequence on the interaction and potential next steps and options	What happened as a consequence on the interaction and potential next steps and options

(as in stakeholder workshops; see Chapter 17) and using contextual inquiry (Chapter 15). Each team represented on the blueprint needs to be involved in its creation. Service blueprints can reveal areas of overlap, duplication and where things are missing, and can be used to coordinate people and resources (Stickdorn and Schneider, 2014).

References and further reading

Adaptive Path (2017) Mapping Experiences. http://mappingexperiences.com/ (archived at https://perma.cc/6LYC-EX8G) (last accessed: 12 June 2017)

Boag, P (15 January 2015) All you need to know about customer journey mapping. Smashing Magazine. www.smashingmagazine.com/2015/01/all-about-customer-journey-mapping/ (archived at https://perma.cc/6M72-NLR4) (last accessed: 12 June 2017)

Churruca, S (17 March 2013) Experience maps, user journeys and more. UX Lady. www.ux-lady.com/experience-maps-user-journey-and-more-exp-map-layout/ (archived at https://perma.cc/7YF7-AVPA)

Government Digital Service (April 2017) Creating an experience map. GDS Service Manual. www.gov.uk/service-manual/user-research/creating-an-experience-map (archived at https://perma.cc/BG4N-PQRA) (last accessed: 12 June 2017)

Grocki, M (16 September 2014) How to create a customer journey map. UX Mastery. http://uxmastery.com/how-to-create-a-customer-journey-map/ (archived at https://perma.cc/S8GM-2J78) (last accessed: 12 June 2017)

Interaction Design Foundation (July 2017) A simple introduction to lean UX. www.interaction-design.org/literature/article/a-simple-introduction-to-lean-ux (archived at https://perma.cc/5CJY-2YFW) (last accessed 26 August 2017)

Ivey-Williams, K (21 April 2016) How to make a user journey map. GDS Design Notes Blog. https://designnotes.blog.gov.uk/2016/04/21/how-to-make-a-user-journey-map/ (archived at https://perma.cc/E9BD-RYXQ) (last accessed: 12 June 2017)

Risdon, C (30 November 2011) The anatomy of an experience map. Adaptive Path. http://adaptivepath.org/ideas/the-anatomy-of-an-experience-map/ (archived at https://perma.cc/5HS4-22CZ) (last accessed: 12 June 2017)

Stickdorn, M and Schneider, J (2014) *This is Service Design Thinking*, BIS Publishers, Amsterdam

32

Using scenarios and storyboards to represent the user journey

TABLE 32.1

Method summary
Method suitability: any user research.
Use if you want to: scenarios are hypothetical stories created with sufficient detail to meaningfully explore an aspect of the service, experience (or product usage). Scenarios describe the stories and context behind why a specific user group comes to your product/ service and can be depicted as plain text, videos or storyboards.
Storyboards are a series of drawings/pictures that visualize a sequence of events (a journey or a scenario) where the service is used. Storyboards can be used for existing journeys or the hypothetical implementation of a new product/service. They allow stories about user experience to be bought into the design process. They can be used to represent both what is currently happening and what should be happening (issues and recommendations).
These methodologies are suitable for agile and lean ways of working.

Scenarios and storyboards are often combined with personas to put the user at the heart of the design and development process (Stickdorn and Schneider, 2014; US Department of Health and Human Services, 2017).

How to create scenarios

Good scenarios are concise and include the following elements:

- *Who is the user?* Each persona will have different motivations and behaviours when using your product/service.

- *Why does the persona use your product/service?* What motivates the user to come to you and what are their expectations upon arrival?
- *What goals do they have?* What does the user want to achieve? And what does your product/service have to do to provide a satisfactory experience?

You may also want to include how the users can achieve their goals. Identify the various possibilities and any potential barriers; more specifically, for each persona consider:

1 *Goals.* What is the user trying to accomplish? How do the user's actions fit into the objectives of the organization?

2 *Process.* What are the steps the user will follow? How does information flow from one step to the next? What are the various roles (such as creator, contributor, editor or approver) that are involved?

3 *Inputs and outputs.* What materials and information will users need to successfully use the thing (eg interface)? What will they need from the interface to continue with their overarching goals?

4 *Experience.* What similar things has the user done in the past? How has the organization survived without this design in the past?

5 *Constraints.* What physical, temporal, or financial constraints are likely to impose themselves on the user?

6 *Physical environment.* How much room do the users have to do what they need to do? What materials are on their desk? What access do they have to necessary information (such as user manuals)? What notes are taped to their monitor?

7 *Tools in use.* What tools does the user currently use?

8 *Relationships.* What are the interconnections between the primary user and other people who are affected by the tool? (US Department of Health and Human Services, 2017; Wechsler, 2010).

How to create storyboards

Storyboards are a great way to step through a potential experience for our emerging personas: to further understand their context, needs, motivations and behaviours. You can get small groups to sketch the scenes of a future scenario (story) across six to ten boxes (or more if required); blanks are shown in Figure 32.1. When filling in your storyboard, caption and title every scene to help explain what is happening, and convey emotion and dialogue through speech/thought bubbles and emoticons.

(This section is based on and adapted from work done by Lagom Strategy, 2016).

Useful pointers

Each scenario should focus on one persona: 'This is yy's story about using the xx...'. You may want to give the groups specific questions to cover in their storyboard:

- What triggers and motivates them to come to xx? What needs do they want to address?
- What do they already know about how to solve their need/s?
- How do they expect the xx to help them?
- How many times do they come to the xx during their story?
- What do they do on the xx? What content do they look at? Do they interact with anything?
- Which sites and sources (on- and offline) do they visit during their story?
- Who else helps or influences them during their story?
- What encourages and discourages them from using the product or service?

FIGURE 32.1 Blank storyboard template

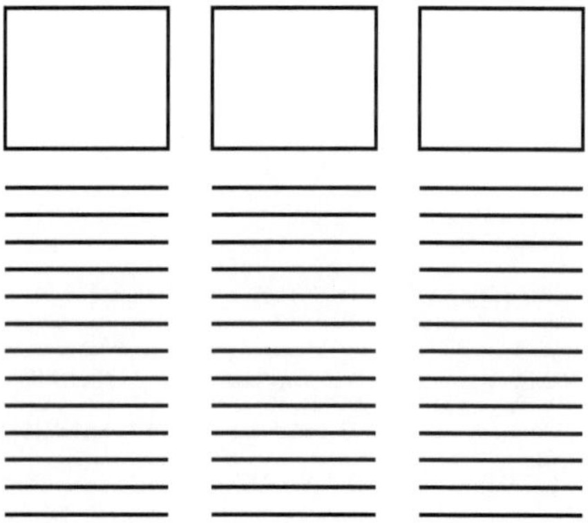

- How does the site eventually help them solve their need/s?
- When does their story end and what do they consider to be a successful user experience?

Remember to consider these questions:

- What is motivating them at each stage?
- What emotions are they feeling at each stage?
- What are their key decision points?
- What is the interplay of off- and online activity in their story?
- What are their hurdles and pain points? How do they overcome them?

References and further reading

Lagom Strategy (2016) www.lagomstrategy.net/ (archived at https://perma.cc/8UUA-KAR6)

Lichaw, D (2016) *The User's Journey: Storymapping products that people love*, Rosenfeld Media, New York

Stickdorn, M and Schneider, J (2014) *This is Service Design Thinking*, BIS Publishers, Amsterdam

US Department of Health and Human Services (12 June 2017) Scenarios. Usability. gov. www.usability.gov/how-to-and-tools/methods/scenarios.html (archived at https://perma.cc/K8MU-FDD7) (last accessed: 12 June 2017)

Wechsler, J (30 November 2010) Using scenarios. UX Think. http://jaxwechsler.com/using_scenarios/ (archived at https://perma.cc/F3SX-EW8W) (last accessed: 12 June 2017)

33

Using infographics to translate numerical and statistical data

TABLE 33.1

Method summary
Method suitability: you can use infographics for a wide variety of data you've collected:

- Quantitative surveys
- Quantitative usability testing
- IA validation
- A/B testing
- Card storing
- Quantitative user testing

Use if you want to: infographics can be used to visualize journeys, patterns and trends, hierarchies and architectures, concepts and plans.

How to make effective infographics

An effective infographic:

- has a clear purpose and is engaging;
- makes sense to its intended audience;
- does not distort or misrepresent the data or the truth;
- is in a fit-for-purpose format (Parry, 2015).

The experience maps discussed in Chapter 31 are an example of an infographic. The kind of infographic you need depends on the objectives of your research, your intended audience and what story you want to tell.

•

If you aren't an analyst or graphic designer, try to collaborate with them. You could hold a workshop to come up with the most useful ways to visualize your data. If this isn't possible, you could start by doing some rough sketches of the visualizations you think may be useful. Show them to some colleagues and ask them what they get from the data; this will help you to understand if each visual is effectively conveying what you want it to. If the visuals don't do this, iterate and try again.

Here are a few useful rules to help you make effective graphics:

- *Show don't tell.* If you need a lot of text to explain what's going on, your infographic isn't likely to be effective. That doesn't mean there can't be any text; rather, you need a balance between the textual and the visual within the infographic.

- *Stick to three colours.* Choose three primary colours. Of the three, one should be the background colour (usually the lightest), and the other two should break up the sections. If you need to add other colours, use shades of the three main colours. This will keep the palette cohesive and calming, rather than jarring.

- *Stick to two fonts and three sizes* (heading, sub-heading and body). Typography can be used to highlight facts and figures.

- *Give your main point prominence in the graphic.* Every good infographic has a hook or primary take-away that makes the viewer say, 'Aha!' What is the thing you most want people to remember?

- *Keep it simple and focused.* Try not to overload your infographic: tell one coherent story in one infographic. It may be that to tell your complete story you need more than one, or an infographic plus other kinds of analysis and presentation.

- *Consider the flow of the graphic.* In the same way you check your written reports and stories, see if the presentation flows. Does it convey the information in the right order? Placement of information will, to a certain extent, determine the order in which people consume the data.

- *Be consistent.* Stick to one theme.

Some bad practices:

- Dominant dark colours do not translate well on infographics.

- Avoid white as a background whenever possible. Infographics are often shared on multiple websites and blogs, most of which have white backgrounds. If your infographic's background is also white, deciphering where it begins and ends could be difficult.

- Some data should not be simplified to use in an infographic. Taking really complicated data and over-simplifying it can cause misunderstanding and defeat the purpose of any research done. An infographic may not be a great format to explain the intricacies of string theory, for example.

Making use of available tools

Often you don't have to create visualizations/infographics yourself. Many of the tools that have been highlighted in the various chapters of this book have visualization options to help you make sense of your data. For instance, Optimal Workshop has a visualization option for tree testing results (IA validation/Treejack), for card sorting results and for the various other tests it offers.

Its card sorting data visualization is known as a Similarity Matrix (Figure 33.1). The matrix clusters together the strongest card groups along the diagonal edge; the darker the colour the more related the cards are, helping you identify obvious clusters and groupings, and things participants don't consider to be related. Figure 33.2 is another example of a card sort data visualization known as a Dendrogram, which is used to visualize content groups and the top labels by participants.

The IA validation (tree test) visualization known as a pie tree (see Figure 33.3) depicts detailed path analysis. Figure 33.4 shows you the choices your participants made to find content and where they all selected their final answers

UserZoom also offers tree test and other UX metrics visualizations to help you understand your data. Many tools such as Survey Monkey and SurveyGizmo offer analysis, visualization and interactive/graphic options for your survey data. Some A/B testing tools will also provide visualization options for your data, such as Google's Data Studio, Visual Website Optimizer and Kissmetrics.

FIGURE 33.1 Similarity matrix visualization

Similarity matrix (values read from the lower-triangular grid). Row and column items are numbered as follows:

1. BananaCom's contact phone number
2. The email address to use for BananaCom help
3. BananaCom's freephone number
4. Career opportunities at BananaCom
5. How to set up my BananaCom email address
6. What to do when my cell phone has been broken or stolen
7. How to transfer my home phone number to my new house
8. Add-on services for my home phone
9. International calling rates for my home phone
10. Deals for home internet and phone bundles
11. The price of 3G Broadband data
12. A table of prices for cell phone plan options
13. A tool to calculate the best cell phone plan for me
14. 3G coverage map
15. Internet connection speed test
16. Change my home internet plan online
17. An online form to request a plan upgrade

Item	1	2	3	4	5	6	7	8	9	10	11	12	13	14	15	16
2	79															
3	75	69														
4	44	41	40													
5	40	48	39	25												
6	38	42	30	21	57											
7	30	28	26	11	57	58										
8	11	8	14	10	14	14	38									
9	11	10	16	8	13	17	30	46								
10	6	12	11	9	11	10	21	41	49							
11	11	12	13	4	11	16	12	19	41	48						
12	9	8	12	7	11	24	15	29	38	41	42					
13	10	12	15	12	20	26	24	29	34	35	40	58				
14	12	15	17	11	18	22	20	20	24	25	53	40	40			
15	8	16	12	10	26	25	20	20	25	34	35	57	11	24		
16	11	18	9	7	23	17	35	40	24	25	53	40	34	15	26	
17	16	20	19	14	21	14	38	23	23	30	25	34	23	31	25	46

SOURCE Optimal Workshop, 2017

FIGURE 33.2 Dendrogram visualization

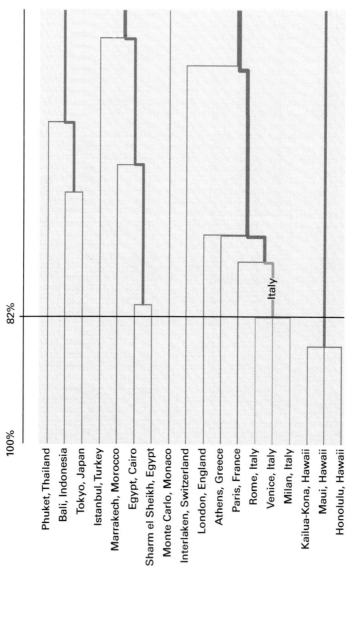

100%   82%

Phuket, Thailand
Bali, Indonesia
Tokyo, Japan
Istanbul, Turkey
Marrakech, Morocco
Egypt, Cairo
Sharm el Sheikh, Egypt
Monte Carlo, Monaco
Interlaken, Switzerland
London, England
Athens, Greece
Paris, France
Rome, Italy
Venice, Italy
Milan, Italy
Kailua-Kona, Hawaii
Maui, Hawaii
Honolulu, Hawaii

Italy

SOURCE Optimal Workshop, 2017

FIGURE 33.3 Pie tree visualization

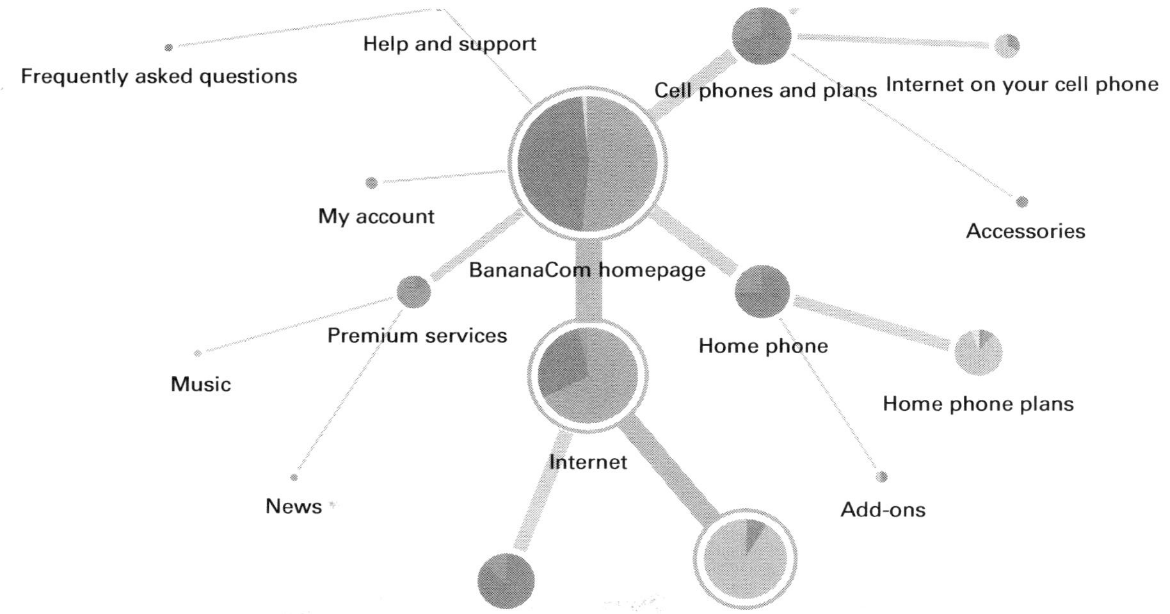

Internet on your cell phone

Accessories

Home phone plans

Add-ons

Cell phones and plans

Home phone

BananaCom homepage

Internet

Help and support

Premium services

My account

News

Frequently asked questions

Music

SOURCE Optimal Workshop, 2017

FIGURE 33.4   Another IA validation (tree test) visualization; showing the success rate of an individual task.

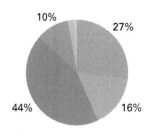

		Direct				
▨	Success	Direct	29	46	27%	43%
		Indirect	17		16%	
▨	Fail	Direct	47	58	44%	54%
		Indirect	11		10%	
▨	Skip	Direct	2	3	2%	3%
		Indirect	1		1%	

SOURCE   Optimal Workshop, 2017

References and further reading

Balliet, A (14 October 2011) The dos and don'ts of infographic design. Smashing Magazine. www.smashingmagazine.com/2011/10/the-dos-and-donts-of-infographic-design/ (archived at https://perma.cc/N6Z9-8PYA) (last accessed: 12 June 2017)

Bowmast, N (2017) Bowmast.com www.bowmast.com/about/ (archived at https://perma.cc/KX4R-VVU8) (last accessed: 12 June 2017)

Cheng, K (2012) *See What I Mean: How to use comics to communicate ideas,* Rosenfeld Media, New York

Easel.ly (15 June 2015) The 6 best practices for designing an infographics. https://easel.ly/blog/the-6-best-practices-for-designing-an-infographics/ (last accessed: 12 June 2017)

McCandless, D (2017) Information is beautiful. www.informationisbeautiful.net/ (archived at https://perma.cc/V78B-F8NA) (last accessed 26 August 2017)

Meyer, A (29 April 2015) Best (and worst) practices for infographics. Marketer Gizmo. www.marketergizmo.com/whats-the-deal-with-infographics/ (archived at https://perma.cc/QV6G-G9H3) (last accessed: 12 June 2017)

Optimal Workshop (2017) www.optimalworkshop.com (archived at https://perma.cc/XQ7E-LHZV)

Parry, G (5 June 2015) When and how to create an effective infographic. PwC Digital New Zealand. https://digital.pwc.co.nz/ideas/when-and-how-to-create-an-effective-infographic/ (archived at https://perma.cc/7D35-FVRD) (last accessed: 12 June 2017)

Patel, N (6 January 2015) 12 infographic tips that you wish you knew years ago. Kissmetrics Blog. https://blog.kissmetrics.com/12-infographic-tips/ (archived at https://perma.cc/BQY5-UKBQ) (last accessed: 12 June 2017)

Rum, J (05 July 2016) How to make beautiful and effective infographics. Social Media Today. www.socialmediatoday.com/marketing/how-make-beautiful-and-effective-infographics (archived at https://perma.cc/JW67-YHVJ) (last accessed 26 August 2017)

Tufte, E (2001) *The Visual Display of Quantitative Information*, Graphics Press, Cheshire, CT

Usability.gov (2017) System Usability Scale (SUS). US Department of Health & Human Services. www.usability.gov/how-to-and-tools/methods/system-usability-scale.html (archived at https://perma.cc/4DWR-AK66) (last accessed 21 May 2017)

Zhang, D (23 September 2015) 10 infographic best practices. W Promote. www.wpromote.com/blog/10-infographic-best-practices/ (archived at https://perma.cc/NZF3-WGFC) (last accessed: 12 June 2017)

34

How to recommend changes to visual, interaction and information design

TABLE 34.1

Method summary
Method suitability: IA validation, card sorting, A/B testing, quantitative and qualitative usability testing. This methodology is suitable for agile and lean ways of working.
Use if you want to: visually explain the improvements you are recommending.

If the research you are doing is focused on improving a product, for example, you'll probably want to make recommendations on how aspects of the design can be made better as part of the report or presentation. As mentioned previously, any suggestion of potential changes you make should be agreed with those who will make them. There is no point making suggestions that aren't technically possible, for example. We've already thought about other useful ways to visualize what you are talking about, for instance:

- infographics to depict the numbers from the research;
- maps and models to visualize the gaps and opportunities in an experience; and
- personas to synthesize and depict the user group as actual people.

In this vein, if you are suggesting changes to interaction, visual design or the information architecture, it can be useful to depict the specific changes or the options you are recommending.

Tools

You can use software and apps to 'sketch' your recommendations. Examples include Balsamiq (which I have used to do the sketches in this book). You can use it to sketch out ideas and create simple clickable low-fidelity prototypes (https://balsamiq.com). Axure is a more powerful prototyping tool, in which you can create both low- and high-fidelity interactive prototypes (https://www.axure.com). There are many different prototyping tools available with varying functionality, costs and ease of use. I've highlight these two as I have had experience with them, but as with all the tools I have mentioned in this book, what's out there is ever changing and easily searchable online.

PowerPoint, Keynote and Google Slides generally have enough functionality to create simple sketches. If you are recommending changes to an information architecture, you can also utilize various tools to visualize the changes. You can make use of the tools already mentioned; others you may want to consider are:

- Excel and other spreadsheet programmes: cells, columns and rows lend themselves nicely to representing your new information architecture.
- There are specific information architecture tools out there and you can also make use of process mapping tools if they are available to you (Bigby 2017).
- If you have made use of the tools in Optimal Workshop to test your existing IA, you can also use of them to visualize your recommended IA: https://www.optimalworkshop.com/.

Of course there is always pen, pencil and paper. These are especially useful for when you are figuring out your initial concepts. Depending on who you need to share these with you may be able to keep your recommendation on paper. You know your audience best and you'll know if it's worth spending some time and effort making you recommendations look 'professional'. The infamous idiom is often true in user research: a picture can be worth a thousand words.

References and further reading

Bigby, G (30 April 2017) 22 awesome information architecture (IA) tools for creating visual sitemaps. Dyno Mapper. https://dynomapper.com/blog/13-create-sitemaps/269-22-of-the-best-information-architecture-tools-for-creating-sitemaps (archived at https://perma.cc/VE9N-PVJC) (last accessed: 12 June 2017)

Optimal Workshop (2017) www.optimalworkshop.com (archived at https://perma.cc/CRU2-ZL5X). (last accessed: 12 June 2017)

Conclusion

I hope you have found this to be a helpful and practical book to support you in doing user research yourself, or in being a better customer when buying in from user research services.

You may find that you get to know certain methods of research and analysis better than others, depending on what your organization's product/service requires. You may get to know certain methods so well you don't need this book any more. That's great; although it's good to remind yourself of the key principles now and again. Once you start to become experienced in certain aspects of user research, you will come to understand that the methods you are more practised in aren't necessarily the most appropriate, especially when a new situation arises. I hope when that happens you will come back to this book for guidance on selecting a different but suitable method of user research that will help you understand your users better.

There are some user research techniques that are not considered in this book that may be relevant to your needs. As long as this book is, it's not exhaustive. You may want to find out about task analysis, multivariate testing, desktop research, expert reviews, competitor benchmarking and content audits, to name a few examples. You may also want to look into using segmentation rather than personas. The main thought I want to leave you with, which by now you already know but I'm going to say it again, is that user research is an iterative process. It's something you'll need to come back to, and hopefully *want* to come back to again and again.

Please let me know what you do and don't find useful in this book; it will help me learn. You never stop learning with user research. I'm always interested when people adapt methods in different ways or use them in new ways, so I'd love to hear about that too. Find me on Twitter @Steph_Marsh81. I look forward to hearing from and talking to you.

Further reading

Albert, W and Tullis, T (2013) *Measuring the User Experience: Collecting, analyzing, and presenting usability metrics,* 2nd edn, Morgan Kaufmann, Burlington, MA

Baxter, K, Courage, C and Caine, K (2015) *Understanding Your Users: A practical guide to user research methods,* 2nd edn, Morgan Kaufmann, Burlington, MA

Buley, L (2013) *The User Experience Team of One: A research and design survival guide,* Rosenfeld Media, New York

Garrett, J J (2002) *The Elements of User Experience: User-centered design for the web,* Peachpit Press, San Francisco, CA

Goodman, E, Kuniavsky, M and Moed, A (2012) *Observing the User Experience: A practitioner's guide to user research,* 2nd edn, Morgan Kaufmann, Burlington, MA

Krug, S (2005) *Don't Make Me Think: A common sense approach to web usability,* 2nd edn, New Riders Publishing, San Francisco, CA

Sauro, J and Lewis, J R (2016) *Quantifying the User Experience: Practical statistics for user research,* 2nd edn, Morgan Kaufmann, Burlington, MA

Walter, A (October 2011) *Designing for Emotion. A book apart.* https://abookapart. com/products/designing-for-emotion (archived at https://perma.cc/QMH3-ARDX)

Young, I (2015) *Practical Empathy: For collaboration and creativity in your work,* Rosenfeld Media, New York

INDEX

A/B (comparative) testing 91, 94, 186–90
  combining research methodologies 206–13
  content testing 122–23
  description of 186
  effort required to do this kind of
    research 188
  how to do A/B testing 189–90
  tools for 190
  what it is good for 186–87
  what it is not good for 187–88
  when to use A/B testing 188
accessibility 54–55
  automated accessibility testing 54
  getting specialists to audit your work 55
  manual accessibility testing 54
  usability testing with assistive
    technologies 55
actionable findings 285–86
actionable insights 270–72
activity theory 256–57
affinity diagramming (identifying
    themes) 215, 227–32
  advantages of 232
  description of 227–28
  disadvantages of 232
  how to do affinity diagramming 228–31
  outcomes from 227
  suitable data for 227
  tools for 231
affinity mapping *see* affinity diagramming
agencies 84–86
agile, definition of 13
agile analysis 216, 236–40
  description of 236
  face-to-face synchronous
    analysis 236–38
  outcomes 236
  rainbow spreadsheet method 238–40
  suitable data for 236
agile UX (user experience), role of user
    research 23–24
agile working 13, 18, 95, 110, 115, 175,
    276, 278, 280–81, 287, 292, 294,
    300, 312

aims and objectives of research 15
alpha phase of development 275, 277, 278
atomic research 272–74
attitudinal (subjective) data 92, 93, 94
automated accessibility testing 54
Axure 313

Balsamiq 313
behavioural (objective) data 92, 93, 94
best practice in user research 26–56
  accessibility 54–55
  asking the right kind of questions 44–54
  avoid using key words in questions and
    tasks 46, 52
  difference between behaviour and
    opinion 41–44
  difficult or unhelpful participants 29
  identifying appropriate user
    groups 26–27
  importance of observation 41–44
  incentivizing people to take part 34–41
  inclusion 54, 55–56
  inclusive language 44
  know when to break some of the
    rules 52–54
  limitations of demographics 29–30
  non-responsive participants 53
  payment of participants 34–35
  recruiting the right participants 27–34
  recruitment brief 28–31
  recruitment screener 28, 31–34, 35–41
  use neutral open-ended questions 44–45
beta phase of development 275, 277, 278
Boulton, Emma 73–74
Breeze, Nick 266
budget for user research
  large budget 85–86
  medium budget 85
  outsourcing aspects of the
    research 84–86
  small budget 85
  very small budget 84
  ways to spend it 84–86
budgeting for research 78–79

Bulery, Leah 74

C-inspector tool 171
California Consumer Protection Act
        (CCPA) 58
card sorting 91, 94, 125–37
    case study example 130–31
    combining research
        methodologies 206–13
    description of 125
    effort required to do this kind of
        research 128
    how to do card sorting 128–36
    iterative approach 137
    moderated face-to-face and remote card
        sorting 128–36
    number of participants 130, 131
    preparing your cards 128–30
    tools for 136–37
    types of 126–27
    unmoderated face-to-face and remote
        card sorting 128, 136
    what it is good for 125
    what it is not good for 125–26
    when to use it 126–27
case studies
    card sorting 130–31
    combining quantitative and qualitative
        data 95
    contextual inquiry 180–81
    difference between behaviour and
        opinion 43
    ethnography in airport design 175
    guerrilla research example 207–08
    knowing when to stop a research session
        early 147–48
    paired interviewing 152–53
children, doing research with 84
conceptual models 260
Condens 225
content analysis 215, 219–25
    advantages of 224
    codifying and categorizing of qualitative
        data 219–20
    description of 219–20
    disadvantages of 225
    how to code your qualitative
        data 220–22
    how to do content analysis 222–24
    outcomes from 219
    semiotic analysis 224
    suitable data for 219
    tools for 225
content testing 91, 94, 119–23

A/B (comparative) testing 122–23
check the assumed reading age 121
cloze testing 121–22
combining research
        methodologies 206–13
comprehension testing 121
creating good content 119
effort required to do this kind of
        research 120
guerrilla content testing 123
highlighting content 123
how to test the effectiveness of
        content 120–23
let people choose their own words 122
what it is good for 119
what it is not good for 120
when to use 120
contextual inquiry 91, 94, 179–84
    case study 180–81
    combining research
        methodologies 206–13
    description of 179
    effort required to do this kind of
        research 181
    how to do contextual inquiry 181–84
    recording data 183, 184
    tools for 184
    what it is good for 179
    what it is not good for 180
    when to use 180
coronavirus pandemic, impact on how user
        research is done 20
contracts 84–86
CRB (Criminal Records Bureau) checks 84
cultural differences, awareness of 83
customer journey mapping and experience
        mapping 284, 294–98

Dalai Lama XIV 52
data, definition of 269
data analysis
    actionable insights 270–72
    affinity diagramming (identifying
        themes) 215, 227–32
    agile analysis 216, 236–40
    atomic research 272–74
    cataloguing and prioritizing issues 216
    choice of method 215
    content analysis 215, 219–25
    creating a user needs backlog 216
    creating personas 216, 251–57
    definition of data 269
    definition of findings 269
    definition of insight 269–70

identifying and prioritizing issues and
        user needs 242–49
insight taxonomy 271
planning for 23
preparing your data 217–18
skills required for 216–17
thematic analysis 216, 233–34
timescale for 275–81
triangulation of evidence 270, 271,
        272, 273
turning findings into insights 269–74
usability analysis 242–49
using mental models 216, 259–67
data collection
    informed consent of participants 61–66
    storage and processing statement 64
Data Controllers 59
data management 74–77
    access to participants' personal
        details 76–77
    file naming conventions 74–76
    helping your colleagues keep track 76
    participant data management 76–77
data privacy statement 64
data processing agreements (DPAs) 79
Data Processors 59
data protection
    defining personal data 59
    definition of 58–59
    General Data Protection Regulation
        (GDPR) 58, 66
    handling personal information 60–61
    legislation 58–61
    protecting participants' privacy 68–69
data protection officer (DPO) 79–80
data types
    objective (behavioural) data 92, 93, 94
    qualitative data 92, 93–95
    quantitative data 92, 93–95
    subjective (attitudinal) data 92, 93, 94
demographics, limitations of 29–30
Dendrogram 306, 308
diary studies 91, 94, 156–64
    combining research
        methodologies 206–13
    description of 156
    digital diaries 162–64
    effort required to do this kind of
        research 158
    how to do a diary study 158–61
    paper diaries 162
    post-study interview 161
    tools for 162–64

what they are good for 156
what they are not good for 156–57
when to do 157–58
digital diaries 162–64
drawing tools 313

ethical issues 67–68
    gathering data 93
    Market Research Society
        principles 67–68
ethnography 91, 94, 174–77
    case study (airport design) 175
    combining research
        methodologies 206–13
    description of traditional
        ethnography 174
    effort required to do this kind of
        research 175
    how to do ethnography 176–77
    mobile ethnography 176–77
    tools for 177
    what it is good for 174
    what it is not good for 175
    when to use ethnography 175
    see also contextual inquiry
Excel 313
executive summaries 283, 287–91
experience mapping 284, 294–98

facilities for user research 84–86
feature creep, avoiding 15
findings
    actionable finding 285–86
    communicating see user experience (UX)
        storytelling
    definition of 269
    turning into insights 269–74
formative research 91, 94
Forrester, Nick 266

General Data Protection Regulation
        (GDPR) 58, 66
generative research 91, 94
getting started with user research
    admin 78–79
    budgeting for research 78–79
    communicating with participants 77–78
    data management 74–77
    eight pillars of user research 71–74
    incentives 78
    setting up for success 71–80
    tools and infrastructure 79–80
Google Data Studio 306

Google Slides 313
Government Digital Service (UK) 18, 22, 54,
        55, 69, 85–86, 119, 245, 266, 295
Government Digital Service Manual 276,
        277
guerrilla research 91, 94, 95, 202–05
    approach to 205
    case study 207–08
    combining research
            methodologies 206–13
    combining with desktop research 208
    content testing 123
    description of 202
    effort required to do this kind of
            research 203
    how to do guerrilla research 203–04
    situations where it is not
            appropriate 208
    tools for 205
    use to kick-start the research
            process 206–08
    ways to use guerrilla research 203–04
    what it is good for 202
    what it is not good for 202–03
    when to use guerrilla research 203

Hemmingway app 121

incentives 78
inclusion 55–56
inclusive language 44
infographics 284, 304–10
information architecture (IA) validation 91,
        125, 166–71
    combining research
            methodologies 206–13
    deciding what to test 168–71
    definition of information
            architecture 166
    effort required to do this kind of
            research 167
    how to do an IA validation 168–71
    online tools for 171
    tree testing 168–71
    visualization 306, 308–10
    what it is good for 166
    what it is not good for 167
    when to do IA validation 167
informed consent, participants 61–67
    age of participants 61–62
    before the research session starts 62
    consent explanation 64–65
    creating a consent form 80
    features of valid consent 61

GDPR and 66
    online surveys 66
    recruiting participants 66–67
    use of digital signatures 62
    ways to ask for consent 62–64
    when you don't need a consent form 64
    withdrawal of consent 65
insight
    actionable insights 270–72
    definition of 269–70
insight taxonomy 271
interviews see user interviews

journey mapping 284, 294–98

Keynote 313
Kissmetrics 306

lean UX (user experience), role of user
        research 23–24
lean working 23–24, 95, 219, 224, 227, 236,
        243, 247, 251, 259, 287, 292,
        294, 300, 312
legal issues
    data protection legislation 58–61
    informed consent 61–67
    recruiting participants 66–67
location of your research 18–20
logistics 82–84
    safety first 82–83

Market Research Society (MRS) 67–68
mental models 216, 259–67
    case study (Smashing Magazine
            cartoon) 261
    case study (web browser URL and search
            bars) 261
    changing people's mental models 261–62
    comparison with conceptual
            models 260
    creating your own mental model (version
            one) 262–63, 264
    creating your own mental model (version
            two) 263, 265–67
    description of 259
    outcomes 259
    purpose of 259–62
    representing user experience 259–62
    suitable data to use 259
Miro 225, 231, 243
Mural 231

new product/service, incorporating user
        research into workflows 275–81

Nielsen, Jakob 93, 261
non-responsive participants 53
numerical data, use of infographics to
        explain 284, 304–10
NVivo 225

objective (behavioural) data 92, 93, 94
observation of participants 41–44
observers, group analysis and debrief after
        completion 23
observing user research 21–22
opportunity framing 15–15
Optimal Workshop 225, 231, 243
    visualization tools 306, 307–10, 313

participants
    communicating with 77–78
    confidentiality 288–89
    difficult or unhelpful participants 29
    incentivizing people to take part 34–41
    informed consent 61–66
    lack of objectivity in responses 41–44
    non-responsive participants 53
    observation of 41–44
    payment of 34–35
    protecting their privacy 68–69
    self-reporting by 42–44
Patel, Salma 233
payment of participants 34–35
personal data, definition of 59
personas, creating 216
    advanced method using activity
            theory 256–57
    advantages and disadvantages of
            personas 254
    anti-personas 254
    definition of a persona 251–52
    example of a basic persona 256
    framework of personal elements 257
    how many personas to create 257
    how to present your personas 254–56
    outcomes 251
    suitable data for 251
    use with scenarios and
            storyboards 300–03
    what to avoid 253
    what to include in your personas 252–54
pilot testing your research methodology 21
planning for analysis and sharing of
        work 23
planning for user research 15–24
    when working agile or lean 23–24
PowerPoint 287, 313

privacy, protecting participants'
        privacy 68–69
problem framing 14–15
problem scenarios 89–90
product lifecycle stage 91, 92
prototyping tools 313
purpose of the research 14–15

qualitative data 92, 93–95
qualitative research, phases and timescale
        of 278, 279
quantitative data 92, 93–95
quantitative research, phases and timescale
        of 278
questions
    asking the right kind 44–54
    closed questions 44
    neutral open-ended questions 44–46

rainbow spreadsheet method 238–40
recruiting participants 23
    ethical and legal issues 66–67
    finding the right participants 27–41
recruitment agencies 85
recruitment brief 28–31
recruitment screener 28, 31–34
    example 35–41
remote research
    advantages and disadvantages 21
    options for 20–21
reports 283, 287–91
research findings see findings
research labs 18, 19
research methods see user research methods
research operations (ReOps) 71–80
    development of the field 71
    eight pillars of user research 72–74
    setting up for success 71–74
research question
    defining 89–92
    problem scenarios 89–90
results, communicating see user experience
        (UX) storytelling

safety of researchers and participants
        82–83
scenarios and storyboards 284, 300–03
self-reporting by participants 42–44
semiotic analysis 224
service lifecycle stage 91, 92
sharing research results see user experience
        (UX) storytelling
sketching tools 313

spreadsheets 231, 243
    programmes 313
    rainbow spreadsheet method 238–40
stakeholder workshops 91, 94, 192–99
    combining research
            methodologies 206–13
    definition of stakeholders 192
    description of 192
    digital workshop tools 199
    effort required to do this kind of
            research 194
    face-to-face workshop tools 198–99
    how to run a workshop 194–98
    tools for 198–99
    types of workshops 196–97
    what they are good for 192–93
    what they are not good for 193
    when to use workshops 193–94
    who needs to be there 197
stakeholders, observing user research 21–22
statistical data, use of infographics to
            explain 284, 304–10
Stoks, Amy 216, 227
storyboards and scenarios 284, 300–03
storytelling see user experience (UX)
            storytelling
subjective (attitudinal) data 92, 93, 94
summative research 91, 94
Survey Monkey 28, 306
SurveyGizmo 306
surveys 91, 94, 139–44
    combining research
            methodologies 206–13
    description of 139
    effort required to do this kind of
            research 140
    how to do surveys 141–44
    incentives for participants 144
    inclusion in survey design 140–41
    pilot testing 144
    recruiting your target user group/
            audience 143
    tools for 144
    what they are good for 139
    what they are not good for 140
    what to avoid asking about 142
    what you can ask about 141–42
    when to do a survey 140
    when to do the recruitment yourself 143
    when to use recruitment agencies 143
    writing questions 142

thematic analysis 216
    description of 233–34
    example 234

outcomes 233
    suitable data for 233
    see also affinity diagramming
timescale for user research 275–81
timing of user research 13–14
Towsey, Kate 80
tree testing 94
    data visualization 306, 308–10
    deciding what to test 168–71
Treejack tool 171
Trello 76, 225, 231, 243
triangulation of evidence 270, 271, 272, 273

Uber insight framework 271
UK Data Service 69
usability analysis 242–49
    cataloguing issues from qualitative
            data 242–47
    cataloguing issues from quantitative
            data 247–49
usability testing 91, 94, 97–116
    building confidence in small
            samples 116
    combining research
            methodologies 206–13
    description of 97–98
    moderated 97, 98–109, 116
    observation of participants 42
    unmoderated 97–98, 109–16
    using assistive technologies 55
    see also content testing
user-centred development cycle 91, 92
user-centric approach 2, 13, 18, 207,
user characteristics, creating
            personas 251–57
user experience (UX) storytelling 283–84
    actionable findings 285–86
    anonymised participant details 288–89
    customer journey mapping and
            experience mapping 284, 294–98
    detailed reports 283, 287–91
    executive summaries 283, 287–91
    infographics 284, 304–10
    making recommendations 285–86
    numerical and statistical data 284,
            304–10
    planning for sharing results 23
    protecting participants' privacy 68–69
    prototyping tools 313
    recommending design
            improvements 284, 312–13
    refining the design 284, 312–13
    scenarios 284, 300–03
    storyboards 284, 300–03
    video playback 284, 292–93

user experience mental models *see* mental
    models
user interviews 91, 94, 146–55
    case study (knowing when to stop a
        research session early) 147–48
    case study (paired interviewing) 152–53
    combining research
        methodologies 206–13
    description of 146
    effort required to do this kind of
        research 147–48
    how to do user interviews 148–55
    interview structure 149–50
    length of the interview 154–55
    moderating interviews (individual
        participants) 150–52
    moderating interviews (two participants,
        paired interviewing) 152–53
    question design 148–49
    recording the data 154
    scheduling interviews 15–18
    tools for interviewing 155
    types of interview 148
    what they are good for 146
    what they are not good for 146–47
    when to do user interviews 147
    see also contextual inquiry
user needs backlog 216
user research
    aims and objectives 15
    appearance and perception when doing
        face-to-face research 83
    benefits from using 3–4
    cultural awareness 83–84
    definition of 1
    distinction from market research 1
    fundamentals 11–86
    further developing your skills 315
    groups who would benefit from
        using 2–3
    incorporation into workflows 275–81
    learning the skills of 4
    location of 18–20
    need for 3
    planning for 15–24
    purpose of 3, 14–15
    remote research options 20–21
    research with children 84
    role of data analysis 216–17
    timescale for 275–81
    timing of 13–14

    venue for 18–20
    what good research looks like 11–86
user research methods
    A/B (comparative) testing 91, 94,
        122–23, 186–90
    card sorting 91, 94, 125–37
    combining research
        methodologies 206–13
    content testing 91, 94, 119–23
    contextual inquiry 91, 94, 179–84
    defining your research question 89–92
    diary studies 91, 94, 156–64
    ethnography 91, 94, 174–77
    formative research 91, 94
    generative research 91, 94
    guerrilla research 91, 94, 95, 123,
        202–05
    information architecture (IA)
        validation 91, 125, 166–71
    objective (behavioural) data 92, 93, 94
    pilot testing 21
    product/service lifecycle stage 91, 92
    qualitative data 92, 93–95
    quantitative data 92, 93–95
    range of methods 90–95
    scenarios using combined
        methodologies 208–13
    selecting an appropriate method 89–95
    stakeholder workshops 91, 94, 192–99
    subjective (attitudinal) data 92, 93, 94
    summative research 91, 94
    surveys 91, 94, 139–44
    tree testing 94
    usability testing 91, 94, 97–116
    user interviews 91, 94, 146–55
    where to start with user
        research 206–08
user researcher role 1–2
user testing *see* usability testing
UserZoom 306

video playback, presenting research
        results 284, 292–93
Visual Website Optimizer 306

websites *see* information architecture (IA)
    validation
WeWork 272
workflows, incorporating user research
        into 275–81
workshops *see* stakeholder workshops